Diplomacy

Also by G. R. Berridge

BRITISH DIPLOMACY IN TURKEY, 1583 TO THE PRESENT: A Study in the Evolution of the Resident Embassy

THE COUNTER-REVOLUTION IN DIPLOMACY and Other Essays

DIPLOMACY AT THE UN (*co-editor with A. Jennings*)

DIPLOMATIC CLASSICS: Selected Texts from Commynes to Vattel

DIPLOMATIC THEORY FROM MACHIAVELLI TO KISSINGER (*with Maurice Keens-Soper and T. G. Otte*)

A DIPLOMATIC WHISTLEBLOWER IN THE VICTORIAN ERA: The Life and Writings of E. C. Grenville-Murray

ECONOMIC POWER IN ANGLO-SOUTH AFRICAN DIPLOMACY: Simonstown, Sharpeville and After

EMBASSIES IN ARMED CONFLICT

GERALD FITZMAURICE (1865–1939), CHIEF DRAGOMAN OF THE BRITISH EMBASSY IN TURKEY

INTERNATIONAL POLITICS: States, Power and Conflict since 1945, Third Edition

AN INTRODUCTION TO INTERNATIONAL RELATIONS (*with D. Heater*)

THE PALGRAVE MACMILLAN DICTIONARY OF DIPLOMACY, Third Edition (*with Lorna Lloyd*)

THE POLITICS OF THE SOUTH AFRICA RUN: European Shipping and Pretoria

RETURN TO THE UN: UN Diplomacy in Regional Conflicts

SOUTH AFRICA, THE COLONIAL POWERS AND 'AFRICAN DEFENCE': The Rise and Fall of the White Entente, 1948–60

TALKING TO THE ENEMY: How States without 'Diplomatic Relations' Communicate

TILKIDOM AND THE OTTOMAN EMPIRE: The Letters of Gerald Fitzmaurice to George Lloyd

Diplomacy

Theory and Practice

5th edition

G. R. Berridge
Emeritus Professor of International Politics, University of Leicester, UK
Senior Fellow, DiploFoundation

First published 2015 by
PALGRAVE MACMILLAN

Palgrave Macmillan in the UK is an imprint of Macmillan Publishers Limited, registered in England, company number 785998, of Houndmills, Basingstoke, Hampshire RG21 6XS.

Palgrave Macmillan in the US is a division of St Martin's Press LLC, 175 Fifth Avenue, New York, NY 10010.

Palgrave Macmillan is the global academic imprint of the above companies and has companies and representatives throughout the world.

Palgrave® and Macmillan® are registered trademarks in the United States, the United Kingdom, Europe and other countries.

ISBN: 978–1–137–44550–6 hardback
ISBN: 978–1–137–44551–3 paperback

This book is printed on paper suitable for recycling and made from fully managed and sustained forest sources. Logging, pulping and manufacturing processes are expected to conform to the environmental regulations of the country of origin.

A catalogue record for this book is available from the British Library.

Library of Congress Cataloging-in-Publication Data

Berridge, G. R.
    Diplomacy: theory and practice / G.R. Berridge, Emeritus Professor of International Politics, University of Leicester, UK, Senior Fellow, DiploFoundation. – Fifth edition.
        pages cm
        ISBN 978–1–137–44550–6 (hardback)
        1. Diplomacy. I. Title.
JZ1405.B475 2015
327.2—dc23   2015002996

In memory of my mother

Contents

List of Boxes

Preface and Acknowledgements

This edition of *Diplomacy: Theory and Practice* has been both refreshed and extended. It has been brought up to date at the time of writing (November 2014), and tightened and corrected where necessary. In places, it has also been extensively reorganized: for example, Chapter 8 is now based on a classification of the types of embassy that raise the main public policy questions; elsewhere, I have clarified some rather dense passages by reducing them to bullet points; and I have removed a number of boxes containing detail now readily available on the Internet. The book has also been significantly broadened in scope, with two new chapters in Part II: 'Secret Intelligence' and 'Economic and Commercial Diplomacy'. In abject surrender to the popularity of the term, I have retained 'Public Diplomacy' as the title of the chapter on propaganda.

In order to give better guidance on further reading at the end of each chapter, I have tried to be more selective in making recommendations and, here and there, annotated them. Other things being equal, I have also given preference to sources freely available on the Internet. As in earlier editions, I have avoided providing URLs for such sources, partly because they are often so long, partly because they tend to rot or die, and partly because it is usually easy enough to find a web resource via a search engine; I simply add '[www]' to a reference available on the Internet at the time of writing. Also for reasons of economy, and because I dislike the on-page clutter produced by the Harvard referencing system, I have eliminated many of the source citations that were a feature of earlier editions, as a rule confining these to quotations and statements that might otherwise raise an eyebrow. The sources for unreferenced recent events are usually serious news websites such as Reuters and *Al-Monitor*, and online versions of newspapers or weeklies like the *Guardian*, *Der Spiegel*, the *New York Times*, the *Washington Post*, and the *Huffington Post*; for other points in the text, the sources are my own earlier writings or works listed in 'Further reading' that should be fairly obvious. When listing books here and in the 'References' at the end, I note only the first place of publication; it is also an idiosyncrasy of mine that I put the name of the publisher before place of publication, because I find this intuitive and because publishers have been doing the same thing on the title pages of their books for well over half a century.

(Students, beware! You will probably incur the wrath of your tutors if you follow my example.)

For valuable observations on parts of the text of this edition, I am grateful to Katharina Höhne, Milan Jazbec, Larry Pope, Kishan Rana, and Max Schweizer. Shim Yangsup, the first-rate translator of the previous edition into Korean, also helped me greatly to clarify the text of this edition at numerous points. The responsibility for remaining blemishes is mine alone. In the production process, I am grateful for the assistance of Hannah Kaspar at Palgrave Macmillan and the staff of Newgen Knowledge Works in Chennai. As usual, I compiled the Index.

Online Updating

For each chapter in the book there is a corresponding page on my website. These pages contain further reflections and details of recent developments on the subject in question. Among other things (including a free PDF of my latest monograph), the website also has a page on resources for students of diplomacy, reviews of recent books, and suggestions for dissertation topics. Please visit http://grberridge. diplomacy.edu/

List of Abbreviations

ABM	anti-ballistic missile
AU	African Union [formerly Organization of African Unity]
BDOHP	British Diplomatic Oral History Programme
BZ	Ministerie van Buitenlandse Zaken (Netherlands Ministry of Foreign Affairs)
CAT	Convention Against Torture and Other Cruel, Inhuman or Degrading Treatment or Punishment
CHOGM	Commonwealth Heads of Government Meeting
DCM	Deputy Chief of Mission
DWA	deportations with assurances
EC	European Community
EU	European Union
FAC	Foreign Affairs Committee [British House of Commons]
FAOHC	The Foreign Affairs Oral History Collection of the [US] Association for Diplomatic Studies and Training
FCO	Foreign and Commonwealth Office
FDI	foreign direct investment
FRUS	*Foreign Relations of the United States*
G7/8	Group of Seven/Eight ['G7' when Russia is cold-shouldered; 'G8' when not]
G20	Group of Twenty ['major advanced and emerging economies']
GATT	General Agreement on Tariffs and Trade
GCHQ	Government Communications Headquarters [British]
GRU	Glavnoye Razvedyvatelnoye Upravleniye [Russian – formerly Soviet – military intelligence]
IAEA	International Atomic Energy Agency
ICRC	International Committee of the Red Cross
ILC	International Law Commission
IMF	International Monetary Fund
ISC	Intelligence and Security Committee [British]
LE	locally engaged
MIRV	multiple independently targetable re-entry vehicle
MoU	memorandum of understanding
NGO	non-governmental organization
NPT	Nuclear Non-Proliferation Treaty

NSA	National Security Agency [US]
OAS	Organization of American States
OECD	Organisation for Economic Co-operation and Development
OGDs	other government departments [i.e. other than the foreign ministry]
OIG	Office of Inspector General [US State Department]
OSCE	Organization for Security and Co-operation in Europe
P5	Permanent 5 [on the UN Security Council: Britain, France, PRC, Russia, United States]
P5+1	P5 plus Germany
PLO	Palestine Liberation Organization
PNGed	declared *persona non grata* – no longer welcome
PRC	People's Republic of China
QDDR	Quadrennial Diplomacy and Development Review [US]
SALT I	Strategic Arms Limitations Talks [first negotiations, 1969–72]
SIAC	Special Immigration Appeals Commission [UK]
SIGINT	signals intelligence
SIS	Secret Intelligence Service [British; aka MI6]
SMEs	small and medium-sized enterprises
SVR	Sluzhba Vneshney Razvedki [successor to the KGB – Russian External Intelligence Service]
TPO	trade promotion organization
TRNC	Turkish Republic of Northern Cyprus
TTIP	Transatlantic Trade and Investment Partnership [EU–USA]
UN	United Nations
UNMOVIC	UN Monitoring, Verification and Inspection Commission
UNSCOM	UN Special Commission
USIA	United States Information Agency
USINT	US Interests Section Cuba
VCCR	Vienna Convention on Consular Relations (1963)
VCDR	Vienna Convention on Diplomatic Relations (1961)
WMD	weapons of mass destruction
WTO	World Trade Organization [formerly General Agreement on Tariffs and Trade]

Introduction

Diplomacy is an essentially political activity and, well resourced and skilful, a major ingredient of power. Its chief purpose is to enable states to secure the objectives of their foreign policies without resort to force, propaganda, or law. It achieves this mainly by communication between professional diplomatic agents and other officials designed to secure agreements. Although it also includes such discrete activities as gathering information, clarifying intentions, and engendering goodwill, it is thus not surprising that, until the label 'diplomacy' was affixed to all of these activities by the British parliamentarian Edmund Burke in 1796, it was known most commonly as 'negotiation' – by Cardinal Richelieu, the first minister of Louis XIII, as *négociation continuelle*. Diplomacy is not merely what professional diplomatic agents do. It is carried out by other officials and by private persons under the direction of officials. As we shall see, it is also carried out through many different channels besides the traditional resident mission. Together with the balance of power, which it both reflects and reinforces, diplomacy is the most important institution of our society of states.

Diplomacy in its modern form has its immediate origins in the Italian peninsula in the late fifteenth century AD. Nevertheless, its remote origins are to be found in the relations between the 'Great Kings' of the Near East in the second, or possibly even in the late fourth, millennium BCE (Liverani: Introduction; Cohen and Westbrook: 1–12). Its main features in these centuries were the dependence of communications on messengers and merchant caravans, of diplomatic immunity on codes of hospitality, and of treaty observance on terror of the gods under whose gaze they were confirmed. However, although apparently adequate to the times, diplomacy during these centuries remained rudimentary. In the main this would seem to be because it was not called on very often

1

and because communications were slow, laborious, unpredictable, and insecure.

In the Greek city-state system of the fourth and fifth centuries BCE, however, conditions both demanded and favoured a more sophisticated diplomacy. Diplomatic immunity, even of the herald in war, became a more entrenched norm, and resident missions began to emerge, although employing a local citizen. Such a person was known as a *proxenos*. In medieval Europe, the development of diplomacy was led first by Byzantium (the Eastern Roman Empire) and then, especially, by Venice, which set new standards of honesty and technical proficiency. However, diplomacy remained chiefly in the hands of special envoys, limited by time and task.

It was in the Italian city-states system in the late fifteenth century AD, when conditions were particularly favourable to the further development of diplomacy, that the recognizably modern system first made its appearance. The hyper-insecurity of the rich but poorly defended Italian states, induced by the repeated invasions of their peninsula by the ultramontane powers after 1494, made essential a diplomacy that was both continuous and conducted with less fanfare. Fortunately, no great barriers were presented by language or religion, and although communications still depended on horsed messengers, the relatively short distances between city states made this less of a drawback. It is not surprising, therefore, that it was this period that saw the birth of the genuine resident embassy; that is to say, a resident mission headed by a citizen of the prince or republic whose interests it served. This Italian system, the spirit and methods of which are captured so well in the despatches of Niccolò Machiavelli, evolved shortly into the French system that, in the middle of the twentieth century, was praised so highly by the British scholar-diplomat Harold Nicolson. This was the first fully developed system of diplomacy and the basis of the modern – essentially bilateral – system (see Chapter 8).

In the early twentieth century the French system was modified but not, as some hoped and others feared, transformed. The 'open diplomacy' of *ad hoc* and permanent conferences (notably the League of Nations) was simply grafted onto the existing network of bilateral communications. As for the anti-diplomacy of the Communist regimes in Soviet Russia and subsequently in China, this was relatively short-lived. Why did diplomacy survive these assaults and continue to develop to such a degree and in such an inventive manner that, at the beginning of the twenty-first century, we can speak with some confidence of a world diplomatic system of unprecedented strength? The reason is that the conditions that first encouraged the development of diplomacy have for some decades obtained perhaps more fully than ever before. These are a balance of power between a plurality of states, mutually impinging interests of an unusually urgent kind, efficient and secure international communication, and relative cultural toleration – the rise of radical Islam notwithstanding.

As already noted, diplomacy is an important means by which states pursue their foreign policies, and in many states these are still shaped in significant degree in a ministry of foreign affairs. Such ministries also have the major responsibility for a state's diplomats serving abroad and for dealing (formally, at any rate) with foreign diplomats at home. It is for this reason that this book begins with the foreign ministry. Following this, it is divided into three parts. Part I considers the art of negotiation, the most important activity of the world diplomatic system *as a whole*. Part II examines the channels through which negotiations, together with the other functions of diplomacy, are pursued when states enjoy normal diplomatic relations. Part III looks at the most important ways in which these are carried on when they do not.

Further reading

Adcock, F. and D. J. Mosley, *Diplomacy in Ancient Greece* (Thames & Hudson: London, 1975): pt 2.

Berridge, G. R. (ed.), *Diplomatic Classics: Selected texts from Commynes to Vattel* (Palgrave Macmillan: Basingstoke, 2004).

Berridge, G. R. and Lorna Lloyd, *The Palgrave Macmillan Dictionary of Diplomacy*, 3rd edn (Palgrave Macmillan: Basingstoke, 2012).

Berridge, G. R., M. Keens-Soper and T. G. Otte (eds), *Diplomatic Theory from Machiavelli to Kissinger* (Palgrave Macmillan: Basingstoke, 2001).

Bull, Hedley and Adam Watson (eds), *The Expansion of International Society* (Clarendon Press: Oxford, 1984).

Cohen, Raymond and Raymond Westbrook (eds), *Amarna Diplomacy: The beginnings of international relations* (Johns Hopkins University Press: Baltimore, MD, 2000).

Dictionary of the Middle Ages, Volume 4 (Scribner's: New York, 1984): chs by Queller and Wozniak.

Durrell, Lawrence, *Esprit de Corps: Sketches from diplomatic life* (Faber and Faber: London, 1957): for light relief.

Frodsham, J. D. (trans. and ed.), *The First Chinese Embassy to the West: The journals of Kuo Sung-T'ao, Liu Hsi-Hung and Chang Te-Yi* (Clarendon Press: Oxford, 1974).

Hamilton, Keith and Richard Langhorne, *The Practice of Diplomacy*, 2nd edn (Routledge: London, 2011): chs 1–4.

Jones, Raymond A., *The British Diplomatic Service, 1815–1914* (Colin Smythe: Gerrards Cross, 1983).

Lanzac, Abel and Christophe Blain, *Weapons of Mass Diplomacy*, trans. from the French by E. Gauvin (SelfMadeHero: London, 2014). A satire on diplomacy in the lead-up to the Iraq War by French author and diplomat Antonin Baudry ('Lanzac' is a pseudonym); it is presented as a comic illustrated by Blain.

Liverani, Mario, *International Relations in the Ancient Near East* (Palgrave: Basingstoke, 2001): intro. and ch. 10.

Mattingly, G., *Renaissance Diplomacy* (Penguin: Harmondsworth, 1965).

Meier, S. A., *The Messenger in the Ancient Semitic World* (Scholars Press: Atlanta, GA, 1988).

Mösslang, M, and T. Riotte (eds), *The Diplomats' World: A cultural history of diplomacy, 1815–1914* (Oxford University Press: Oxford, 2008).

Munn-Rankin, J. M., 'Diplomacy in Western Asia in the early second millennium B.C.', *Iraq*, 1956, Spring 18(1).

Nicolson, Harold, *The Evolution of Diplomatic Method* (Constable: London, 1954).

Peyrefitte, Alain, *The Collision of Two Civilisations: The British expedition to China 1792–4*, trans. from the French by J. Rothschild (Harvill: London, 1993).

Sharp, Paul and Geoffrey Wiseman (eds), *The Diplomatic Corps as an Institution of International Society* (Palgrave Macmillan: Basingstoke, 2007).

Queller, D. E., *The Office of Ambassador in the Middle Ages* (Princeton University Press: Princeton, NJ, 1967).

1
The Foreign Ministry

It is difficult to find a state today that does not have, in addition to a diplomatic service, a ministry dedicated to its administration and direction. This is usually known as the ministry of foreign affairs or, for short, foreign ministry. It is easy to forget that this ministry came relatively late onto the scene. In fact, its appearance in Europe post-dated the arrival of the resident diplomatic mission by nearly three centuries. This chapter will begin by looking briefly at the origins and development of the foreign ministry, and then examine its different roles.

Until the sixteenth century, the individual states of Europe did not concentrate responsibility for foreign affairs in one administrative unit but allocated it between different, infant bureaucracies on a geographical basis. Some of these offices were also responsible for certain domestic matters. This picture began to change under the combined pressure of the multiplying international relationships and thickening networks of resident embassies that were a feature of the seventeenth and eighteenth centuries. The first of these trends increased the possibilities of inconsistency in the formulation and execution of foreign policy, and this demanded more unified direction and better preserved archives. The second trend – foreign policy execution by means of resident missions – increased vastly the quantity of correspondence flowing home. This added the need for attention to methods of communication with the missions, including the creation and renewal of their ciphers. It also meant regard to their staffing and, especially, their financing – including that of their secret intelligence activities, because separate secret service agencies did not appear until very much later (see Chapter 10). All of this demanded better preserved archives as well, not to mention more clerks and messengers. In sum, the rapid increase abroad in what was called 'continuous negotiation' by Cardinal Richelieu, the legendary

5

chief minister of the French King Louis XIII, required not only continuous organization at home but also one bureaucracy, rather than several in competition.

It has often been assumed that it was in France that the first foreign ministry began to emerge when, in 1589, Henry III gave sole responsibility for foreign affairs to one of his secretaries of state, Louis de Revol, an administrative innovation that – after some regression – was confirmed by Richelieu in 1626. But there might well be other candidates, within and beyond Europe, for the title of first foreign ministry. Moreover, the office of the French secretary of state for foreign affairs in Richelieu's time was little more than a personal staff: it was not even an outline version of a modern foreign ministry, with an organized archive and defined bureaucratic structure. This had to wait until the last years of the reign of Louis XIV at the beginning of the eighteenth century (Picavet: 39–40).

Indeed, it was only during the eighteenth century that a recognizably modern foreign ministry became the general rule in Europe, and even then the administrative separation of foreign and domestic business was by no means watertight. Britain came late, having to wait until 1782 for the creation of the Foreign Office. The US Department of State was established shortly after this, in 1789 (Box 1.1). It was the middle of the nineteenth century before China, Japan, and Turkey followed suit.

Box 1.1   'Department of Foreign Affairs' to 'Department of State'

A Department of Foreign Affairs was established by the Continental Congress on 10 January 1781. This title was also initially employed for the foreign ministry of the United States itself under legislation approved by the House and Senate on 21 July 1789 and signed into law by President Washington six days later. In September, the Department was given certain *domestic* duties as well, which subsequently came to include management of the Mint, fulfilling the role of keeper of the Great Seal of the United States, and the taking of the census. No longer charged solely with *foreign* tasks, it was for this reason that, at the same juncture, the department's name was changed to 'Department of State'. Despite surrendering most of its domestic duties in the nineteenth century, the Department found itself stuck with the name.

Even in Europe, however, it was well into the nineteenth century before foreign ministries, which remained small, became bureaucratically sophisticated. By this time, they were divided into different administrative units on the basis either of specialization in a particular function (for example, protocol and treaties), or – more commonly – geographical regions. In addition to the foreign minister, who was its

head = foreign minister → headed by an official w/ great policy influence
high edu. reqs ↔ "upper class"

temporary political head, the typical foreign ministry had by this time also acquired a permanent senior official to oversee its administration. As time wore on, this official also acquired influence over policy, sometimes very great. Entry into the foreign ministry increasingly demanded suitable educational qualifications, although the pool from which recruits came was limited to the upper reaches of the social hierarchy until well into the twentieth century.

opponents
↓

The foreign ministry still had rivals for influence over the formulation and execution of foreign policy in the nineteenth century. Among these were the monarchs or presidents, chancellors or prime ministers, who felt that their positions gave them special prerogatives to dabble in this area, as also the war offices with their nascent intelligence services. Nevertheless, if the foreign ministry had a golden age, this was probably it. It did not last long. Distaste for both commerce and popular meddling in foreign policy was entrenched in most foreign ministries, which were essentially aristocratic in ethos, and this soon put them on the defensive in the following century. World War I itself was also a tremendous blow to their prestige because it seemed to prove the failings of the old diplomacy over which they presided. Much of the growing dissatisfaction with the way ministries such as these were staffed and organized, as well as with the manner in which they conducted their affairs, focused on the administrative (and in some instances social) divisions within the bureaucracy of diplomacy.

Problems

Despite the intimate link between those in the foreign ministry and the diplomats serving abroad, both their work and the social milieux in which they mixed were very different. Persons attracted to the one sphere of activity were not, as a rule, attracted to the other, and they were usually recruited by different methods. Foreign ministry officials had more in common with the civil servants in other government ministries than with their own, glittering diplomats, whom in any case they rarely met and had good grounds for believing looked on them as social inferiors. They also tended to develop different outlooks. American diplomats, who closed ranks in the face of frequent ridicule at home (notably in the Middle and Far West), developed a particularly strong 'fraternal spirit' (Simpson: 3–4). The result was that, except in small states, it became the norm for the two branches of diplomacy – the foreign ministry and its representatives abroad – to be organized separately and have distinct career ladders. Between them there was little if any transfer. It was also usual for the representatives abroad to be themselves divided into separate services, the diplomatic and the consular – and, later on, the commercial as well.

FM & diplo abroad = organized separately / different career ladders
↖ little transfer ↗
also divided into separate services

Box 1.2 Foreign ministries: formal titles making a point, and some metonyms

Most foreign ministries are loosely described as the 'Ministry of Foreign Affairs', but in their formal titles many of them add some words in order to advertise a priority of the moment, acknowledge a recent merger with another ministry, or make some other point. For example, in March 2007 the Austrian ministry was renamed 'Federal Ministry for *European* and International Affairs', which signalled that Vienna did not regard other EU members as foreigners, and, in March 2014, its title was changed again, to 'Federal Ministry for Europe, *Integration* and Foreign Affairs', thereby providing a standing reminder of Austria's enthusiasm for the European project. For analogous reasons, the Senegalese ministry for a time added 'African Union' to a title already signalling a priority: 'Ministry of Foreign Affairs, African Union and Senegalese Abroad'. It is reassuring, if – on the face of it unnecessary – that the word 'Cooperation' should be introduced by so many, as when in 2009 the South African ministry replaced altogether its former title, 'Department of Foreign Affairs' (see below). For short, some foreign ministries are often referred to by the names of buildings or streets with which they are associated (metonyms). The following list illustrates the variety of titles given to foreign ministries at the time of writing (2014), together with some metonyms:

Afghanistan:	*Ministry of Foreign Affairs*
Australia:	*Department of Foreign Affairs and Trade*
Austria:	*Federal Ministry for Europe, Integration, and International Affairs*
Belgium:	*Ministry of Foreign Affairs, Foreign Trade, and Development Cooperation*
Benin:	*Ministry of Foreign Affairs, African Integration, la Francophonie and Beninese Abroad*
Botswana:	*Ministry of Foreign Affairs and International Cooperation*
Brazil:	*Ministry of External Relations ('Itamaraty')*
China, People's Republic of:	*Ministry of Foreign Affairs*
Croatia:	*Ministry of Foreign and European Affairs*
France:	*Ministry of Foreign Affairs and International Development ('Quai d'Orsay')*
India:	*Ministry of External Affairs ('South Block')*
Italy:	*Ministry of Foreign Affairs ('Farnesina')*
Japan:	*Ministry of Foreign Affairs ('Gaimusho')*
Malaysia:	*Ministry of Foreign Affairs ('Wisma Putra')*
Mauritius:	*Ministry of Foreign Affairs, Regional Integration and International Trade*
Senegal:	*Ministry of Foreign Affairs and Senegalese Abroad*
South Africa:	*Department of International Relations and Cooperation*
Spain:	*Ministry of Foreign Affairs and Cooperation*
Syria:	*Ministry of Foreign Affairs and Expatriates*
United Kingdom:	*Foreign and Commonwealth Office ('Foreign Office' or 'FCO')*
United States of America:	*Department of State ('Foggy Bottom')*

The gradual unification during the twentieth century of the bureaucracy of diplomacy, including that of the diplomatic and consular services (see Chapter 9), no doubt played its part in enabling the foreign ministry to resist the later challenge to its position that came from advances in telecommunications. Freedom from the conservative reflexes likely to have been produced by close relationships with powerful domestic interests also assisted the foreign ministry by making it easier to adapt to changing circumstances (Hocking and Spence: 6). There is no doubt, however, that it is the continuing importance of the tasks discharged by the foreign ministry that has ensured its survival as a prominent department of central government in most states. What are they?

Staffing and supporting missions abroad

The efficiency of the *administrative* departments that carry out the numerous tasks falling under this sub-heading is of great importance, not least in foreign ministries where the traditional glitter of the diplomatic career has been tarnished and the loss of experienced staff in mid-career is a constant risk. These tasks include the following:

- Providing the personnel for the state's diplomatic and consular missions abroad, including posts at the permanent headquarters of international organizations. This means not only their recruitment and training, sometimes in a fully-fledged diplomatic academy such as the Rio Branco Institute in Brazil, but also the sensitive job of selecting the right persons for particular posts, which is of special importance in the case of mini-embassies (see pp. 128–9).
- Supporting the diplomats and their families, especially when they find themselves in hardship posts or in the midst of an emergency. Because of the murderous attacks on its embassies in recent decades, the US Department of State has had to devote considerable energy and resources to giving them greater protection, and now even has to have an Office of Casualty Assistance.
- Providing the physical fabric of the missions abroad, which means renting, purchasing, or even constructing suitable buildings; and then providing them with equipment and furnishings, regular maintenance, guards, and secure communications with home.
- Performance measurement of missions against stated objectives, including periodic visits of inspection. The reports that follow such visits are usually valuable, provided they are conducted by persons

commanding professional respect. The *Semiannual Reports* of the Department of State's Office of Inspector General (OIG), which has a hotline for whistleblowers, are available on the Internet. These are unclassified summaries of detailed individual reports of inspections, although some of the latter – rightly in parts redacted – are also available. Among the most recent is an audit of the emergency action plans for the US missions in Pakistan. By contrast, the *quantitative* performance measurement popular in recent years is generally worse than useless: not only is it unsuited to judging missions' core functions of policy advice and implementation but it also tends to frustrate staff and magnify the importance of their commercial and consular services simply because they are more amenable to measurement (FAC 2011: 9, 31, 48–51).

Policy-making and implementation

The foreign ministry has traditionally had the main role in policy-making, issuing the appropriate instructions to missions, and ensuring that they are carried out. However, communications technology now allows missions to contribute more to policy, and some argue it should be their responsibility alone (Advisory Committee: 68). The foreign ministry should certainly engage its missions abroad in lively dialogue on the bilateral relationships in which they are at the sharp end (Browne: 78), but it is important that it should not surrender too much influence to them. If it does, it risks foreign policy being infected either by localitis, a resident mission's adoption of the host state's point of view, or clientitis, the sacrifice of objective reporting to what some important client in its own metropolis wants to hear, a tendency made more likely by the ease with which missions can now join electronically in debates at home (Smith 2009: 849–51).

It is in regard to policy advice that what are sometimes known as the 'political departments' come in. Most of these are arranged either along geographical or functional lines, although in an acute crisis a special section within the ministry might take over (Box 1.3). *Geographical* departments normally concentrate on regions or individual states of particular importance, while *functional* departments (sometimes called 'subject' or 'thematic' departments) deal typically with high-profile general issues such as climate change, drugs and international crime, human rights, and energy security.

Box 1.3   Crisis management

The foreign ministries of states that have to deal regularly with crises with national security implications tend to have a crisis section that is permanently operational. In the Israeli foreign ministry, for example, this is called the 'Situation Room', while in the US Department of State its name is the 'Operations Center'. Significantly, both are located within the office with overall coordinating functions within their ministry, the Coordination Bureau and the Executive Secretariat respectively. Most states handle crises of this sort by means of temporary arrangements, for which they have more or less precise plans, although increasing numbers have permanent units ready to respond to consular emergencies abroad.

Historically, the geographical departments dominated foreign ministries and so, until relatively recently, had more prestige. Among those in the British Foreign Office, the Eastern Department was for many years before World War I the most prestigious and aristocratic; it covered the Ottoman Empire and its predatory Russian neighbour, and was thus much absorbed with the famous 'Eastern Question' (whether to prop up or carve up the Ottoman Empire). In the US Department of State, an attempt in the 1950s and 1960s to give more prominence to functional departments at the expense of the regional bureaus was made more difficult by personnel distinctions remaining from the pre-Wriston reform era: the functional departments were staffed by civil servants, while the geographical ones were staffed by diplomatic officers (Simpson: 19).

Even issue-oriented functional departments, however, had some historical pedigree. The British Foreign Office's Slave Trade Department, for example, which was its first department of this kind, was created in the early nineteenth century and for many years was actually its largest. Departments such as these concentrate technical expertise and advertise the fact that the foreign ministry is seized with the current international problems of greatest concern. (Hiving off a major function, such as development aid, from the foreign ministry and making it the subject of a separate ministry is an even better way of doing this, but can lead to problems of coordination.) More in harmony than geographical departments with the concept of 'globalization', functional departments now tend to be at least as prominent, and usually more so.

It is, however, highly unlikely that functional departments will replace the geographical departments completely and – except on the part of small, poor states with very limited bilateral ties of any importance – it would be a mistake to pursue this course. Apart from the fact that the disappearance of geographical departments would weaken the case for a separate foreign ministry (since the international sections of 'other government departments' – OGDs – might be regarded as capable of taking over their functional work), there are two main reasons for this. First, the conduct of bilateral relations with an important individual state or region by half a dozen or more functional departments, each with a different global agenda, is hardly likely to be well coordinated. Second, functional departments inevitably have little – if any – of the kind of specialist knowledge of the languages or history of the world's regions essential for judicious policy advice; an internal FCO report laid much of the blame on country ignorance for the failure of British policy in Iran prior to the fall of the Shah in 1979 (Browne: chs 10, 11; FAC 2011: 11, 68–70; *Seventh Report*).

It is chiefly for one or both of these reasons that, in the late 1970s, major reforms in the French foreign ministry restored administrative divisions on geographical lines after decades of advance by the functional principle; that geographical departments still actively jostle functional departments in the FCO; and that the State Department's six regional bureaus remain 'the heart' of its operations, even if they might look 'a mere bump on its impossibly complex and horizontal wiring diagram' (Pope: 20). It is also reassuring that, even among small states, it is not difficult to find foreign ministries where geographical departments are prominent in their structures; Botswana and Mauritius are good examples. With the rise in importance of international organizations, most foreign ministries now have *multilateral* departments as well, some of which also have a geographical focus in so far as they deal with regional bodies such as the African Union (AU).

Some foreign ministries also have departments known by names such as 'intelligence and research' or 'research and analysis'. These specialize in general background research and in assessing the significance of information obtained by secret intelligence agencies (see Chapter 10). Although chiefly a consumer of the product of these agencies, the foreign ministry sometimes plays a key role in its assessment in high-level inter-departmental committees.

If policy is to be well made and implemented properly, the foreign ministry's institutional memory must be in good order. This applies especially to the details of promises made and received in the past, and potential promises that have been long gestating in negotiations. This is why such an important section of even the earliest foreign ministries was their archive (later, 'registry') of correspondence and treaties, as well as maps, reports, internal memoranda, and other important documents.

Before separate foreign ministries were created, such archives were kept by other secretaries of state or palace officials. They even existed in the palaces of the Great Kings of the ancient Near East (Meier: 212). Preserving securely, organizing systematically, and facilitating rapid access to their archives by indexing are key foreign ministry responsibilities. A related task in some foreign ministries is determining carefully what sensitive documents – and parts of sensitive documents – can be released to the public upon application under freedom of information legislation. Many foreign ministries also have a small historians' section that is responsible, among other things, for selecting and publishing periodically hitherto secret documents of historical interest. In America, under the title *Foreign Relations of the United States* (FRUS), these have appeared since 1861.

Since foreign policy should be lawful and, sometimes, be pursued by resort to judicial procedures, and since agreements negotiated by exhausted diplomats need to be scrutinized for sloppy language, internal inconsistencies, and incompatibility with existing agreements, legal advice and support is always necessary – although whether it is taken is another matter. In some states, it has been traditional to provide this from a law ministry (or ministry of justice) serving all government departments. Nevertheless, the predominant pattern is now for a major foreign ministry to have its own legal (or treaties) division, headed by an officer usually known as the legal adviser or, in French-speaking states, *directeur des affaires juridiques*. It is also now more common for the members of this division to be lawyers specializing in this work and not diplomats with a legal education who are rotated between the legal division and general diplomatic work in posts abroad. It is interesting, and perhaps hopeful for the strengthening of international law, that since the end of the 1980s informal meetings of the legal advisers of the foreign ministries of UN member states have been held on a regular basis at the organization's headquarters in New York.

The foreign ministries of the developed states, and a few others, also have a policy planning department. Very much a product of the years following World War II, this was a response to the frequent criticism of unpreparedness when crises erupted and was inspired in part by the planning staffs long-employed by military establishments. It is no accident that the State Department was given its first planning staff when a former soldier, General George C. Marshall, became secretary of state after World War II (Simpson: 23, 79, 85), and that its Quadrennial Diplomacy and Development Review (QDDR) – the first of which was completed at the end of 2010 – is modelled on the Pentagon's Quadrennial Defense Review. The best planning units – in regular contact with outside bodies such as scholarly research institutes – are chiefly concerned with trying to anticipate future problems; identifying the type, quantity, and disposition of the resources needed to meet them; and, in the process, challenging conventional mind-sets. The FCO's planners, like those in the State Department, appear not to look much beyond the medium term of four to five years, although others are more ambitious. Their potential value was acknowledged following the failure of British diplomacy to anticipate the fall of the Shah in 1979. Thus, one proposal made by the secret FCO report to help avoid such embarrassments in the future was that the planning staff should regularly suggest 'improbable scenarios' for political risk countries and challenge the embassy and the geographical department to refute them. This was also one of the report's recommendations accepted by the British ambassador to Iran at the time, Sir Anthony Parsons, who believed that his failure was not one of information but of imagination (Browne: 79, 85). A recent, radical report on Dutch diplomacy maintains that the most important element of the professional expertise of its ministry of *buitenlandse zaken* (BZ) should be its 'ability to predict future developments' (Advisory Committee: 73).

Foreign ministry planners are usually given freedom from current operational preoccupations but are not left so remote from them that they become 'too academic' (Coles: 71, 87–8). With such a strategic brief and supposed to provide independent judgements, it is not surprising that they are usually permitted to work directly under the ministry's executive head. However, it is often difficult to get busy foreign ministers and senior officials, who must inevitably give priority to current events, to focus on discussions of even the medium term, while the operational departments might well be obstructive. Moreover, as one former policy planner has observed, although they always *say* they want 'a strong institutionalized challenge' to their assumptions, 'in reality they prefer a quiet life' (Cowper-Coles 2012: 142). The result is that the policy planners often feel they are wasting their time, which was certainly true of George Kennan. The first director of the State Department's planning staff, he resigned after Dean Acheson, who had replaced Marshall as secretary of state, began to make him feel like a 'court jester' and the operational units began to insist on policy recommendations going up through the 'line of command' (Kennan: 426–7, 465–6). Today's State Department policy planners, who provide 'mostly a speechwriting shop', probably feel the same, although they have only themselves to blame: the first QDDR was at once turgid and other-worldly, 'drew nothing but yawns' in the White House, and is best forgotten (Pope: 39).

The foreign ministry's influence on government policy varies from one state to another. It is usually highest in those with both a constitutional mode of government and long-established foreign ministries with the reputation of being one of the 'great offices of state', as in France and Britain. This is one of the reasons why a major problem faced by Tony Blair (British prime minister from 1997 until 2007) when re-shuffling his cabinets was that everyone wanted to be foreign secretary and, once they had it, wanted to cling on to it 'until the end of time, or at least the end of the government...' (Blair: 270, 340). However, even in such states the foreign ministry is at a permanent disadvantage relative to the military-intelligence complex if acute military insecurity is ingrained, as in Israel.

In the same state, foreign ministry influence can fluctuate markedly over time. One reason for this is the inevitable variation in the degree to which prejudices embedded among officials chime with those of the political leadership. For example, the pro-Indian tendency of the State Department at the time in the early 1970s when – for reasons of China policy – the Nixon White House was 'tilting' to Pakistan reduced further this foreign ministry's influence. Another reason is the equally inevitable variation in the political weight of individual foreign ministers, on the one hand, and the level of experience and interest in foreign affairs of individual leaders, on the other. When the former is great and the latter limited, a perfect surge in foreign ministry influence is to be expected – as in the case of the FCO, following the appointment of William Hague as foreign secretary and David Cameron as prime minister after the British general election in 2010 (Seldon; FAC 2011: 43–4).

Coordination of foreign relations

Despite the foreign ministry's continuing role in foreign policy advice and implementation via its missions abroad, it is rare for it now to have its former authority in the direct, general conduct of foreign relations, which in many cases was far from absolute anyway. What the foreign ministry is now inclined to aspire to instead is a coordinating role in foreign relations.

In all states today the OGDs – notably commerce, finance, transport, environment, the central bank, and, above all, defence – engage in *direct* communication not only with their foreign counterparts, but also with quite different agencies abroad, and do so to an unprecedented degree. Indeed, the extent of this 'direct dial diplomacy' is now so great that the OGDs commonly have their own international sections. As a result, it is no longer practical – or, indeed, advisable – for the foreign ministry to insist that, in order to ensure consistency in foreign policy and prevent foreigners from playing off one ministry against another, it alone should have dealings with them.

Direct dial diplomacy was the result of a growing list of increasingly complex international problems during the twentieth century, the diminishing ability of the generalists in the foreign ministry to master them, and the increasing ease with which domestic ministries could make contact with both counterpart ministries abroad and the multiplying number of interested non-state actors – from multinational corporations to civil society organizations. But this development was by no means as menacing to the foreign ministry as some observers thought and its enemies hoped. This is because direct dial diplomacy threatened the overall coherence of foreign policy. So, too, did other trends: pursuit of the same or related negotiations through multilateral as well as bilateral channels, unofficial as well as official channels, and backchannels as well as front ones. The chaos in the conduct of foreign relations that this promised could only be reduced by some authoritative body charged with *coordinating* the foreign activities of the OGDs: enter the resilient foreign ministry.

It has been noted earlier in this chapter that foreign ministries have had coordination very much in mind in reasserting the geographical principle in their internal administration, but how do they try to promote coordination beyond their own doors? Their strategies include the following:

- retaining control of all external diplomatic and consular missions, and insisting that officials from other ministries attached to them report home via the ambassador;
- placing senior foreign ministry personnel in key positions on any high-level committee specifically charged with the coordination of foreign and national security policy – attached to the office of a head of government, such committees are often known by such titles as 'cabinet office', 'prime minister's office', or 'national security council';
- exploiting similarly the great potential of the lower-level interdepartmental or inter-agency committee focused on a particular aspect of policy;
- securing for the foreign ministry the position of 'lead department' in as many negotiations on global issues as possible, which is not

realistic on financial matters but is in more areas than might be imagined (Woolcock and Bayne: 389, 395; FAC 2011: 52–8);

- requiring written clearance from the foreign minister of other ministries' policies on key questions with an overseas dimension and securing the legal prerogative of vetting all international treaties entered into by them;
- requesting prior notice of any proposed official trip abroad by a senior government employee;
- exchanging staff on a temporary basis with other ministries;
- finally, and most radically, housing key functions under the same ministerial roof. The favoured option here is the foreign ministry's absorption of the ministry dealing with trade, and perhaps with development cooperation (some examples are mentioned in Box 1.2), although this does not solve the problem of coordinating the foreign activities of the remaining OGDs.

Such strategies are by *no means* always successful (Barder: 126–9), especially in the case of the US State Department.

Dealing with foreign diplomats at home

Senior foreign ministry officials periodically find themselves having to respond to a *démarche* on a particular subject made by a foreign ambassador; occasionally, too, foreign ministers will summon a head of mission to listen to a protest of their own. When something of this nature occurs, the foreign ministry is engaged in a function already discussed; namely, policy implementation. However, it has other responsibilities relative to the diplomatic corps resident in its capital.

Well aware of the capacity of diplomats for intrigue, as well as their legitimate role as observers, governments have treated their official guests with suspicion since the inception of resident missions in the second half of the fifteenth century. In some states, notably China in the 100 years or so following the mid-nineteenth century and latterly in Saudi Arabia and North Korea, foreign missions have even been firmly steered to a particular quarter of the capital – the better to keep their activities under close scrutiny, and avoid contamination of the population with degenerate foreign habits and subversive ideas. Today, most states are more relaxed about the political activities and moral character of diplomats but there remains a concern that they will abuse their immunities from the criminal and civil law.

US : Protective Liaison Division

Indeed, this concern has grown since the 1950s, chiefly because the explosion in the number of states since that time has greatly increased both the size of the diplomatic corps and the size and frequency of special missions. Accordingly, all foreign ministries must have either a separate protocol department or one that embraces protocol together with a closely related function. Such departments contain experts in ceremonial and in diplomatic and consular law. Among other things, they serve as bridges between the diplomatic corps and the local community and oversee arrangements for visiting dignitaries. For its part, the Chinese government still takes a particularly close interest in the activities of the diplomatic corps, with a vast Diplomatic Service Bureau affiliated to the foreign ministry, as well as a Protocol Department. Among other things, the bureau provides service staff for the diplomatic and consular missions in Beijing. Old habits also die hard in Russia, where an analogous organization – the Main Administration for Service to the Diplomatic Corps (GlavUpDK) – still survives. In some states, too, the foreign ministry is responsible for assisting in both the physical protection of certain visiting dignitaries and foreign missions. In the United States, for example, special agents in the Protective Liaison Division of the State Department's Bureau of Diplomatic Security are charged with coordinating the protection of all foreign officials and their missions across the country.

Building support at home

For much of the period following World War II, foreign ministries and their diplomatic services were frequently targets of attack from politicians and commissions of inquiry, and persistently sniped at by the tabloid press. It is not difficult to see why: they had acquired reputations for social exclusiveness in recruitment and for high living abroad, and faced a growing challenge to their very *raison d'être*. It was, therefore, an acute weakness that they had no domestic political base on which to fall back for support. Education ministries had teachers, agriculture ministries had farmers, defence ministries had the armed forces – but foreign ministries had only foreigners, a political base worse than useless.

The foreign ministries in many countries belatedly responded to this situation with some success. They now nurture their national media at least as carefully as they cosset foreign correspondents in the capital, and actively cultivate parliamentarians and domestic interests.

They stress the fact that their officers abroad are the country's 'first line of defence', and cost only a fraction of the military's budget. They

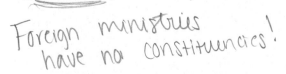

Foreign ministries have no constituencies!

seek popular approval, as well as greater efficiency, by recruiting more women and members of ethnic minorities, and, at least in the West, by flinging open their doors to the representatives of NGOs, academics, and others, even attaching them to conference delegations; a few – from Britain to Mongolia – go so far as to open their doors literally by having 'open days'.

On their websites, foreign ministries advertise their value by providing up-to-date information on foreign travel destinations, including advice on personal safety. These sites also highlight the consular services available to their nationals should they find themselves in need of assistance abroad (see Chapter 9). A logical bureaucratic extension of arrangements of this sort, also much hyped by numerous foreign ministries and particularly poignant in the case of Syria (Box 1.2), is a separate department devoted to the welfare needs of nationals permanently resident abroad, including the facilitation of their return. Foreign ministries also take every opportunity to impress on exporters and agencies seeking inward investment the value of the commercial diplomacy of their overseas missions and the top priority they now give to this (see Chapter 14). And, in the small number of cases where foreign ministries have actually merged with trade ministries, they have not only promoted coordination but also moved directly to capture a key political constituency, namely businessmen.

In short, it is now widely recognized that it is as important for head office to engage in 'outreach' at home as it is for its missions to undertake this abroad.

Summary

In most states today, the foreign ministry must formally share control over the making of foreign policy with other ministries and executive agencies – and to a growing extent with its missions abroad. Nevertheless, it tends to retain significant influence via its broader perspective, geographical expertise, control of the diplomatic service abroad, investment in public diplomacy (discussed in Chapter 13), nurturing of domestic allies, and acceptance by outsiders that it is well positioned to make a major contribution to the coordination of the state's multidimensional international relationships. Most of these relationships issue, from time to time, in the activity of negotiation, which – even narrowly conceived – represents the most important function of diplomacy. It is therefore appropriate to turn next to this subject.

Further reading

Advisory Committee on Modernising the Diplomatic Service, *Modernising Dutch Diplomacy: Progress Report, Final Report* (May 2014) [www].

Anderson, M. S., *The Rise of Modern Diplomacy, 1450–1919* (Longman: London, 1993): 73–80, 110–19.

Browne, N. W., 'British Policy on Iran, 1974–1978' (FCO: ca. 1980): chs 10 and 11 and the rejoinder by Sir Anthony Parsons in the Appendix [www]. This highly influential internal FCO report on the failures of the British embassy in Iran prior to the fall of the Shah in 1979 is available as a downloadable PDF.

Burke, Shannon, 'Office of the Chief of Protocol: Following protocol is this office's charter', *State Magazine*, January, 1999 [www].

Cowper-Coles, Sherard, *Ever the Diplomat: Confessions of a Foreign Office mandarin* (HarperPress: London, 2012): chs 4 (includes his time in policy planning), 13.

FAC, 'The Role of the FCO in UK Government', Seventh Report of Session 2010–12, Volume I, 12 May 2011, HC 665 [www]. See also the government's response at 'Seventh Report...' lower down this list.

FCO Historians, 'Slavery in Diplomacy: The Foreign Office and the suppression of the transatlantic slave trade', *History Note*, 17 [www].

Fitzmaurice, Gerald G., 'Legal advisers and foreign affairs', *American Journal of International Law*, 59, 1965: 72–86.

Fitzmaurice, Gerald G., 'Legal advisers and international organizations', *American Journal of International Law*, 62, 1968: 114–27.

Gates, Robert M., *Duty: Memoirs of a Secretary at War* (Knopf: New York, 2014): on Hillary Clinton as secretary of state.

Kennan, George E, *Memoirs, 1925–1950* (Hutchinson: London, 1967): 325–7, 426–7, 465–6: on formation of the policy planning staff in the State Department.

Kissinger, Henry A., *Years of Upheaval* (Weidenfeld & Nicolson, and Michael Joseph: London, 1982): 432–49: on the Department of State and the Foreign Service.

Kurbalija, Jovan (ed.), *Knowledge and Diplomacy* (DiploFoundation: Malta, 1999): ch. by Keith Hamilton.

Neilson, Keith and T. G. Otte, *The Permanent Under-Secretary for Foreign Affairs, 1854–1946* (Routledge: New York, 2009).

OIG, US Department of State [www]: an exceptionally valuable site.

Pope, Laurence, *The Demilitarization of American Diplomacy: Two cheers for striped pants* (Palgrave Macmillan: Basingstoke, 2014): chs 2–3.

Rana, Kishan S., *21st Century Diplomacy: A practitioner's guide* (Continuum: London, 2011): ch. 6.

Rana, Kishan S., *Asian Diplomacy: The foreign ministries of China, India, Japan, Singapore and Thailand* (DiploFoundation: Malta, 2007).

Rice, Condoleezza, *No Higher Honor: A memoir of my years in Washington* (Crown: New York, 2011): ch. 21: interesting reflections on the State Department, including policy planning; previously National Security Advisor, Rice was Secretary of State, 2005–9.

Seldon, Anthony, 'Power returns to the Foreign Office', *The House Magazine*, July 2013.

Seventh Report from the Foreign Affairs Committee Session 2010–12. The Role of the FCO in UK Government. Response of the Secretary of State for Foreign and Commonwealth Affairs, July 2011, Cm 8125 [www].

Many foreign ministries have their own websites, most of which provide at least a list of the different departments (sometimes even an 'organigram'), while a few go so far as to give a detailed history of the ministry. In the last regard, the website of the Canadian foreign ministry is outstanding. The back copies of *State Magazine*, available via the US State Department's website, are also useful.

Part I
The Art of Negotiation

Introduction to Part I

In international politics, negotiation consists of discussion between officially designated representatives with the object of achieving the formal agreement of their governments to a way forward on an issue that has come up in their relations. Negotiation, as noted in the Introduction to this book, is only one of the functions of diplomacy and, in some situations, not the most urgent; in traditional diplomacy via resident missions, neither is it the activity to which most time is now generally devoted. (Although when diplomats 'lobby' some agency of the state to which they are accredited, the only differences from negotiation are that the dialogue is configured differently and successes are not formally registered.) Nevertheless, negotiation remains the most *important* function of diplomacy. This is, in part, because the diplomatic system now encompasses considerably more than the work of resident missions, and because negotiation becomes more and more its operational focus as we move into the realms of multilateral diplomacy, summitry, and that other growth sector of the world diplomatic system – mediation. Furthermore, it hardly needs labouring that it is the process of negotiation that grapples directly with the most threatening problems, whether they be economic dislocation, environmental catastrophe, global financial meltdown, or – as at the time of writing – brutal civil wars generating millions of refugees and internally displaced persons. It is because negotiation is the most important function of diplomacy that it is to this that Part I of this book is devoted.

Students of negotiations, notably Zartman and Berman, divide them into three distinct stages: those concerned with prenegotiations, formula, and details. The first two chapters of Part I hinge on these distinctions, Chapter 2 dealing with prenegotiations and Chapter 3 with the formula and details stages together – 'around-the-table' negotiations (Saunders).

25

The characteristics of each stage are analysed, including their characteristic difficulties. However, two cautions must at once be registered. First, the concept of sequential stages of negotiation is an analytical construct: in reality, not only do the stages usually overlap but, sometimes, the difficulties of a particular stage are so acute that return to an earlier stage is unavoidable ('back-tracking'). Second, the notion of three-stage negotiations has developed principally out of analysis of talks on issues where the stakes are high, typically between recently or still warring parties; in negotiations between friendly states on matters of relatively low importance the prenegotiations stage will often present few problems and might barely be noticeable at all.

Following discussion of the stages of negotiations, Chapter 4 considers the various devices whereby their momentum might be preserved or – if lost – regained. In Chapter 5, an examination will be found of the different ways in which negotiated agreements are presented to the world and why different situations demand that agreements be differently 'packaged'. Part I concludes with a chapter dealing with the question of how agreements are best followed up in order to ensure that their provisions are actually implemented without the need for recourse to law or force.

Since high-stakes negotiations are of greatest interest and, by definition, most consequential, it is these that are principally in mind throughout this part of the book.

2
Prenegotiations

[handwritten: 1st stage of negotiations
> agree to agenda & procedures for tackling it
> bilateral: informal, not public
> multilateral: formal, public]

Prenegotiations, despite their misleading name, are the first stage of negotiations. Also commonly referred to as 'preliminaries' or 'talks about talks', their job is to establish that substantive, around-the-table negotiations are worthwhile, and then to agree the agenda and the necessary procedures for tackling it. In bilateral relationships, these discussions are usually informal and well out of the public gaze. However, in multilateral diplomacy, where the parties are more numerous and procedure is more complex, a good part of the prenegotiations might be both formal and well advertised. For example, the substantive stage of the Conference on Security and Cooperation in Europe, which had 35 participating states and culminated in the Helsinki Final Act in 1975, was preceded by nine months of preparatory talks that produced a document containing their recommendations (Alexander: 29–34).

Whether formal or informal, public or well hidden, prenegotiations are often far more important and far more difficult than is usually supposed. This is especially true in tense relationships, where prenegotiations are always fragile. This chapter considers, in turn, each of the chief tasks confronting the negotiators in this stage.

Agreeing the need to negotiate

States sometimes engage in prenegotiations, and even substantive negotiations, merely in order to buy time or obtain a good press for being thought accommodating. This is why a party fearing it might fall victim to such procrastination, and also nervous about its hard-liners, often insists on 'preconditions' – key concessions from the other side as a condition for sitting down to substantive talks (Pillar); this has long been a prominent feature of the relations between Israel and its

[handwritten: preconditions - key concessions from the other side as a condition for prenegotiations]

Stalemates = negotiations

3rd parties can create stalemates

Arab rivals. But sometimes even the party most sceptical about the real commitment of the other to talks feels compelled to consider negotiations 'without preconditions,' as the Syrian 'National Coalition' (after many desertions) eventually did, notably by dropping its insistence that President Bashar al-Assad step down before it would agree to turn up for 'Geneva II' in January 2014.

It is, unfortunately, an unusual situation in which the parties to a conflict are *equally* convinced that a stalemate exists or, in other words, that each has a veto over the outcome preferred by the other. It is also an unusual situation in which, even if there is widespread acceptance of a stalemate, all are *equally* agreed that negotiation is the only way forward. One party might believe that time is on its side. This could be because of some anticipated technical or scientific development it hopes will tip the balance of military power in its favour, or because it looks forward to the possibility that more dovish politicians might take over the leadership of its rival. Even if there is widespread agreement that the time is ripe for a negotiated settlement, it is also an unusual situation in which all are *equally* prepared to acknowledge this – suing for peace, after all, is usually a sign of weakness – or, if they are so prepared, *equally* able to devote the time and resources needed to launch a negotiation.

It should not be surprising, therefore, that establishing that negotiations are worthwhile is often a complicated and delicate matter, 'in many cases…more complicated, time-consuming, and difficult than reaching agreement once negotiations have begun' (Saunders: 249). For instance, because establishing the need for negotiations rests fundamentally on establishing that a stalemate exists, any party to whom suspicions of weakness attach might feel compelled to raise the temperature of the conflict while simultaneously probing the possibility of talks. Third parties might be calling for gestures of goodwill, but stepping up the pressure will safeguard the balance of power with its rival and offer protection against domestic hard-liners. If, on the other hand, powerful third parties are positioning themselves to act as mediators (see Chapter 17), they might be able – for example, by regulating the flow of arms to the rivals – to engineer a stalemate.

In bitter conflicts where the stakes are high, as in that between the Indians and the Pakistanis over Kashmir, acceptance of a stalemate nearly always takes a long time. When the issues concern core values and perhaps even survival itself, there will be enormous reluctance to accept that another party has the ability to block achievement of one's aspirations or permanently threaten an otherwise satisfactory status quo. Acceptance of a stalemate in such circumstances requires repeated

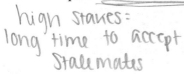
high stakes = long time to accept stalemates

demonstrations of power and resolve by both parties. In the Arab–Israeli conflict, it took four wars (five, including the War of Attrition from 1967 until 1970) before Egypt made peace with Israel, in 1979 – and even then it required the assistance of sustained top-level American mediation and the application of heavy pressure on both sides. It was a further 14 years before the Palestine Liberation Organization (PLO) and Israel reached out for the olive branch. Acceptance of a stalemate might also require each party to lobby the allies of the other because, if these powers concede that there is a stalemate, this is more likely to be accepted by the parties themselves.

If, ultimately, existence of a stalemate is accepted, the parties next have to acknowledge the possibility that a negotiated settlement (although not *any* negotiated settlement) could be better for all concerned than continuing with things as they are. This is, perhaps, the true beginning of prenegotiations. Through direct or indirect contacts between rivals, and through propaganda directed at allies and domestic constituencies, this means conveying three messages:

- that the parties have important interests in common – for example, avoiding nuclear war – as well as interests that divide them;
- that disaster will be inescapable if negotiations are not grasped; and
- that there is a possible solution – this might involve the suggestion that negotiation of the dispute in question be linked to another in which the parties are also on opposite sides, thus increasing the scope for trade-offs.

Indeed, encouraging the belief that negotiations are at any rate worth a try means floating a formula or framework for a settlement. This will have to give something to both sides and, at the least, suggest that enlisting intelligence, imagination, and empathy – that is to say, diplomacy – might be able to produce a solution. It will also have to be fairly vague because a vague formula avoids giving hostages to fortune in a world in which circumstances are constantly changing. Such a formula is also meat and drink to that ubiquitous individual, the wishful thinker; and, at this early stage, when nothing that will help to launch the negotiations can be spurned, the wishful thinker is the negotiator's ally.

When parties to a conflict start to explore the possibility of a negotiated settlement, they do not do this in a political vacuum. A variety of circumstances, at home and abroad, will affect the likelihood that negotiations will be launched successfully. To begin with, it is necessary for the leadership on both sides to be domestically secure. This will give them the confidence that they will be able to ride out any charge that they are proposing to 'sell out' to the enemy. In democracies (even of an imperfect kind), this consideration argues for rapid movement after elections, when a new government can take unpopular action in the reasonable expectation that the voters will either have forgotten or secured compensating blessings by the time they are next able to cast their ballots. Thus, American president Jimmy Carter moved as fast as possible on the Arab–Israeli front after his inauguration in January 1977 because he knew that the kind of settlement he had in mind would cause anguish to the powerful pro-Israel lobby in the United States. Similarly, following his impressive election victory in June 2013, Iranian president Hassan Rouhani injected energy into prenegotiations with the United States on the nuclear question, which had commenced secretly in Oman in March 2013 but then stuttered (Rozen). In autocracies, domestic hard-line opponents have to be dealt with in some other way before negotiations – at least, substantive negotiations – can be launched. Lin Piao, the pro-Soviet minister of defence in the People's Republic of China (PRC) who appears to have opposed any *rapprochement* between Peking and Washington, died in a mysterious air crash in early 1972 (MacMillan: 202–3).

It is a further advantage to the leadership of parties contemplating negotiations if they have a record of hostility towards the other side. Coming from such a background, they are well placed to defend themselves against any charge that they are moved by secret sympathies for the enemy or an inadequate grasp of their own national or ideological priorities; and they are therefore suitably positioned to hold their own conservatives in line. So it was that the reputation for fierce anti-Communism of US President Richard Nixon was a great asset to him in the early 1970s. This was because he had come to the conclusion that it was necessary to make friends with the PRC, improve relations with the Soviet Union, return Okinawa to Japan, and dump South Vietnam – all policies that were anathema to American conservatives. Another leader whose superhawk reputation stood him in good stead when it came to making peace with his enemy was the Israeli prime minister Menachem Begin. Begin, who headed the Likud coalition that triumphed in the elections in mid-1977, was a former leader of the Jewish underground movement, the Irgun, and leader of its political successor, the Herut Party. Herut had a reputation for extremism and Begin's name was traditionally linked to the policy of absolute refusal to surrender territory to the Arabs – 'not one inch' (Weizman: 36–7). This reputation helped him to carry the Israeli parliament, the Knesset, through the negotiations from 1977 to early 1979 that produced the surrender of Sinai to Egypt and an agreement on the West Bank that to many Israeli hard-liners looked like the thin end of the wedge of a future Palestinian state.

Finally, it is worth noting that prenegotiations are most likely to make progress if incidents causing public alarm are avoided. A tragic example is provided by the terrorist attacks on Mumbai on 26 November 2008, which were blamed by India on groups operating in Pakistan and brought talks on improving relations between the weak governments of the two countries to a tense halt. Such occurrences can wreck any stage of negotiations, but prenegotiations are most vulnerable to them. In this stage, relatively little prestige has been tied to a successful outcome, and retreat from negotiations does not generally carry high 'exit costs' (Stein: 482–3). A high premium attaches, therefore, not only to preventing terrorist outrages such as the one in Mumbai, but also to the avoidance of exchanges of fire along any ceasefire line, and the discouragement of hostile popular demonstrations and virulent press campaigns. Such incidents put pressure on leaders to increase their demands; they also give them a pretext, if they want one, to avoid or break off initial contacts with the other party.

⑤ pressure on leaders to increase demand
⑥ pretext to break off contact

Agreeing the agenda

If the need for negotiations is recognized and conditions are propitious, it usually becomes possible to move quickly to discussion of the agenda. This means not only agreeing what will be discussed, but also the order in which the agreed items will be taken. However, in an adversary relationship, difficulties often arise because a proposed agenda might be 'prejudicial' rather than 'neutral' (Young 1968: 378–80). And it is for this reason that, especially with groups such as the Taliban, it is inadvisable to rush ahead with an outline of the points for discussion (Kuehn and van Linschoten).

There are three main reasons why agenda *content* can be prejudicial:

① • It might indicate that one party has already conceded a vital point of substance. For example, when the government of El Salvador and the insurgent coalition it faced began to edge towards negotiations at the end of the 1980s, the former wanted the armed forces item on the agenda to be described as their 'modernization' and the latter their 'future'. Agreement to the first would mean acceptance by the insurgents that the government's forces would be retained (even strengthened), while agreement to the second would signify the opposite. Understandably, this provoked 'serious controversy' (de Soto: 363).

Reason that context might be prejudicial: [handwritten]

② [handwritten]

- Agenda content could also hand a propaganda victory to one side. This is possible because agendas are invariably leaked if not publicly acknowledged. Therefore, a party can suggest agenda items it knows will never produce concessions from the other side simply to publicize its own policies. If, for some reason, the victim of this treatment feels bound to permit their discussion, it will have magnified the effects of its rival's propaganda and disturbed its own friends. This is why the United States resisted the suggestion of Saddam Hussein that the Palestinian question, as well as Iraqi occupation of Kuwait, should feature in their talks in late 1990 and early 1991. Had this proposal been accepted, Washington would not only have fuelled Saddam's implausible campaign to present himself as the sword of Palestine, but also have conceded the principle that his aggression entitled him to some reward, thereby completely compromising the American policy of seeking a low Israeli profile in the crisis.

③ [handwritten]

- Finally, agenda content might be prejudicial if left too vague. This can permit formal discussion of an issue despite the initial wish of one party to refuse it. It is, therefore, precisely for a vague agenda that the other will be likely to press.

thus 1st [handwritten in margin]

The *order* of the agenda can also create difficulties. This is because the parties to any negotiation generally approach them in the expectation that they will have to give concessions on some items in order to receive them on others. It is natural for them to demand that the latter should be discussed first. This creates the impression of strength and avoids trouble at home; in addition, it might lead the other side to be generous with its concessions in the hope that this will be reciprocated further down the agenda. Calculations of this sort were evident during important negotiations between the South African government and the shipping companies in the Europe–South Africa trade in late 1965 and early 1966. Until the very end of three series of negotiations covering 33 formal meetings, the government managed to delay discussion of the issue of an increase in freight rates, which was the major item on which it expected to have to *make* concessions to the companies. In the meanwhile, the government won concession after concession on other items, such as the shipment of arms in national flag vessels (Berridge 1987: 102–8).

The significance of the order in which agenda items are taken is reduced if it is possible to make the grant of early concessions conditional on receipt of later ones; this often happens. On the other hand, conditionality cannot obscure the fact that the party concerned is willing, in principle, to make these concessions, or entirely erase the image of weakness created by their early granting. Furthermore, since the principal beneficiary of negotiations on the first items will generally maintain that it has made some concessions on these points as well, it might not always be easy to secure payment later – and, if conditionality is evoked too forcefully, could lead to a charge of bad faith. In general, then, the sequence in which agenda items are taken is unlikely to be a matter of indifference to either party.

Agreeing procedure Final Step

With the agenda settled, the final task in prenegotiations is agreement on procedure. Fortunately, this is assisted by general rules of protocol, which – although having a reputation for pompous formality – have the virtue of making it unnecessary for diplomats to argue afresh about all of the details of procedure each time they meet (Cohen 1987: 142). Often significant among these rules in negotiations, as also in any social events in their wings, are those governing diplomatic precedence – which diplomats are treated most deferentially, and which least. But there still remain at least five procedural questions to resolve in prenegotiations, not necessarily in the following order: secrecy, format, venue, delegations, and timing.

Secrecy

In current usage, 'secret diplomacy' is a vague term and it is, therefore, as well that prenegotiations should clarify what is intended in this regard. It can mean keeping secret all or any of the following: the contents of a negotiation, knowledge that negotiations are going on, the content of any agreement issuing from negotiations, or the fact that any agreement at all has been reached. Keeping the content, and sometimes the fact, of negotiations secret is important chiefly because a successful negotiation means, by definition, that each side has to settle for less than its ideal requirements, which is another way of saying that certain parties – radical supporters of the governments concerned, some other domestic constituency, or a foreign friend – have, in some measure, to be sold out. If such parties are aware of what is afoot at the time, they might well be able, and would certainly try, to sabotage the talks. The degrees and aspects of secrecy required by a negotiation (not forgetting the prenegotiations) are important not only in their own right, but also because they affect other procedural considerations, notably venue.

Format

Will the negotiations be direct or indirect? It is axiomatic that direct, or 'face-to-face', talks will be employed when the parties have normal relations, and in routine matters it might readily be agreed that an embassy will play a leading role. Direct talks between enemies also have many practical advantages. If negotiations between bitter rivals nevertheless need to be indirect, perhaps because of problems of recognition or worries over loss of prestige, who will be the intermediary? Will it have to be a genuine mediator, or will provision of good offices by a third party be sufficient? (On mediation and good offices, see Chapter 17.) Whatever the role of the third party, can the negotiations be made somewhat easier by taking the form of proximity talks, as in the case of the discussions held in Turkey between Israel and Syria that began in 2007? In such talks, an intermediary is employed but the delegations of the principal parties are prepared to base themselves in more or less close proximity to each other, ideally in the same hotel or conference centre. This makes the mediator's job easier.

If more than two parties are to be involved in the talks, will they be conducted by a series of parallel bilateral discussions, a multilateral conference, or some combination of both? Bilateral discussions have in their favour maximum flexibility, speed, and secrecy. On the other hand, they are likely to inspire suspicion among allies that one or other among their number is seeking a separate deal with the rival; they also lack the propaganda value of a big conference. If a combination of bilateral discussion and multilateral conference is preferred, what powers shall the multilateral plenary conference have relative to decisions made in its bilateral subcommittees? Do the latter merely report to the former as a matter of courtesy, or do they give it a veto? If a key player fears it could be in a minority in the plenary, it is highly unlikely that it will agree to the latter course. Choice of format is thus heavily influenced by the degree of urgency attending a negotiation, the state of relations among allies, and the determination of the most powerful or most resolute among the parties as to which format will best suit its own interests. Weaker states generally prefer to negotiate with the more powerful in a multilateral forum, since the environment is more regulated and their chances of forming coalitions are greater. In early 2009, questions of this nature were very much alive in discussions of the method of 'engaging' Iran and North Korea, where the American preference appeared to be bilateral talks under the 'umbrella' of a multilateral framework of regional players (Haass and Indyk: 51). These were an echo of the serious and complicated problems of negotiating format confronting the Middle East diplomacy of US president Jimmy Carter in the late 1970s, which are still worth recalling.

With the drastic decline in Soviet influence in Egypt preceding the Yom Kippur War of 1973, the United States was firmly in the driving seat as far as negotiations to resolve the Arab–Israeli conflict were concerned. And Washington's view was that, while secret bilateral diplomacy was the only format likely to achieve any real breakthrough, this would only happen if the Geneva Conference format (Box 2.1) were to be employed in some way. Among other things, this would symbolize trends toward making peace and put pressure on the radicals to moderate their demands, minimize the chances of the Soviet Union disrupting the process out of pique at being excluded, and, above all, legitimize direct Arab–Israeli contact. In each of these regards, the Geneva Conference had had some degree of success. However, by the time that Carter inherited the mantle of Middle East brokerage in 1977, circumstances had changed.

Box 2.1 The Geneva Conference format for Middle East peace negotiations

This had its immediate origins in the aftermath of the Yom Kippur War, when the UN Security Council called (in Resolution 338) for immediate talks between the Arabs and the Israelis 'aimed at establishing a just and durable peace in the Middle East'. A conference was duly held in Geneva in late December 1973. It had six notable features: it was held under UN auspices (the venue was the UN's European headquarters, and the secretary-general issued the invitations and presided in the conference's opening phase); it was co-chaired by the United States and the Soviet Union; all interested parties were invited (which meant the Israelis sitting down with the Arabs); it consisted chiefly of 'a battery of public speeches', rather than serious secret negotiation (Kissinger 1982: ch. 17); neither superpower would be present in negotiations at the sub-committee level (Quandt: 143); and the plenary conference was to have no right of veto over decisions taken in any subsequent bilateral negotiations. This conference was in direct line of descent from earlier multilateral conferences on regional questions chaired by major powers from opposite sides of the Cold War, and, for that matter, also held in Geneva. These included the Geneva Conference on South-East Asia (1954), which was co-chaired by Britain and the Soviet Union and reconvened in 1961–2 in order to discuss Laos.

Carter's reasons for initially supporting a reconvening of Geneva, albeit after significant progress had been made in bilateral talks, were essentially the same as those of former secretary of state Henry Kissinger. These reasons were: protecting the flank of the moderate Arab states on the Palestinian question (there would be 'Palestinian' representation of some kind at Geneva, as well as representation of all Arab states), advertising the peace process, and limiting the potential of the Soviet Union for trouble-making (Quandt: 118–21, 137–43). However, Egypt had moved much further away from Moscow by 1977 and was worried about the influence that the Geneva format might give it over a settlement. This format, especially if it involved a unified Arab delegation, would also reduce Egypt's flexibility in negotiations with Israel. These considerations were by then the more important for Cairo since the relatively easy steps of military disengagement had by then been achieved, and what was left were the big questions; namely, sovereignty over Sinai and the future of the West Bank, in that order. Geneva might help Egypt but, as it was shaping up, it was more likely to prove a trap. In the event, the delay in reconvening Geneva – caused in part by the difficulty of agreeing on how the Palestinians should be represented – gave Egyptian president Anwar Sadat the pretext for sabotaging this route by making his spectacular journey to Jerusalem in November 1977. After this, the Geneva format was a dead letter, despite the fact that much of the diplomacy of 1977 had been concerned with preparing for it.

Venue

In a friendly bilateral relationship, especially when issues of relatively low importance are coming up for negotiation and the lead is left to an embassy or a special mission supported by an embassy, the selection of venue should present few difficulties. The choice for each is home or away, and a tradition might even have been established as to which capital is normally employed. For example, as with many states with pride in its own diplomats, Britain has usually preferred to negotiate through its own embassies rather than through a foreign embassy in London. This gives it greater assurance that its messages to the foreign government are delivered quickly and securely to the right people, and are not distorted en route. For example, in its negotiations with Turkey, which in any case did not have resident embassies abroad on a regular basis until the early nineteenth century, Anglo-Turkish negotiations were almost always conducted in Constantinople, later in Ankara (Berridge 2009: 34, 210–11, App. 9). In more difficult relationships, however, particularly when the stakes are high, attitudes to venue tend to be different.

In such circumstances, choice of the format of negotiations sometimes goes a long way towards dictating where they will take place. For instance, had the Arab–Israeli talks of the Carter years in fact followed the Geneva Conference format (Box 2.1), it is unlikely to have caused surprise if they had taken place in Geneva. Indeed, the American proposal was that, as in 1973, the UN secretary-general should once more issue the invitations, and there is no suggestion in the public record that an alternative venue was ever seriously considered. In November 1991, when the next international conference on the Middle East – co-chaired by the superpowers and, in most essentials, resembling the 1973 Geneva Conference – actually took place, it did not convene in Geneva but in Madrid. Why is venue often a contentious point in prenegotiations between bitter rivals?

Venue is important because, if a state is able to persuade its rival to send a delegation to its own shores, this will be a great practical convenience. For this reason, it will also suggest that it is the more powerful of the two. In consequence, the travellers will have suffered a loss of face. It is hardly surprising, therefore, in light of the speed and efficiency with which images and other kinds of information can be flashed across the world, that this happens only rarely, and that alternative solutions are the subject of discussion in the prenegotiations stage. In fact, there are three common strategies for getting over this problem: neutral ground, meeting 'halfway', and alternating home venues (rotating them, if there are more than two parties).

Some venues are chosen for negotiations because, either by convention or law, they are neutral ground. This explains the popularity of venues in Switzerland and Austria, both permanently neutral states in international law. Vienna, the capital of Austria, has the added advantage of unique historical association with the development of modern diplomacy, from the Congress of Vienna in 1815 to the UN Conferences on Diplomatic Intercourse and Immunities (1961) and Consular Relations (1963) (see Chapters 8 and 9 respectively). The Hague, which was chosen as the site of the Iran–United States Claims Tribunal in 1981, provides another example. Although the Netherlands is a North Atlantic Treaty Organization (NATO) member, The Hague is home to the International Court of Justice and also the Permanent Court of Arbitration, which, indeed, provided the Iran–United States Claims Tribunal with its first quarters in the city.

Another traditional device for saving face is to choose a venue roughly equidistant between the capitals of the rival states. Since compromise is the essence of diplomacy, it is appropriate, as well as face-saving, if the parties agree to meet somewhere geographically halfway between their own countries. This was another part of the appeal of Vienna during the Cold War, since it is roughly equidistant between Moscow and the capitals of the European members of NATO. And it was the whole of the appeal of Wake Island in the Pacific Ocean as the venue for the highly sensitive and subsequently controversial talks in October 1950 between US President Harry Truman and Douglas MacArthur, a particularly troublesome general. MacArthur was virtually the American 'emperor' of Japan and, therefore, an independent power in his own right. He had not visited the United States since 1938, and Truman had never met him (Miller: 314–20). A state might even be content to forgo neutral ground and meet a rival on the territory of the latter's ally – provided it is halfway between them. Thus, when in 1986 the Soviet leader, Mikhail Gorbachev, proposed a US–Soviet summit 'somewhere halfway' to prepare for the one already arranged in Washington, he mentioned as possibilities either London or Reykjavik, although both Britain and Iceland were NATO members. In the event, they settled on Reykjavik.

Finally, states can avoid any loss of prestige over the issue of venue by agreeing – should there be a need for lengthy negotiations – to alternate between their respective capitals. Since someone has to be the first to travel, however, taking it in turns is a solution that is generally acceptable only after some diplomatic breakthrough and general improvement in relations. There has to be, in other words, reasonable confidence that a sequence will be established, that each will share the benefits of negotiating at home. For example, after the initial superpower summits in the 1950s and early 1960s, which were held on neutral ground (Geneva and Vienna), a rough pattern of alternation was established in the early 1970s (on these serial summits, see Chapter 12). At about the same time, it was agreed that American and Chinese diplomats would meet alternately in their embassies in Warsaw (Berridge 1994: 88). Following the settlement of the Angola/Namibia conflicts in 1988, the venue of the regular meetings of the joint commission created to consolidate the agreement rotated between the capitals of the full members. And this is the procedure adopted for summit meetings of the member states of the EU, the European Council.

Venue, however, is not only of symbolic importance because of its implications for prestige; it might also be of symbolic significance because of the ability of a particular venue to assist one or other of the parties in making some point of propaganda. For example, Israel has generally wanted talks with the Arabs to take place in the Middle East, as was the case with some of the negotiations with Egypt after 1977 and also with the PLO after 1993. One of the reasons for this is that it emphasizes the point that Israel is a legitimate member state of the region, rather than a temporary foreign implant. For a similar reason, among others, South Africa was much more enthusiastic about holding the 1988 talks on Angola and Namibia in Africa rather than in Europe or North America and, as it turned out, Brazzaville and Cairo were the settings for some rounds of the negotiations. To return to the Middle East, it seems likely that one of the reasons why Madrid rather than Geneva was chosen for the 1991 conference was the need to underline, for the benefit of Israel, that this would be in no sense a UN-driven conference. Israel had a general aversion to the UN, which went back to the General Assembly's 'Zionism is a form of racism' resolution of the mid-1970s. But it also disliked the UN's identification with the version of the 'international conference' proposal associated with Saddam Hussein and the PLO at the time of the Gulf War. Madrid was also conveniently placed for the PLO, which was headquartered in Tunis, while the Spanish government was currently enjoying a *rapprochement* with Israel following the establishment of diplomatic relations in 1986 and the constitutional recognition of Judaism in 1990.

Practical considerations, as hinted earlier, are also of importance in influencing preferences for the venue of negotiations. It is generally for these reasons, as well as reasons of prestige, that states prefer their rivals to come to them. In true Middle Kingdom tradition, 'the Chinese unquestionably prefer to negotiate on their own territory as it facilitates their internal communications and decision-making procedures and maximizes their control over the ambiance of a negotiation' (Binnendijk: 9). If states, nevertheless, have to send delegations abroad to negotiate, it is generally an advantage if they do not have to send them too far. Proximity usually facilitates communication with home, and also makes it easier to respond quickly to any sudden developments by flying in more senior personnel or recalling negotiators for consultation. If the venue has to be more remote, it is an advantage if it is in a country where the travellers have a sizeable embassy. This will provide them with local back-up and reliable communication facilities. The force of this point was brought home to the American delegation accompanying President Reagan to the summit with Gorbachev in Reykjavik in October 1986. The US embassy's secure room, or 'bubble', was the smallest ever built and could seat only eight people. At one point, this maximum had already been reached when the President himself turned up. Being closest to the door, the US Arms Control Director, Kenneth Adelman, at once surrendered his chair to his chief. 'I then plopped down on the only square foot of unoccupied floor space,' he reports, 'leaning solidly against the President's legs and with nearly everyone's shoes touching my legs' (Adelman: 46).

Some venues also have air services, conference facilities, hotels, entertainment, and security vastly superior to those available to others. Some also have better climates. The Mozambique capital of Lourenço Marques (now Maputo) was quite rightly rejected as the venue for a major conference on southern African transport in the early 1950s, partly on the grounds that the weather in the chosen month, February, was intolerably hot and humid.

An interesting footnote to the practical implication of venue is illustrated by the Israeli attitude to the negotiations on discrete subjects that it was agreed at Madrid in 1991 should subsequently be held with their Arab rivals. Different venues were proposed for each subject by the Israelis in order to make Arab coordination more difficult, although in the event they failed to achieve this point and all of the 'bilateral tracks' were pursued in Washington (Ashrawi: 153–4).

Delegations

Further points requiring agreement in prenegotiations usually concern the level, composition, and size of delegations. The last aspect is not normally controversial, unless a state proposes to send a delegation so small that it implies lack of seriousness of purpose, or so large that difficult problems of accommodation and security are raised. Level and composition of delegations is, however, another matter.

The level at which talks are held (including who exactly is to be the lead negotiator) is very important because the higher it is the more priority they can be expected to attract and, perhaps, the more rapid progress in them reasonably anticipated. (Sometimes, lower-level talks can be better because it is easier for delegates to throw out ideas 'speaking personally'.) For example, in the 1950s, the South African government, ever anxious to persuade Britain to signal strong commitment to defence talks on Africa, was constantly urging London to conduct negotiations at senior ministerial level. By contrast, the British government, which did not share the enthusiasm of Pretoria for this subject and was also keen to avoid over-identification with its racial policies, was generally adamant that they should be 'written down' to the level of officials.

In some regimes, the line between 'officials' and 'ministers' has little, if any, meaning, although who it is important to have on the other side of the negotiating table will remain fairly obvious. In this respect, the contented report of the Australian Department of Foreign Affairs and Trade on free trade agreement prenegotiations with China in May 2005 is revealing. This chose only to highlight confirmation that 'the Chinese negotiating team will be led by Zhang Xiangchen, an experienced negotiator and Deputy Director General of WTO Affairs in the Chinese Ministry of Commerce' (Australian Government 2005).

The greater ease of foreign travel has weakened the excuse that senior people cannot afford the inconvenience of taking part in a negotiation abroad, and seems to have much reduced interest in level of delegation as an issue in prenegotiations. (The Chinese–Australian free trade area negotiations rotated between Beijing and Canberra and involved large and very mixed delegations.) A marked disparity in status between the states in question is also likely to render the issue less troublesome. Micro-states know that, as a general rule, matters to which they are happy to have their president attend cannot command the personal attention of the leader of a superpower.

Who is to lead delegations might be agreed but problems of composition remain; that is, what departments, factions, named individuals, and so on, are to be included in it. For example, the refusal of Israel to have anything whatever to do with the PLO, together with the Arab insistence that talks on the future of the West Bank and Gaza would be meaningless without it, led to a horrendous wrangle over the question of a Palestinian delegation in 1977. As in the case of the issue of the agenda, this served to illustrate that prenegotiations can, in fact, disguise discussion of the most vital points of substance. The Israeli view was that if the 'so-called' Palestinians were to be represented at all, it should be as part of a Jordanian delegation, since it was a widely held view in Israel that the Palestinians were 'really' Jordanians. If, instead, they had conceded a separate Palestinian delegation, they would have conceded a separate Palestinian identity – and thus, on grounds of national self-determination, the right of the Palestinians to their own state.

Timing

The final procedural question is timing. The issue of whether or not there should be a deadline for concluding the talks – and, if so, what sort it should be – is so important to the question of diplomatic momentum that it is better to leave this discussion until Chapter 4. But when should the negotiations commence? The possibility that favourable circumstances are unlikely to last for ever argues for a prompt start, but pressing for this suggests weakness. Other commitments on the part of key negotiators have to be considered as well, practical arrangements made, and time allowed for the preparation of briefing papers and for appropriate consultations. The more parties are involved and the more sensitive the issues at stake, the longer all of this is likely to take. However, it is unusual today for the timing of the opening of a negotiation to be as difficult as it was for the Congress of Münster and Osnabrück summoned to end the Thirty Years War. This was originally called for 25 March 1642, then put back to the start of July 1643, and did not officially open until 4 December 1644 (Satow: vol. II, 5–6).

The practical difficulties of finding a mutually convenient date for the start of negotiations nevertheless remain considerable in the modern world, even for those that in principle can be planned well ahead. For example, the General Council of the World Trade Organization (WTO) agreed in January 2001 to accept the invitation of the government of Qatar to hold its next ministerial conference at its capital, Doha, in early November. However, the WTO found subsequently that these dates clashed with a summit meeting in Rome of the Food and Agriculture Organization. The government of Qatar then pointed out that it could not host the meeting after 9 November due to the commencement of Ramadan, which would not end until about 16 December, while this – unfortunately for others – was too close to Christmas. As for bringing it forward, there was the problem of the summit of the Asia-Pacific Economic Cooperation forum expected to be held in mid-October in China.

Because of such difficulties in finding a practicable starting date for negotiations, it would be surprising to learn that one that *also* coincides with favourable astrological portents is sometimes sought. However, this cannot be altogether ruled out, since – still alarming to recall – astrology penetrated the White House itself during the Reagan years (Regan). By contrast, there can be more certainty that dates on the calendar that evoke strong memories – good or bad – are taken seriously. Among inauspicious dates, it can safely be assumed that 30 January, the anniversary of 'Bloody Sunday' in 1972, is avoided with great care in the planning of any negotiations touching on Northern Ireland; and that 14 May, the anniversary of the creation of the state of Israel in 1948, is never thought to be a good occasion on which to start negotiations between Palestinians and Israelis.

Summary

In prenegotiations, states and others first have to agree that it may be in their mutual interests to negotiate at all. Having agreed that negotiating might be better than not negotiating, they then have to agree an agenda and all of the multifarious questions that come up under the heading of 'procedure'. This being so, it might be thought surprising that, in tense relationships, states ever get round to substantive negotiations at all. That they do is testimony not only to the remorseless logic of circumstance, but also to the fact that diplomacy is a professionalized activity.

Further reading

Alexander, Michael, *Managing the Cold War: A view from the front line*, ed. and introduced by Keith Hamilton (RUSI: London, 2005): 29–34.

Cohen, R., *Negotiating across Cultures*, 2nd edn (US Institute of Peace Press: Washington, DC, 1997): 67–82.

Cradock, P., *Experiences of China* (John Murray: London, 1994): chs 16–18.

Hampson, Fen Osler, with Michael Hart, *Multilateral Negotiations: Lessons from arms control, trade and the environment* (Johns Hopkins University Press: Baltimore, MD, 1995).

Kazuo, Ogura, 'How the "inscrutables" negotiate with the "inscrutables": Chinese negotiating tactics vis-à-vis the Japanese, *China Quarterly*, 79, September 1979: 535–7, 541–2, on agendas.

Pillar, Paul, 'The preconditions game and talks with Iran', *The National Interest*, 31 January 2012 [www].

Quandt, W. B., *Camp David: Peacemaking and politics* (Brookings Institution: Washington, DC, 1986): chs 3–7.

Rozen, Laura, 'Three days in March: New details on how US, Iran opened direct talks', *Al-Monitor*, 8 January 2014 [www].

Saunders, H., 'We need a larger theory of negotiation: The importance of prenegotiating phases', *Negotiation Journal*, 1, 1985.

Stein, Janice G. (ed.), *Getting to the Table: The process of international prenegotiation* (Johns Hopkins University Press: Baltimore, MD, 1989).

Young, Kenneth T., *Negotiating with the Chinese Communists: The United States experience, 1953–1967* (McGraw-Hill: New York, 1968): ch. 15.

Zartman, I. W. and M. Berman, *The Practical Negotiator* (Yale University Press: New Haven, CT, 1982): ch. 3.

3
'Around-the-Table' Negotiations

If prenegotiations are successfully concluded, the next task for the negotiators is to move into around-the-table mode. This stage is generally
more formal, and there is usually more public awareness of what, in
broad terms, is going on. After wrapping up any outstanding procedural
points, first comes the task of trying to agree on the basic principles of
a settlement: the formula stage. If this is successfully completed, the
details then have to be added. This chapter will begin by looking at the
formula stage and conclude with an examination of the details stage.
The latter is often more difficult, not least because it is the moment of
truth for the negotiators.

The formula stage

For the broad principles of a settlement there are many deliberately
anodyne synonyms, among the more common of which are 'guidelines',
'framework for agreement', and 'set of ideas'. Zartman and Berman prefer
'formula' and, since it is short and clear, so do I. A classic example of a
successful formula was the 'one country, two systems' idea that shaped
the settlement achieved in 1984 between Britain and China over Hong
Kong. This had evolved in the course of Chinese thinking about Taiwan
and was originally resisted by the British, who wanted to retain administrative control of their colony after relinquishing sovereignty. Other
instructive examples of agreed formulas include those on Cyprus and
the Arab–Israeli conflict. The high-level agreements on Cyprus of 1977
and 1979 amounted to a deal in which the Turks would give up some
of the territory seized following their intervention in 1974 provided
the Greeks would admit replacement of the unitary constitution of the

island state by a federal one, thereby granting Turkish Cypriots sovereignty over some of their affairs in a defined geographical zone: the *land for federation* formula. As for the Middle East, in UN Security Council Resolution 242 of November 1967, passed following the Six-Day War, it was agreed that Israeli forces would withdraw 'from territories [not, famously, from *the* territories] occupied in the recent conflict' provided the Arab states would recognize the state of Israel and end the condition of belligerency with it: the *land for peace* formula.

The chief characteristics of a good formula are simplicity, comprehensiveness, balance, and flexibility. Simplicity is important because this makes the formula a straightforward guide for the negotiators to follow. It also lends itself to publicity, and it is often the intention of at least one of the parties to broadcast the formula to the world; this rallies supporters, unnerves rivals, and makes it more difficult for the other side to wriggle out of its undertakings. When, in 1939, the British government was desperate to claim progress in constructing an anti-Axis 'peace front' in the Balkans and the Mediterranean but found itself unable to rush a nervous Turkey into signing up, it persuaded Ankara to agree to an early, joint declaration of the *principles* of Anglo-Turkish solidarity. This produced cheers in the House of Commons and relief in the press (Box 3.1) – although, as it turned out, little else.

Box 3.1   Formula for an Anglo-Turkish Alliance, 12 May 1939

On 12 May 1939, as reported in Hansard, the British prime minister Neville Chamberlain said to applause in the House of Commons:

It is agreed that the two countries will conclude a definitive long-term agreement of a reciprocal character in the interests of their national security. (Cheers.) Pending the completion of the definitive agreement his Majesty's Government and the Turkish Government declare that *in the event of an act of aggression leading to war in the Mediterranean area they would be prepared to cooperate effectively and to lend each other all the aid and assistance in their power*. (Cheers.)' [emphasis added]

This enabled *The Times* to announce on the following day:

DEFENSIVE AGREEMENT WITH TURKEY
A COMMON DECLARATION

———

MUTUAL UNDERTAKINGS IN THE MEDITERRANEAN
LONG-TERM PACT TO FOLLOW

The best formula will also be comprehensive; that is, it will promise solutions to all major points of dispute between the parties. However, this is often not practical politics, and a formula is not vitiated if this is impossible. Some issues might be registered but postponed for later consideration, as was the case with Taiwan following agreement between the PRC and the United States on the wording of their Shanghai Communiqué in February 1972. Others might be fudged if simplicity's price in embarrassment is too high, as with the question of a state for the Palestinian Arabs in the Camp David Accords of September 1978, another well-known formula. Others might be omitted altogether, as with multiple independently targetable re-entry vehicles (MIRVs) in the interim agreement on the limitation of offensive arms produced at the end of the Strategic Arms Limitation Talks (SALT I) in May 1972. Whichever strategy is employed will depend on the priorities of the moment and the nature of the external pressure on the parties. It was, for example, unnecessary for the United States and the Soviet Union to fudge or pretend to have made progress on MIRVs in SALT I since neither party was under overwhelming pressure on this particular score. By contrast, Egyptian leadership of the Arab world turned on whether or not there appeared to be *something* for the Palestinians in the Camp David Accords; in the event, it was not enough.

As for the balance and flexibility of a good formula, this means that it must promise roughly equal gains to all parties when the all-important details are fixed.

How is a good formula obtained?

The nettle of general principle might be grasped immediately by the negotiators once they are seated around the table. This is sometimes described as the 'deductive approach' (Zartman and Berman: 89) and requires little further comment. Going from the general to the particular is the logical way to proceed in negotiations. Alternatively, the nettle of principle can be approached with caution – by stealth, perhaps from its flank, always slowly, and with thickly gloved hands. Sometimes described as the 'inductive approach' (going from the particular to the general), this is more commonly known as step-by-step' diplomacy. The most advertised case of this method was the Middle East diplomacy of Henry Kissinger in the years following the Yom Kippur War of October 1973, but it was not a Kissinger invention. It was, for example, the key tactic of the functionalist – as opposed to the federalist – movement for European integration following the end of World War II (Mitrany). The step-by-step approach is suited to the negotiation of a dispute marked by great complexity and pathological mistrust. In such

[handwritten: a build up of progress]

[handwritten: limited negotiations w/ agenda & uncontroversial items]

circumstances it normally makes sense to begin the negotiations with an agenda limited in scope and restricted to relatively uncontroversial items. This makes the negotiation more manageable, which is especially important if the diplomatic resources of the parties are also limited. Additionally, it permits mistrust to be gradually broken down, builds faith in the efficacy of diplomacy by making early successes more likely, and familiarizes the parties with the procedures involved in dealing with each other. The idea is that, as confidence builds, the more difficult questions can gradually be broached with a greater prospect of success. If the initial negotiation is predicated on the hope that more recalcitrant parties will be drawn in later, the step-by-step approach also has the advantage of establishing precedents. Thus it was Kissinger's hope in 1973 – in the event, justified – that having negotiated a limited disengagement agreement between Israel and Egypt, the Syrians would be emboldened to risk a similar step. *[handwritten: PROBLEMS w/ step by step:]*

The step-by-step approach, however, is not without its problems.

It can mislead by suggesting a relative lack of concern over the bigger questions; it carries the danger of 'paying the whole wallet' for just one item (Zartman and Berman: 178); above all, it takes time. Because it takes time, the favourable circumstances that made launching the negotiations possible might change for the worse and the moment might be lost. There might have been no alternative to employing the step-by-step approach, but this is the risk it carries.

If and when a formula is agreed, states often wish to give maximum publicity to the event, as already indicated. However, if the formula is based on 'linkage' – that is, the trading of concessions in unrelated or only remotely connected issues – such a course of action has its drawbacks, and the negotiations might at this point run into difficulties. (This could have happened earlier if the deal was suspected from the nature of the agreed agenda.) The reason for this is that, while linkage, or negotiating on a broad front, is more likely to break an impasse by increasing the scope for imaginative solutions, it is also offensive to those who believe that issues should be treated on their merits, especially if their interests are harmed in the process without any quid pro quo on their own issue. This is why Kissinger's problems with members of the anti-defence spending lobby were magnified when it became clear, early in the first Nixon administration, that he was contemplating trading US concessions in arms control negotiations for Soviet help in places such as Damascus and Hanoi. The issue of nuclear weapons, they believed, should be dealt with on its merits. It is also why many members of the OAU (now the African Union) were enraged when it became clear, in the early 1980s, that the Americans and the South Africans were insisting on Cuba's departure from Angola as the price for South Africa's withdrawal from Namibia. Cuban troops were in Angola at the invitation of the recognized government, it was argued, whereas the occupation of Namibia was illegal and South Africa was obliged to get out anyway. Nevertheless, in a formula based on linkage, there are winners as well as losers; this helps.

The details stage

Final Stage

If a formula is agreed by the parties to a negotiation, the final stage involves fleshing it out – agreeing the details. This is by no means as simple as it sounds. Indeed, in so far as it is possible to generalize in this matter, the details stage is a strong candidate for the dubious honour of being called the most difficult stage of all. This is well illustrated by the details stage of the negotiations over Iran's nuclear programme (Box 3.2). Why is the details stage often so difficult and why, as a result, do talks often founder here?

Box 3.2   Nuclear talks with Iran: the details stage

Negotiations on Iran's nuclear programme between the government in Tehran and varying combinations of outsiders anxious about the programme's military potential – most recently, the permanent members of the UN Security Council, plus Germany ('P5+1'), not forgetting the International Atomic Energy Agency (IAEA) – have been protracted and fitful. An acceptable formula for a comprehensive settlement of the question had long been well understood; namely, Iran's acceptance of effective methods to guarantee that its nuclear programme would be 'exclusively peaceful', *in return for* the lifting of all UN and other economic sanctions. But among the many 'specifics' that had to be agreed were the *precise* limits on Iran's uranium-enrichment capacity; the *precise* means by which its genuine concerns for national security and legitimate interest in preserving industrial secrecy were to be reconciled with verification methods efficient enough to reassure the P5+1; and the *precise* timetable for the removal of sanctions. Significant progress in these talks was eventually marked when, in November 2013, an agreed 'Joint Plan of Action' was announced in Geneva, but this still had to be followed by three rounds of technical-level talks before implementation of the six-month interim agreement, together with further detailed talks, could commence on 20 January 2014. In the following July, the deadline for a comprehensive agreement had to be extended for a further four months, to 24 November; and then for another seven months to 1 July 2015.

Difficulties

The first reason for difficulty in the details stage is that it is, by definition, complicated. It might not be more complicated than prenegotiations – although it usually is – but it is invariably more complicated than the formula stage. In addition to presenting a difficulty in itself, complexity also means, as a rule, that larger teams of negotiators are required in the details stage; and this produces greater scope for disagreement inside them. It is, for example, a commonplace of American commentary on the detailed Soviet-American arms control talks in the 1970s that the really tough negotiations took place not in Vienna or Helsinki but, rather, between the various agencies of the administration in Washington – so-called 'double-edged diplomacy' (Box 5.3).

Second, it is in the details stage that careful thought has to be given to establishing a common language. This is necessary to avoid misunderstanding, but can be extremely problematical because some definitions serve the interests of some parties better than others. Definitions proved to be a nightmare in the same US–Soviet arms control negotiations, where wrangles over some terms (chiefly concerning categories of weapon) lasted for years. It was, for example, not until 1986 – 16 years after SALT I began in 1969 – that Soviet negotiators abandoned their insistence that 'strategic weapons' were those capable of reaching the territory of a potential adversary irrespective of their location (Adelman: 52). On such a definition, US forward-based systems such as those in Western Europe would be included in any regime to limit 'strategic weapons', while Soviet missiles targeted at Western Europe but unable to reach the United States would not.

Third, because the details stage of negotiation is complicated and time-consuming, and usually requires the participation of specialists, the negotiating teams are normally composed of individuals of lower authority than those involved – or, at any rate, leading – in the negotiations during the formula stage. This often causes further delay because of the greater likelihood that they will need periodically to refer home for guidance, and stall until replies are formulated. In high-profile negotiations, the stickiness of the details stage can be compounded further because government ministers involved in the formula stage, having returned home, will usually find themselves under less pressure from the other side and more from their own constituencies. This might lead to a reversion to a tougher attitude and cause hard-line instructions to be issued to the negotiators saddled with fleshing out the formula. This is precisely what happened after the Camp David formulas had been agreed in the rarefied atmosphere of the American presidential retreat in September 1978 (Quandt: 259). Indeed, it was only after the resumption of top-level participation in the talks, not least by President Carter himself, that at least an Egypt–Israel peace treaty was finally produced five months after the 'framework' had been agreed.

A fourth reason why the details stage is often particularly difficult is that it presents an opportunity to shift the balance of advantage in the agreed formula; and, because of the complexity of this stage, this might not be easy to detect.

Finally, the details stage is the last stage: the moment of truth. What is agreed here has to be acted on; so, if the negotiators get it wrong, they will suffer. When the details stage is concluded, it could mean soldiers surrendering positions in defence of which they have lost brothers, settlers giving up land in which they have sunk roots, exporters abandoning prized markets, or workers losing their livelihoods. As a result, there should be no vagueness and no inconsistencies, and the deal should be defensible at home. Magnanimity is generally at a discount in the details stage of negotiations.

Negotiating strategies

Detailed agreements are negotiated by one of two means, or – more usually – by some combination of both. The first method is to compromise on individual issues; for example, by splitting the difference between the opening demands of the parties on the timetable for a troop withdrawal. This is what happened in regard to the Cuban troops in Angola during the American-brokered negotiations in 1988. The South Africans wanted them out as soon as possible, and had in mind a timetable of months. By contrast, the Marxist government of Angola, anxious to retain the protection afforded by Fidel Castro's 'internationalist military contingent' for as long as possible, was thinking of a timetable for its withdrawal in terms of three or four years. In the end, they compromised on a year and half, which was spelled out in detail in an annex to the agreement. A similar compromise is possible in the Iran nuclear talks, by splitting the difference between the number of centrifuges Tehran wants to retain (tens of thousands) and the number to which the P5+1 wishes to restrict them (the low thousands), but at the time of writing this has not been achieved.

The second method for making concessions is to give the other side more or less what it wants on one issue in return for satisfaction on a

Homan's Theorem

separate one; in principle, this is the same as linkage (p. 47), except that here the issues, while separate, are of the same species. This works best when each party is able to acquire from the other something it considers of greater value than what has to be surrendered in return. This was elaborated by the sociologist George Homans in a work published in 1961, and is thus sometimes known as 'Homans's theorem' (Zartman and Berman: 13–14, 66, 175–6). A simple example would be the exchange of a packet of rich biscuits for a piece of lean steak, where the former was held initially by a meat-loving weight-watcher and the latter by a vegetarian with a sweet tooth.

A variant on Homans's theorem is a deal in which one party seeks to trade something which it values highly but which it knows it is going to have to surrender anyway, irrespective of whether or not it gets a quid pro quo from the other side. In principle, both parties can do this as well. The trick here is to make sure that the other side does not share the same information. This is where liberal democracies are at a severe disadvantage compared with authoritarian regimes, which was a constant lament of Henry Kissinger in the 1970s. Thus, in seeking to trade a US freeze in the deployment of anti-ballistic missiles (ABMs) in return for Soviet limitations on offensive nuclear forces, Kissinger was seriously hampered by the obvious determination of Congress to kill off the ABM programme anyway (Kissinger 1979: 194–210, 534–51). Neither did it help him in his negotiations with the North Vietnamese in Paris that, under even more fierce Congressional pressure, his major trump card – US military power in South Vietnam – was slipping inexorably from his grasp with every fresh public announcement of further troop withdrawals. For similar reasons, it is not surprising that, in 2014, the P5+1 appeared insufficiently impressed by indications that Iran was willing to cooperate in the effort to destroy the so-called 'Islamic State' if, in return, it was offered more concessions in the nuclear talks; for reasons of its own, Iran was already engaged in this struggle anyway. When the other party knows that history is on its side, it has little incentive to pay for 'concessions'.

Should negotiators be accommodating or tough in their general approach? Each has advantages and disadvantages, and, since the circumstances of different negotiations vary so enormously, generalization in this area is a hazardous business. Nevertheless, at the risk of inviting the charge of banality, the following might be ventured:

- First, extremes of flexibility and rigidity are both inconsistent with the logic of negotiation.

- Second, it is usually best to make concessions in one fell swoop. This avoids the impression given by making small ones incrementally that there are always more for the asking.
- Third, major concessions should not be made at the beginning of negotiations, since this leaves little room for later bargaining. This mistake was made by British prime minister Tony Blair when, not long after the attacks on the Twin Towers in September 2001, he effectively committed Britain to join any US-led attack on Iraq *before* securing American agreement to important British 'conditions', among them a serious effort first of all to pursue 'the UN route' to get rid of Saddam Hussein's alleged weapons of mass destruction (WMD): 'We were getting too little in return for our public support,' the British ambassador in Washington complained to London in July 2002 (Meyer 2005: 248).
- Fourth, if points have to be conceded one after another, the impression of weakness might be reduced by exploitation of various tactical expedients. Among these are making the concessions contingent on a final package deal, periodically suspending the talks in order to remind the other party that too much pressure might lead to their collapse, and raising the question of the formula again.
- Fifth, a tough attitude in negotiations is most appropriate to parties confident that they can walk away without major loss, which helps to explain the attitude of the Begin government during the Camp David negotiations. It is equally appropriate to regimes based on religious fanaticism or police terror, because the governments of such states are relatively indifferent to the costs imposed by diplomatic failure on their own people.

Whichever strategy, or combination of them, is adopted for making and seeking concessions will depend on circumstances and the established style of the negotiators. When the negotiators come from different cultural traditions, there can be problems.

Summary

Negotiation is generally a lengthy and laborious process, proceeding through prenegotiations and a formula to the details phase. In each stage, there is a risk of breakdown, although this is probably most acute in the first, because here the exit costs are low, and in the last, because this is the negotiators' moment of truth. The momentum of the negotiations might thus falter, even if both parties in a bilateral negotiation, or a majority of parties in a multilateral negotiation, are serious about making them a success. How diplomatic momentum might be sustained is a serious question, and it is to this that we must next turn.

Further reading

Arms Control Association, 'History of Official Proposals on the Iranian Nuclear Issue', January 2014 [www].

Bellaigue, Christopher de, 'The Politics of Dignity: Why nuclear negotiations with Iran keep failing', The Atlantic, 23 May 2012 [www].

Bellaigue, Christopher de, 'Talk like an Iranian', The Atlantic, 22 August 2012 [www].

Blair, Tony, Evidence of to the Iraq Inquiry, 29 January 2010 [www]: 45–63.

Brahimi, L., 'Conversations with History: Interview with Lakhdar Brahimi' (Institute of International Studies, UC Berkeley: 2005) [www].

Cohen, R., Negotiating across Cultures, 2nd edn (US Institute of Peace Press: Washington, DC, 1997).

Durrell, Lawrence, Bitter Lemons (Faber: London, 1957): 47–74 ('How to Buy a House').

International Atomic Energy Agency, 'IAEA and Iran' [www].

Joint Plan of Action, Geneva, 24 November 2013 [www].

Kazuo, Ogura, 'How the "inscrutables" negotiate with the "inscrutables": Chinese negotiating tactics vis-à-vis the Japanese', China Quarterly, 79, September 1979.

Meyer, Christopher, DC Confidential: The controversial memoirs of Britain's Ambassador to the U.S. at the time of 9/11 and the Iraq War (Weidenfeld & Nicolson: London, 2005): ch. 22.

Quandt, W. R, Camp David: Peacemaking and politics (Brookings: Washington, DC, 1986): chs 8–12.

Ross, Dennis, Statecraft: And how to restore America's standing in the world (Farrar, Straus and Giroux: New York, 2007): chs 8–9.

Solomon, Richard H. and Nigel Quinney, American Negotiating Behavior: Wheeler-dealers, legal eagles, bullies, and preachers (US Institute of Peace: Washington, DC, 2010).

Straw, Jack, Evidence of to the Iraq Inquiry, 21 January 2010 [www]: 31–6, 44–52.

Touval, S., 'Multilateral negotiation: an analytic approach', Negotiation Journal, 5(2), 1989.

Vance, C., Hard Choices: Critical years in America's foreign policy (Simon & Schuster: New York, 1983).

Zartman, I. W. and M. Berman, The Practical Negotiator (Yale University Press: New Haven, CT, 1982), chs 4–6.

4
Diplomatic Momentum

The momentum of a negotiation might falter, even if the parties are serious about proceeding. This was a recurring problem with the Uruguay Round of the General Agreement on Tariffs and Trade (GATT) negotiations, which started in September 1986 and was not finally completed until April 1994. Why might momentum falter? Why is it serious? And what might be done to prevent it?

Some reasons for a loss of momentum, particularly in the difficult details stage of negotiations, have already been mentioned. Among these is the need for frequent reference home on contentious points. But talks can also be slowed down – or even temporarily interrupted – by a host of other factors. For example, the illness of key personnel, the outbreak of disputes within delegations, the re-igniting of bad feeling caused by a serious incident, and a hope that patience will see the replacement of a hard-line by more dovish government and thereby improve the prospects for a settlement – a hope that may or may not be fulfilled.

If there is a lull in the talks, the great danger is that it will drag on and become permanent. This is because an absence of progress can demoralize the negotiators and, just as important, demoralize their supporters. Such a development will also provide the enemies of negotiations with fresh opportunities for sabotage and provide them with further ammunition: 'We told you this approach wouldn't work!' Furthermore, because, in a lull in negotiations, both parties are likely to remain on relatively good behaviour, one or other might conclude that perhaps the status quo is not so bad after all. Finally, and potentially most fatal of all, a lull in the talks permits the attention of key personnel to be drawn to other items on the crowded international agenda. This, at one time, seemed to be the likely fate of the Uruguay Round in early 1991, when the Gulf War literally blew up at just the point when a pre-Christmas crisis left the talks drifting aimlessly and urgently in need of top-level attention. In such circumstances, what can be done to sustain momentum, and to regain it if lost?

One method is to employ the step-by-step approach discussed in the previous chapter. A good example is provided by the Joint Plan of Action on Iran's nuclear programme of November 2013 (Box 3.2). This was an interim agreement, the preamble of which emphasized that it was a 'reciprocal, step-by-step process' on which faith was being placed to achieve the 'final step' of a comprehensive solution. It also made provision for monitoring by a Joint Commission of the parties, as well as the International Atomic Energy Agency, in order to ensure that all the scheduled steps were promptly taken.

If ratification of any initial achievements is contingent on a package deal, the step-by-step approach also gives the negotiators a vested interest in driving the talks towards a final conclusion. After all, they will not normally wish to see their achievements thrown away and have to admit their time has been wasted. This approach, however, is rarely able to maintain momentum unaided, not least because it has a downside: its unavoidable slowness, together with the impression it gives of ducking the main issues, can generate exasperation. It is, then, perhaps the step-by-step approach that is the strategy of negotiation most in need of special assistance in the maintaining of momentum. How can this be provided?

Deadlines

A traditional device is to employ deadlines; that is, calendar dates by which either some partial, interim, or final agreement must be reached. Deadlines must allow sufficient time for the negotiations to be concluded. If they are too tight – especially when a multilateral convention is being negotiated under the lash of a coalition of NGOs and 'like-minded' states – the support of key parties could be lost. This has happened with the treaties banning anti-personnel landmines and establishing the International Criminal Court. But, as well as being realistic, deadlines must also be real: real penalties must be expected to flow from failure to reach agreement by the specified date, including the clear risk that one or more of the parties concerned will have to pay a higher price for a settlement, or that the opportunity for a settlement will slip away altogether. The reality of deadlines, and thus their effectiveness in preserving diplomatic momentum, varies chiefly according to whether they are self-imposed or imposed by events external to the negotiation.

Self-imposed deadlines

Self-imposed deadlines are those agreed by the negotiators themselves, either by forming a best estimate of the time required for a negotiation, or by simply plucking a date from the air. A deadline of the first sort has a good chance of proving realistic, and can also help to keep a negotiation on schedule, especially if its subject is one of wide interest and the deadline has been made known to the public. This is because allowing such a deadline to slip by invites political attacks – from the negotiation's supporters, charging failings on the part of the diplomats; and, more dangerously, from its hard-line opponents, seizing the opportunity to parade the slippage as conclusive evidence of their political naivety. Such were the risks courted by the self-imposed deadline of 20 July 2014 for the conclusion of a comprehensive settlement of the Iranian nuclear question, with the readiness of hard-liners both in Tehran and Washington (and in Israel) to pounce being a particular worry should it be missed – although it was (Box 3.2), and their attacks were shrugged off.

In fact, except in special cases (Box 4.1), self-imposed deadlines rarely carry heavy penalties for being missed. They are, after all, under the control of the negotiating parties and can, therefore, simply be 'extended' if they cannot be achieved. This possibility in regard to the 20 July deadline on the Iran nuclear question was actually written into the Joint Plan of Action on Iran's nuclear programme, although only coyly and indirectly (EU; US Department of State 2014b), and at the end of July it was extended to 24 November 2014; when that was missed, it was extended again. The best deadlines, therefore, are those forced on the negotiators by outside circumstances.

Box 4.1   The Chinese 'deadline' on Hong Kong

A party to a negotiation confident that it has much the stronger hand can announce a deadline without any discussion, and accompany it with the threat to take unilateral action on the issue if a settlement is not reached by this date. In effect, this is an ultimatum, and the weaker party might well conclude that, if it wishes to retain some influence over events, it has no alternative but to adapt to this timetable. An example is provided by the Sino-British negotiations over the restoration of Hong Kong to China. In September 1983, a few months after the start of the negotiations, the PRC government announced that if a settlement were not achieved within a year – that is, by September 1984 – it would simply make known its own decisions on the future of the island. The British fell in with this timetable, and the Joint Declaration on Hong Kong was initialled in the same month. A natural deadline also stimulated progress in these talks: the expiry of the 99-year lease on the so-called 'New Territories' (which comprised 92 per cent of the territory of the colony of Hong Kong) on 30 June 1997 (Cradock: 162, 189–90, 196–7).

External deadlines

There is little doubt that external deadlines (also known as 'natural' or 'practical' deadlines) are usually the most valuable for sustaining diplomatic momentum. These include deadlines imposed by events *outside the control* of the negotiating parties; for example, scheduled elections, the opening of other conferences where the same subject is high on the agenda, the expiry of the negotiating authority of a key party, or the expiry of a ceasefire agreement. Other deadlines of this sort include events that can be cancelled, but only at considerable cost; for instance, summit meetings (discussed in Chapter 12) and even family holidays. It is true that external deadlines might leave insufficient time to perfect an agreement, but an imperfect agreement is usually better than no agreement at all.

Significant natural deadlines are imposed by the US electoral cycle on American diplomacy, especially that in which the president plays a personal role. Only in the first year of the office-holder's maximum of two four-year terms is the president relatively free of the pressure of electoral deadlines and, during these months, much emphasis is inevitably placed on prenegotiations. In the second year, the president begins to look for diplomatic breakthroughs in advance of the mid-term elections for Congress in November. In the third year, it is not long before the White House begins to worry about the effects of its diplomacy on the notoriously protracted nominating process for presidential candidates. And in the fourth year, unless it is the incumbent's second term, there is an inevitable anxiety about the general election in November.

It is, therefore, not altogether accidental that it was just two months before the mid-term elections in 1978 that President Carter devoted 13 days to promoting peace between Israeli leader Menachem Begin and Egyptian leader Anwar Sadat at Camp David. Nor is it accidental that his 'clear priority after Camp David was to conclude the [detailed] treaty negotiations as quickly as possible, literally within days' (Quandt: 260). His sense of urgency was also heightened by an even tighter practical deadline: the ninth Arab League summit, scheduled to meet in Baghdad in late October. For it was feared that the 'moderate' states of Jordan and Saudi Arabia would both come under intense pressure at this event from the 'radical' Arab states to denounce the Camp David Accords, and that this would cause Sadat to lose his nerve. By the beginning of 1979, at which point the details stage of the Egypt–Israel negotiations had still not been completed, Carter was in his third year.

The prospect of a presidential election in the United States can also act as a spur on America's negotiating partners. This is almost inevitable if they expect to get a worse deal from the rival presidential candidate than from the incumbent, and especially if there is a real possibility that the former might win. This was the calculation at work on the Iranians in the negotiations at the beginning of 1981 over the hostages held at the US embassy in Tehran. Apprehensive of the attitude of the new, conservative Republican administration of Ronald Reagan but, at the same time, determined to complete their humiliation of Jimmy Carter, they finally settled on the very day of the new president's inauguration, 20 January 1981.

Symbolic deadlines

Symbolic deadlines include potent anniversaries and the dates of religious festivals. They are a special case of external deadlines because they cannot be shifted, although they are not quite the same because they can usually be bypassed.

The pressure exerted on negotiators by a deadline chosen for its emblematic significance derives from the fact that dates of this sort are ideal pegs on which the mass media is able to hang news items. And, with increasing media attention focused on the negotiations by the approach of such a date, concluding them successfully by this time shows proper respect for the event commemorated, while failure to meet it implies the opposite: the prize is a propaganda victory, the penalty a propaganda defeat.

A good example of such a deadline was the proposal of the Cuban government in May 1988, endorsed by both Washington and Moscow, that the Angola/Namibia negotiations should be completed by 29 September (Crocker 1999: 229). The appeal of this was that it was the tenth anniversary of the passing of UN Security Council Resolution 435 on the arrangements for the independence of then South African-controlled Namibia. Not taking this deadline seriously, therefore, would imply not taking seriously the question of Namibian independence – a 'motherhood' issue (Berridge 1989: 475–6).

The usefulness of a symbolic date as a deadline varies with the importance attached to the event it commemorates, and is significantly reduced if forced by mediators on a party whose own estimation of the event is not as high as that of the others. This was the case with the proposed deadline regarding the Angola/Namibia negotiations. This is because South Africa itself – a key player – could hardly have been expected to shudder at the prospect of being seen to be indifferent to the UN's passing of what was a transparently anti-South African resolution. In the event, at South Africa's suggestion, the deadline for these talks was brought forward to 1 September. Nevertheless, the regularity with which symbolic deadlines are employed in negotiations is testimony to the value attached to them.

Overlapping deadlines

It will be self-evident that the best deadlines of all are those that are at once self-imposed, external, and symbolic. These might be rare, but deadlines that overlap in at least the first two respects are not. Two examples will illustrate these points.

The symbolic significance of the start of the Easter weekend in 1998 as a deadline for the negotiations that produced the Good Friday Agreement on Northern Ireland was itself potent (Box 4.2). However, this was also an external deadline because any agreement would need to be confirmed by referendums and then followed by the election of a new Northern Ireland Assembly. This would take a minimum of two months; so, if a settlement were not to be reached by the middle of April, the whole process could easily fall foul of the North's 'marching season', when community tensions are always raised by sectarian parades; these start every year at Easter and climax in early July. As it turned out, with the deal concluded on 10 April it was possible to hold referendums in both the North and the South in May. The results of these referendums expressed overwhelming popular acceptance of the Good Friday agreement, and it was possible to elect the new assembly in late June.

Box 4.2 The Good Friday Agreement, 1998

The target date of midnight on Thursday 9 April 1998 was deliberately promoted by George Mitchell, the American mediator, for a settlement of the internal conflict in Northern Ireland, in part because it was the start of the Easter holiday. 'As I studied the calendar,' he wrote later, 'Easter weekend leaped out at me. It had historical significance in Ireland. It was an important weekend in Northern Ireland, a religious society' (Mitchell: 143). His deadline did slip, but only by hours: agreement was finally reached at about 5.30 p.m. on 10 April, Good Friday. Not surprisingly, this settlement was immediately dubbed the 'Good Friday Agreement'. Spin doctors were in seventh heaven.

As for the 20 July 2014 deadline for a comprehensive settlement of the Iran nuclear question, this was at once self-imposed *and* roughly coincident with what appears to have been seen as a critical practical deadline: the date when it was estimated that, failing a settlement, Iran might have sufficient weapon-grade uranium to 'break out' and make an atom bomb (Albright and Walron). Furthermore, not far behind was another external deadline: the mid-term elections in early November for the US Congress. These carried the threat (which in fact materialized) that a surge in support for the more anti-Iranian Republicans would add control of the Senate to their control of the House of Representatives, and thereby severely impede the ability of President Obama's Democratic Party administration to make a deal with Tehran.

It often happens that deadlines – overlapping or not – are passed by much larger margins than the one for the negotiations producing the Good Friday Agreement. The Angola/Namibia negotiations were not concluded for almost four months after 1 September 1988, the Egypt–Israel Peace Treaty was still unsigned at the time of the American mid-term elections and the Arab League Summit in early November 1978, and the Uruguay Round plodded on for over three years following December 1990. Nevertheless, it seems reasonable to suggest that, in light of the urgency these deadlines visibly injected into all of these negotiations, in their absence they would have taken even longer and might not have been concluded at all. Even in the Iran nuclear negotiations, real progress had already been made by the time the 20 July 2014 deadline was missed (Sherman) – and more, by general agreement reported in the press, by the point when the next was overshot, on 24 November.

Metaphors of movement

Our conceptual system mediates the manner in which we both think and act, and it is now uncontroversial that this system is fundamentally a metaphorical one.

Metaphors, which are representations of one thing in terms of another (for example, 'time is money'), have their effect by highlighting and organizing certain aspects of our experience while hiding those inconsistent with it (Lakoff and Johnson: 3, 10, 156–8). Moreover, although most of the metaphors that shape the lives of peoples and governments alike do so unconsciously, they can be deliberately chosen and manipulated. 'War' and 'battle' are common metaphors employed by governments to encourage their citizens to 'close ranks' and make exceptional 'sacrifices' in situations that bear no resemblance to real warfare. The 'war on poverty' and the 'battle against climate change' are familiar metaphors that come to mind here. It is hardly surprising, therefore, that metaphors should also be deliberately employed by those seeking to preserve the momentum of negotiations, and that these metaphors should chiefly be metaphors of *movement*.

A common instance of such a metaphor used in negotiations is that of the automobile. Negotiations are often said to be 'driven forward' and thus, by implication, to be capable, like a car, of high speeds and an easy ability to manoeuvre around potholes, bumps, and other obstacles in 'the road' (US Department of State 2013). If they come to a stop despite a 'green light', this is because they have 'stalled', a condition usually caused by the sort of embarrassing incompetence best corrected as soon as possible. In case the drivers of the talks are in any doubt about the direction in which they should be headed, a 'road map' of the sequence in which points should be agreed and implemented is routinely provided. Notable instances of this language are to be found in reference to the Action Group for Syria Final Communiqué of 30 June 2012 – 'a very concrete road map', said US Secretary of State Hillary Clinton (*Al-Jazeera*); and to the Joint Plan of Action on Iran, with which the reader will by now be familiar – 'We have [here] a clear roadmap', said a senior State Department official (US Department of State 2014a).

Even more common in the language of negotiations than the automobile metaphor is the metaphor of the train, perhaps because trains have far fewer opportunities to make detours. If the negotiation is like a train, it will be perilous for all concerned if it does not stay 'on the track' – if, that is to say, it is 'derailed' – which is, in any case, a very rare occurrence. It will also be dangerous for anyone 'to get off' before it 'pulls into the station'; and general exasperation will ensue if the talks get 'shunted into a siding'. The train metaphor is particularly useful because it can cope with lulls in a negotiation: trains, after all, stop in stations – but only briefly. Trains also run to timetables, so the metaphor reinforces the use of deadlines. And only rare and terrible disasters prevent them from eventually arriving at their terminus. Complicated negotiations are also commonly described as 'dual track' or 'multi-track', and negotiations by unofficial bodies and individuals as 'track two' diplomacy (see Chapter 17). 'Back-tracking' is the worst of all sins in negotiations.

The popularity of the train metaphor is not difficult to understand. In the Angola/Namibia negotiations, the Americans used it repeatedly (see the section on 'Publicity' below). And so they appear to have done again in setting up the conference on the Middle East at Madrid in 1991, when James Baker, US Secretary of State at the time, reports telling the Palestinians that 'the train was moving and they'd better not miss it' (Baker: 200).

Metaphors of movement of the kind just described help to prevent loss of momentum in negotiations by stimulating all of the participants, together with their supporters, to believe that they are on something fated to forward motion. In consequence, they are also encouraged to resign themselves to helping it reach its destination. At this point it will be clear, and needs to be emphasized, that implicit in the metaphor of movement is a further metaphor – the *metaphor of the journey* – and that both are, at the same time, *metaphors of collaboration*. A metaphor of movement sometimes used by negotiators that brings out the collaborative aspect particularly well is the 'race against time'. This is a race against one of the sorts of 'deadline' – themselves now revealed as an instance of this metaphor – that were discussed in the previous section. This kind of race is a race in which the parties collaborate against their common enemy, time, rather than one in which they compete against each other. In the negotiation that is like a race against time there are no prizes for 'not finishing' or 'dropping out early'. Obstacles that are met in the negotiation are 'hurdles', and it is the duty of everyone, including those for whom an early shower might, in reality, be the best option, to 'clear' them. Negotiators of countries on the verge of war, as in the case of the United States and Iraq in early 1991, are now generally expected to go 'the extra mile' for peace.

The importance of the metaphor of the *journey* – which has a point of departure and proceeds through stages to its destination – is stressed by Lakoff and Johnson (89–91). It is true that they use it as an example of a metaphor of argument rather than negotiation, but negotiation is no more than a special variant of this. The production by the US Department of State's metaphor machine of the 'road map' metaphor, an obvious instance of the metaphor of the journey, has already been noted. There is, however, another instance – one that is far more important – as demonstrated by the fact that it is the commanding concept of Part I of this book and, so far, has been taken for granted. This is the concept of 'stages of negotiation', and the related metaphor – also noted by Lakoff and Johnson (90) – of 'step-by-step' diplomacy.

In sum, metaphors of movement, especially those that imply the need for collaboration on a shared journey, are a common device employed by those anxious to preserve the momentum of a negotiation. The extent of their effectiveness in different situations must remain largely speculative, but the revelations of linguistic philosophy and the evidence of the repeated use of these metaphors in negotiations suggest that two conclusions are reasonable. The first is that the influence of these metaphors will often be considerable, and the second is that it will be most significant for the behaviour of those for whom continued negotiation is risky and for whom, therefore, metaphors of movement are a treacherous stimulus – a true siren call. The potency of such metaphors, especially if picked up, embellished and repeated by the mass media, must be difficult to resist. This brings us naturally to publicity.

Publicity

It is a long-established mantra of commentary on diplomacy that publicity is one of the worst enemies of negotiation; this is often true, and invariably so when an attempt is made to conduct it in the open. However, employed judiciously, publicity *about* a negotiation can also help to move it forward. In addition to implanting and constantly emphasizing appropriate metaphors in the course of official statements and press briefings, as we have seen, it can do this in at least three other ways: first, by flying kites to see how the other side will react; second, by mobilizing popular support for a negotiated solution; and third, by 'talking up the talks'. These are among the reasons why the press office is such an important department of heads of government and their foreign ministries.

Floating formulas or flying kites, both publicly and privately, is of special importance in prenegotiations, as already remarked, but is not confined to this stage. For example, during the 14 weeks of substantive negotiations held on Rhodesia at Lancaster House in London in 1979, the head of News Department at the Foreign Office, Sir Nicholas Fenn, often aired suggestions for the press to report (Dickie: 249). Flying kites openly can expedite negotiations by preparing the public for an eventual settlement. It can perhaps do this even more effectively by permitting negotiators to gain greater insight into the ambitions and anxieties of their interlocutors by noting their reactions when the kites soar upwards. An idea *publicly* accepted – or, at least, not dismissed outright – will be regarded as a serious basis for negotiation, because this will be an indication that the party concerned believes it can sell this at home.

Even authoritarian regimes ignore their own popular opinion at their peril – as the Shah of Iran discovered in the late 1970s – and they are, in any case, almost always anxious to influence foreign opinion. As a result, mobilizing the public in support of important negotiations will be a priority for any government committed to them, especially if they appear to be flagging. This was why the Egyptian leader Anwar Sadat took the dramatic step of journeying to the disputed city of Jerusalem in November 1977 to address the Israeli people directly. It was also why the Carter administration decided, shortly afterwards, to 'mount a public campaign' directed at both American and Israeli opinion to bring pressure to bear on the government of Menachem Begin (Quandt: 162).

Another important way of sustaining momentum in negotiations is to give the public the impression that they are nearer to success than is, in reality, the case. 'Talking up the talks' cannot be done repeatedly, or in circumstances when it is manifestly obvious that success is nowhere in sight. This will result in a loss of public credibility. It can also rebound by angering the delegation of the more recalcitrant party, which might find itself unfairly in hot water with its own supporters. Nevertheless, used sparingly and when clear progress in one or other stage of the negotiations has been made, talking up the talks can prove very useful indeed. It was employed by the British Foreign Secretary Lord Carrington at the Lancaster House talks on Rhodesia (Dickie: 250), by the UN mediator in the Afghanistan talks in the 1980s (Harrison: 35), and also by Chester Crocker in the Angola/Namibia negotiations. Crocker's tactic, like that of the other two negotiators, was to sound optimistic at press briefings once it was clear there was a genuine chance of a breakthrough. Any party then deserting the talks or behaving in an obstructive manner would be the target of attack from the many influential quarters that, in the atmosphere of superpower *rapprochement* and war-weariness then prevailing in southern Africa, favoured a settlement. A report written a few days after the final breakthrough at Geneva, in November 1988, summed up this particular ploy very neatly, as well as highlighting the use of the train metaphor in these negotiations:

> Once a little momentum was achieved, Mr Crocker would drive the talks train faster and faster, briefing journalists on how well negotiations were going and how close to agreement they were. If the participants tried to stop the train or get off they would be seen as wreckers. It failed a few times, but each time Mr Crocker put the train back on the tracks and started again. 'If anyone had got off the train when they arrived in Geneva they would have sprained a wrist,' one US official said after agreement was reached on Tuesday night. 'If anyone tries to get off now they will break both legs.' (*Independent*, 17 November 1988)

Raising the level of the talks

A negotiation can lose momentum because those employed in it lack the authority to grant significant concessions. If this happens, the obvious solution is to insert or reinsert more senior personnel. Raising the level of the talks has the added advantage of once more bringing these decision-makers face to face with the realities of the negotiation, and dilutes the influence on them of their home constituencies. It can also provide an opportunity to bring different people with fresh ideas into the process and, providing it is done publicly, will be symbolically significant: raising the level of the talks will indicate that the parties to the negotiation continue to attach high priority to progress. This increases public expectations of success and, in consequence, the pressure for a settlement.

There are various ways of raising the level of negotiations. It can be done in set-piece fashion. For example, following confirmation at the Leeds Castle conference in July 1978 that no further progress in the Egypt–Israel negotiations could be made at foreign minister level, Jimmy Carter decided to propose a summit at Camp David. And in September 2014, in order to inject fresh energy into their negotiations on defence cooperation, the Indian and Japanese leaders held a summit and also agreed to explore actively the possibility of raising to ministerial level (foreign and defence ministers in the so-called 'two-plus-two' format) the level of their regular defence talks.

A more common method is to inject senior personnel into a negotiation in a more *ad hoc* manner. Thus Carter briefly joined the foreign minister level negotiations held at Blair House in Washington in October 1978 in order to flesh out the details of the Camp David Accords agreed the previous month (Quandt: 272). A further method is to create a second channel at a higher level, and often in a different place, while leaving the lower-level channel untouched. This has the advantage of achieving a division of labour on the agenda while retaining the lower-level channel as an all-purpose fall-back in the event of difficulties. For example, US–North Korea talks began to take place at ministerial level in New York following admission of Pyongyang to the UN in September 1991, but counsellor-level talks continued in Beijing.

Finally, it is important to stress a variation on the latter tactic, namely the 'back channel'. This is a higher channel that, on important issues, *secretly* bypasses the lower or front channel. It was the device employed by Henry Kissinger for arms control discussions in Washington with Soviet ambassador Anatoly Dobrynin while the same subject was under formal negotiation in Helsinki and Vienna. Back channels were also notoriously favoured by PLO leader Yasser Arafat. Their advantages are secrecy, speed, and the avoidance of internal bureaucratic battles. Their disadvantages, however, are also numerous. These include the possibility of overlooking key points, damaging the morale of the front channel negotiators when they find out what is going on, and the related difficulty of getting those excluded from the decision-making to support the implementation of any agreement that emerges.

Summary

The momentum of negotiations might falter for any number of reasons, even though the parties remain committed to progress. This is serious because a slow-down can turn into a lull, and a lull can become a full stop. In order to prevent this, negotiators characteristically resort to self-imposed deadlines, and lean especially on such external ones as are to hand. The holy grail is a conjunction of deadlines. They also employ publicity and metaphors of movement, and raise the level of the talks as a last resort. None of these devices is the best for sustaining or regaining momentum in all circumstances: which is the most suitable turns on the nature of the negotiation concerned, the stage it has reached, the personalities involved, and the nature of the threat to its momentum. Many permutations of these points could be made but it would be an idle exercise: in the end, it is a matter of political judgement.

If an agreement is eventually reached, with or without the assistance of these devices (and it will be a rare agreement that requires none of them), it will still need to be packaged and followed up. It is to these questions that we must now turn.

Further reading

Carter, J., *Keeping Faith: Memoirs of a president* (Bantam Books: New York, 1982): 267–429: on the Egypt–Israel negotiations.

Cradock, P., *Experiences of China* (John Murray: London, 1994): chs 16–20, 23: on the negotiations in 1983–4 for the transfer of Hong Kong to Chinese sovereignty.

de Soto, A., 'Ending violent conflict in El Salvador', in C. A. Crocker, F. O. Hampson, and P. R. Aall (eds), *Herding Cats: Multiparty mediation in a complex world* (United States Institute of Peace Press: Washington, DC, 1999).

Harrison, S., 'Inside the Afghan talks', *Foreign Policy*, 1988.

Hiro, Dilip, 'Will the Iran nuclear deal thrive or wither?' *Yale Global Online*, 21 January 2014 [www].

Lakoff, G. and M. Johnson, *Metaphors We Live By* (University of Chicago Press: Chicago and London, 1980): chs 1–3, 11, 16 and 23.

Mitchell, George J., *Making Peace* (Heinemann: London, 1999): 126–83, on the Good Friday agreement on Northern Ireland.

Moore, Christopher, *The Mediation Process: Practical strategies for resolving conflict*, 2nd edn (Jossey-Bass: San Francisco, 1996): 291–300, on deadlines.

Pinfari, Marco, *Peace Negotiations and Time: Deadline diplomacy in territorial disputes* (Routledge: Abingdon, 2013).

Quandt, W. B., *Camp David: Peacemaking and politics* (Brookings Institution: Washington, DC, 1986): esp. ch. 2, on the US electoral cycle.

Ross, Dennis, *Statecraft: And how to restore America's standing in the world* (Farrar, Straus and Giroux: New York, 2007): 205–7, on deadlines.

Samore, Gary, 'Will Iran strike a nuclear deal by July?' *Politico Magazine*, 2 June 2014 [www].

Solomon, Richard H. and Nigel Quinney, *American Negotiating Behavior: Wheeler-dealers, legal eagles, bullies, and preachers* (US Institute of Peace: Washington, DC, 2010): chs 2–3.

Sullivan, J. G., 'How peace came to El Salvador', *Orbis*, Winter, 1994.

5

Packaging Agreements

Diplomatic agreements vary in form to an almost bewildering degree. They vary in title or style, being given such descriptions as treaty, founding act, final act, protocol, exchange of notes, and even plain 'agreement'. They vary significantly in textual structure, language, whether they are written or oral, and whether or not they are accompanied by side letters. They also vary in whether they are publicized or kept secret. The purpose of this chapter is to explain this variation, and to indicate what form an agreement might take depending on its subject matter and the political needs of its authors.

Some international agreements create international legal obligations, while others do not. Some forms of agreement are better at signalling the importance of their subject matter, while others are better at disguising its significance. Some are simply more convenient to use. And some are better than others at saving the face of any parties obliged to make potentially embarrassing concessions in order to achieve a settlement. The form taken by any particular agreement will depend on what premium is attached to each of these considerations by the parties to the negotiation. It will also depend on the degree of harmony between them on these questions, and – in the absence of harmony – the extent to which concessions on form can be traded for concessions on substance.

International legal obligations at a premium

Perhaps because it is relatively unimportant or because it amounts only to a statement of common objectives, the parties to a negotiation might agree that the subject of their agreement is not appropriate to regulation by international law. If, however, they determine to the contrary, then they must put it in the form of a treaty (Box 5.1).

Box 5.1 What is a 'treaty'?

The term 'treaty' derives from the French word *traiter*, to negotiate. It was defined by the Vienna Convention on the Law of Treaties (1969), which came into force in 1980. This stated that a treaty is 'an international agreement concluded between States in written form and governed by international law, whether embodied in a single instrument or in two or more related instruments and whatever its particular designation.' It is important to add to this that, in order to be 'governed by international law', an agreement must (under Article 102 of the UN Charter) 'as soon as possible be registered with the Secretariat and published by it.' This is because unregistered agreements cannot be invoked before 'any organ of the United Nations', which includes the International Court of Justice (Ware: 1). In short, parties who want their agreement to create international legal obligations must write it out and give a copy to the UN; in so doing, they have created a 'treaty'. The Vienna Convention on the Law of Treaties between States and International Organizations or between International Organizations (1986) extended the definition of 'treaty' to include international agreements involving international organizations as parties – although, as yet, it has not entered into force.

In view of the widespread cynicism about the effectiveness of international law, why might the parties to a negotiation want to create an agreement entailing international legal obligations? They do this because they know that such obligations are, in fact, honoured far more often than not, even by states with unsavoury reputations (Henkin: 47). This is mainly because the obligations derive from consent; because natural inhibitions to law-breaking exist in the relations between states that do not obtain in the relations between individuals – notably the greater ability of states to defend their interests, and the far greater likelihood that the fact and the authorship of international law-breaking will be detected; and because a reputation for failing to keep agreements will make it extremely difficult to promote policy by means of negotiation in the future (Berridge 1997: 154–7; Bull: ch. 6).

Signalling importance at a premium

Creating a treaty is one thing; *calling* a treaty a 'treaty' is another. In fact, treaties are more often than not called something quite different. A few of these alternative titles were mentioned at the beginning of this chapter; others include act, charter, concordat, convention (now applied to a multilateral treaty with a large number of signatories), covenant, declaration, exchange of correspondence, general agreement, joint communiqué, memorandum of understanding, *modus vivendi*, pact, understanding, and even agreed minutes. Some treaties are, nevertheless, still called treaties, usually when there is a desire to underline the importance of an agreement. This is because of the term's historical association with the international deliberations of rulers or their plenipotentiaries, and because the treaty so-called is presented in an imposing manner, complete with seals as well as signatures (Box 5.2). Agreements on matters of special international significance that have accordingly been styled treaties include the North Atlantic Treaty of 4 April 1949, which created the West's Cold War alliance; the Treaty of Lisbon of 13 December 2007, which amended the previous constitution-making treaties of the EU and, among other things, established the office of 'High Representative of the Union for Foreign Affairs and Security Policy'; and the various Treaties of Accession of new members to the EU. Agreements ending wars are commonly called peace treaties, as in the case of the Treaty of Peace between the Arab Republic of Egypt and the State of Israel of 26 March 1979. And agreements providing all-important guarantees of a territorial or constitutional settlement are invariably called treaties of guarantee. In this case a good example is the Cyprus Guarantee Treaty of 16 August 1960. These, however, are now rare (see Chapter 6).

Box 5.2 The treaty so-called

The treaty so-called usually has the following characteristics:

- Descriptive title
- Preamble, including the names and titles of the High Contracting Parties, the general purpose of the agreement, the names and official designations of the plenipotentiaries, and an affirmation that the latter have produced their full powers, and so on
- Substantive articles, which are numbered I, II, ..., commonly beginning with definitions, and usually leading from the general to the more specific
- Final clauses, which deal with matters such as the extent of application of the treaty, signature, ratification, accession by other parties, entry into force, duration and provision for renewal
- Clause stating 'in witness whereof' the undersigned plenipotentiaries have signed this treaty
- Indication of the place where the treaty is signed, together with the authentic language or languages of the text, and date of signature
- Seals and signatures of the plenipotentiaries

It is important to note, however, that, as the Foreign Relations Committee of the US Senate has complained, trivial agreements are sometimes sent to it for approval as treaties, while much more important ones are classified as 'executive agreements' and, in consequence, withheld. A trivial agreement sent as a treaty was one to regulate shrimp-fishing off the coast of Brazil (Franck and Weisband: 145). The executive branch presumably does this to make the Senate feel that its constitutional prerogatives in foreign policy-making have not been entirely ignored (executive agreements are discussed later in this chapter).

If an agreement is believed by its authors to be of great political importance but is not of such a character as to warrant the creation of legal obligations, its importance cannot be signalled, neither can its binding character be reinforced by calling it a treaty: it is not a treaty. However, precisely because the parties have rejected the possibility of clothing their agreement in international law but remain politically bound by it, as well as deeply attached to the agreement's propaganda value, it is doubly important to dress it in fine attire of a different kind. Hence the use of imposing titles such as Atlantic Charter (1941) and Helsinki Final Act (1975).

Convenience at a premium

Since states today negotiate on so many matters, an international agreement does not have to be of merely routine character for convenience to be an important consideration in dictating its shape. Convenience argues for informal agreements: treaties not styled as 'treaties', or agreements that, because they remain unpublished or are published but announce that their provisions are 'non-binding', are treaties in neither form nor substance. What inconveniences are avoided by packaging an agreement informally?

First, the complexities of formal treaty drafting and its attendant procedures, such as the production of documents certifying that the plenipotentiaries have full powers, are avoided. This is probably of special benefit to smaller and newer foreign ministries, but is also likely to be regarded as an advantage by the overburdened ministries of the bigger powers as well. Not surprisingly, therefore, exchanges of notes or exchanges of letters, which consist simply of a letter from one of the parties spelling out the terms of the agreement and a reply from the other indicating acceptance, are now the most common form of treaty (Roberts 2009: 552).

The second inconvenience that can usually be avoided by informal packaging is ratification of the agreement. This means avoiding the need for confirmation on the part of the negotiators' political masters that they will honour an agreement negotiated and signed on their behalf. Ratification became normal practice when poor communications made it difficult, if not impossible, for there to be any certainty that negotiators had not wilfully or accidentally misinterpreted their instructions, or that their masters had not changed their minds altogether since dispatching them on their diplomatic errand. The revolution in communications virtually removed this problem, although constitutional rules of one sort or another in liberal democracies usually continue to require it (Lantis: 23–9), and executive branches themselves still sometimes favour a form of agreement that demands ratification – perhaps when one has been negotiated against an over-tight external deadline and is thought likely to benefit from time for second thoughts, or when they feel a particular need to impress the foreign party to the agreement with a demonstration of its popular support.

Mostly, however, governments prefer to avoid the need for ratification because, at best, it is likely to cause delay in the entry of an agreement into force and, at worst, risk its outright rejection – the fate of the Lisbon Treaty signed by the Dublin government in December 2007, but rejected by Irish voters in a referendum six months later. (They finally approved it in October 2009.) And this is not a rare occurrence: treaty failure at the ratification stage, notes one scholar who has given close attention to the subject, is today 'surprisingly common' (Lantis: 10). To prevent this, if ratification cannot be avoided, governments need to engage in what has been loosely called 'double-edged diplomacy' (Box 5.3).

Box 5.3 'Double-edged diplomacy'

If a government cannot sidestep ratification, the obvious way for it to handle possible problems with the process is to carry affected domestic interest groups with it in shaping a negotiating position, and then perhaps co-opt some of their most respected representatives into the negotiating team. Such individuals will then find it difficult to object too strenuously to any agreement subsequently brought home for ratification. This has been called 'double-edged diplomacy', although the term is misleading: foreign service officers will enjoy diplomatic privileges and immunity while negotiating an agreement abroad, but not – no doubt to their great regret – while trying to sell it to other departments, lobbyists, and elected representatives at home.

To return to how ratification can be avoided by informal packaging, a common method is to employ the exchange of notes or exchange of letters, already mentioned. This normally enters into force immediately upon signature and so is popular for this reason as well as because it avoids the formal complexities of the treaty so-called. Informal agreements with other titles might, however, also be so framed in order to avoid pressure for ratification.

In the United States, the answer is to create agreements in a form that, *by definition*, do not require ratification, for only 'treaties' need to be ratified by the Senate. Hence, first, the massive resort to 'executive agreements', which are treaties in the meaning of the Vienna Convention (Box 5.1) but are not *called* 'treaties' (Lantis: 29; Ragsdale: 76–7); and, second, the frequent use of non-binding declarations. The latter are typically statements of commonly held principles or objectives, such as the Atlantic Charter, the Helsinki Final Act, and the Joint Plan of Action of November 2013 on Iran's nuclear programme. The last mentioned was regularly described by the Iranians as 'informal' and a 'non-paper'; it also avoided language of legal intent and was unsigned (Ramsey). Such agreements are expected to be politically effective but, invoking no legal obligations, are treaties neither by name nor as defined by the Vienna Convention (Dalton; Glennon: 267–9).

The final inconvenience that can be avoided by packaging agreements informally is unwanted publicity; that is, publicity on delicate matters that stirs up political opponents at home, or presents intelligence gifts to unfriendly parties abroad. To avoid the former, agreements can be published (and, therefore, become binding) but in such informal style as to be unlikely to attract too much attention. A good example is provided by the Anglo-Argentine agreement of 1971 on better communications and movement of persons between the Argentine mainland and the disputed Falkland Islands/Malvinas. This consisted of a cryptically entitled 'joint statement' initialled by delegation heads, later confirmed by a brief exchange of notes (Grenville and Wasserstein: 11, 433–6).

To avoid presenting intelligence gifts to unfriendly states, the parties to a successful negotiation might not only conclude an informal agreement, but also withhold publication. This means that it is not a treaty. But there are circumstances in which international legal obligations are relatively unimportant; for example, in the case of certain kinds of defence agreements between close allies, bound to each other by urgent common interest and strong ties of sentiment. A now well-known example, the full text of which was not made public until 2010, is the British–US Communication Intelligence Agreement of 1946, later known as the

UKUSA Agreement, which provided the basis for the alliance on electronic interception of communications (signals intelligence or SIGINT) between London and Washington (see p. 164). Another example from the same stable is the UK–US Memorandum of Understanding on British participation in the American 'Strategic Defence Initiative'. This was signed in 1985 but, in Britain, revealed in its details only later, and in confidence, to the Defence Select Committee of the House of Commons (Ware: 3).

Saving face at a premium

In politically sensitive negotiations where publicity for any agreement achieved is unavoidable, and even desirable, what excites special interest in its packaging is the issue of 'face' – reputation for strength and honourable behaviour. This means the necessity to save from excessive embarrassment those parties whose concessions would otherwise make them vulnerable to the wrath of their supporters. Face is a particularly important consideration in shame cultures, such as those of the Arab Middle East (Cohen 1997: 183).

Where face is a vital issue, the composition and structure, as well as the title of any agreement, might not only be an important, but also a controversial element in a negotiation. It will be important because some kinds of packaging will be better than others at disguising the concessions that have had to be made. It is also likely to be controversial because what one side wants to disguise, the other will usually wish to highlight. Settlement of the US Embassy hostages crisis in Iran in 1980–1 was helped by using a form of agreement – a declaration by the Algerian mediators – that suggested Ayatollah Khomeini had made his own concessions to the third party rather than to 'the Great Satan' (see Chapter 17; Grenville and Wasserstein: 11). It is fortunate that this was of no great concern to the diabolical United States. In what other ways can agreements be packaged in order to save face, and therefore ease a settlement?

Both languages, or more

Language is fundamental to nationality, so this is something to which diplomatic agreements must be acutely sensitive. This has not always been the case, in part because nationalism is a relatively modern ideology. Until the seventeenth century, most treaties were written in Latin, thereafter in French, and in the twentieth century chiefly in English. However, since the end of World War II it has become much more common for copies of agreements made between parties speaking different languages to be translated into the language of each. Furthermore, as might be imagined – and as was confirmed by the Vienna Convention on the Law of Treaties – each version is typically described as 'equally authentic' or 'equally authoritative'.

The diplomatic advantage of drafting agreements in the language of each party is that it fosters the impression – whether true or not – that negotiated agreements reflect relationships of equality and contain an equal exchange of concessions. After 1945, to take some examples, agreements between the United States and the Soviet Union were written in English and Russian, and, between the United States and South American countries, in English and Spanish. The Paris Peace Accords of 1973, which ended the Vietnam War, were drawn up in English and Vietnamese. The agreement concluded between Cuba and Angola in 1988, which concerned the withdrawal of the forces of the former from the territory of the latter, was written in Spanish and Portuguese.

It should be added, though, that there is a disadvantage to the foregoing norm. This is because an agreement might be vague or loose at certain points and, in the course of its implementation, it may transpire that one interpretation of these points is favoured more by the language of one text than it is by the language of the other. Where there are only two languages, this is a recipe for trouble. It is for this reason that states sometimes wisely decide to have the text of their agreements also drawn up in a third language – usually English – and accept that this shall prevail in the event of a divergence of interpretation between the other two, as in the case of the Hindi and Russian texts of the India–Russia Agreement on Illicit Trafficking in Narcotics and their Precursors signed in Moscow in November 2007. It is even more likely that this arrangement, provision for which was made in the Vienna Convention on the Law of Treaties, will be used in agreements where an English-speaking state has been employed as a mediator. Many agreements, however, have no master text, thereby perhaps signifying the greater importance generally attached to saving face compared with avoiding possible future misunderstandings. To take but one example, the first of the two 'Angola/Namibia Accords', signed in December 1988 – to which South Africa, Cuba, and Angola were each a party – was signed in English, Spanish, and Portuguese versions, 'each language being equally authentic'. No text was nominated as the one to prevail in the event of disagreement.

Small print

Sensitivity to language only deals with the question of face in the most general way, and negotiators must needs turn to other devices when they are confronted with the problem of disguising a sensitive concession in the text of an agreement. Perhaps the most common way of doing this is to say very little about it, tuck it away in some obscure recess, and pad out the rest of the agreement with relatively trivial detail – a tactic that used to be known as 'throwing dust in our faces'. A good example of this can be found in the UN-brokered agreements of 1988 between the Soviet-backed Afghan Communist government and the American-backed Pakistanis, one of the most important provisions of which concerned the withdrawal of Soviet troops from Afghanistan. The Kremlin was extremely sensitive to any suggestion that it was abandoning its clients in Kabul to the ferocious *mujahedin*. As a result, in the three agreements and one declaration that made up what were popularly known as the Geneva Accords on Afghanistan, only two short sentences were devoted to the Soviet troop withdrawal. Furthermore, they were tacked onto the end of a paragraph that gave no signpost at the beginning as to what was to come at the end. And the agreement of which these two sentences were the most pregnant part was padded out, rather in the manner of a 'final act', with a résumé of the history of the negotiations, the titles of the other agreements reached, and general principles of international law (Berridge 1991: 148–51).

Another 'small print' technique for saving face is to place embarrassing concessions in documentary appendages to the main text. These take many forms: side letters, interpretive notes, appendices, additional protocols, and so on. Whatever their title, the point remains to make the concessions binding by putting them in a written, public agreement, but to do so in such a way as to make them less likely to attract attention and easier to play down for those obliged to grant them. Numerous side letters – exchanges of correspondence which are, figuratively speaking, placed at the side of the main documents – were published to accompany the two main agreements in the Camp David Accords of September 1978 and the Egypt–Israel Peace Treaty of the following March. While most of these served purposes other than face-saving, some were drafted for precisely this reason. These included the anodyne restatement of existing positions on the incendiary question of the status of Jerusalem. The Egyptians wanted the matter dealt with in side letters to obscure the fact that they had made no progress on the issue, while the Israelis happily concurred to hide the fact that they had been prepared to talk about it at all (Carter: 395, 397–9; Vance: 225–6). The Israelis even persuaded the Americans not to restate the substance of their own position on East Jerusalem, which was that it was occupied territory. Instead, they merely stated in their own letter that their position remained that outlined in statements by two former American ambassadors to the United Nations (Quandt: 252).

Tucking sensitive matters away in documentary appendages to the main agreement also has disadvantages. First, in a complex and tense negotiation under great pressure of time, there is more chance of a slip-up. For example, in September 1978 the Americans failed to secure unambiguous written Israeli agreement to a freeze on new settlements in the West Bank and Gaza until the autonomy negotiations had been concluded, which proved to be a serious oversight. It is inconceivable that this could have occurred had this issue been addressed in the general framework accord, rather than by means of a side letter which, as it turned out, the Israelis never signed (Vance: 228). Second, it can subsequently be claimed that ancillary documents do not have the same value as the main text of an agreement. This is what Israeli premier Menachem Begin alleged of the side letter of 17 September 1978 from Sadat to Carter. This was the one in which the Egyptian president indicated his readiness to negotiate on the West Bank and Gaza on behalf of the Palestinians should the Jordanians refuse to assume this responsibility. Begin hoped to persuade the Americans that there was no point in discussing the West Bank at all if Jordan refused to take part (Quandt: 299, 386–7). Naturally enough, Irish republicans also refused to admit that the side letter hurriedly written by British Prime Minister Tony Blair to the Ulster Unionist leader David Trimble (which contained assurances about the British attitude permitting the Unionists, at the last minute, to sign up to the Good Friday agreement) was part of that agreement at all.

Euphemisms

It is notorious that politicians who live by the vote also live by the euphemism, and that the more awkward the positions in which they find themselves the more creative in this regard they become. This is rarely an edifying spectacle. In diplomacy, however, the use of euphemisms is more defensible. Indeed, in the description of concessions, the use of words or expressions more palatable to the party that has made them is another face-saving feature of almost all politically sensitive international agreements, although at some price in terms of accuracy.

A good example of the use of euphemisms is to be found in the Geneva Accords on Afghanistan referred to earlier, in which Soviet sensitivities on the issue of the withdrawal of their troops were so solicitously handled by confining the relevant provisions to the small print. The risk of humiliating the Kremlin was reduced further by the complete absence of any reference whatever to the withdrawal of 'Soviet' troops. What were to be withdrawn instead were 'foreign' troops. It might be added, too, that the agreement containing the provisions on 'foreign' troop withdrawals had a title that was, itself, a masterpiece of euphemistic obscurantism: 'Agreement on the Interrelationships for the Settlement of the Situation relating to Afghanistan' (Berridge 1991: App. 5). Brilliant.

These examples illustrate the fact that euphemistic language can help states to sign agreements providing for the withdrawal of their military forces from situations where their prestige is at stake. Others can be found to demonstrate its usefulness where they are being bought off; that is, induced to surrender some principled position by a delivery of hard cash or payment in kind. Rich states negotiating with poorer ones often find it possible to smooth the road to an agreement by discreetly giving them extremely large amounts of money. Since, however, it would be humiliating to the poorer state if this were to be too obvious, and not present the richer one in a particularly flattering light either, these large amounts of money are never called 'large amounts of money'. Instead, they are usually described by the payer as 'reconstruction aid'. This is what the Americans called the large amounts of money repeatedly offered to the North Vietnamese, from as early as April 1965, to encourage them to negotiate an end to the Vietnam War. Having been finally made a part of the Paris Peace Accords of January 1973, the money was referred to, obliquely, in Article 21: 'In pursuance of its traditional policy, the United States will contribute to healing the wounds of war and to postwar reconstruction of the Democratic Republic of Vietnam and throughout Indochina.' North Vietnam – the payee – had wanted the promised dollars to be called 'reparations', but that was too much for Washington to swallow (Kissinger 1982: 37–43).

'Separate but related' agreements

Where an agreement is based on linkage, it will probably be necessary to obscure this as much as possible, especially if one party has, for years prior to the settlement, insisted that it would have nothing to do with any such deal. This had been the position of the Angolans and their supporters (more so the latter) in regard to the proposal that South Africa would withdraw from Namibia if, in return, Cuba would pull out of Angola. Linkage, as mentioned earlier, is deeply offensive to those who believe that issues should be resolved on their merits. It is, therefore, significant that, when a settlement of the south-west African imbroglio was achieved at the end of 1988 (which was based on this linkage), it was embodied not in one agreement but two. One dealt exclusively with Namibian independence and the other only with the withdrawal of Cuban troops from Angola. Moreover, South Africa was not even presented as a party to the latter, and so did not sign it. The same device had been employed in the Camp David Accords a decade earlier. The draft Egypt–Israel peace treaty was presented as one of two accords published simultaneously, while the other was a much more general 'Framework for Peace in the Middle East', the nub of which dealt with the West Bank and Gaza. Having the two related in this way satisfied the Egyptian president, who was anxious to preserve his position that progress on the Egypt–Israel front was linked to progress on the Palestinian question. Having them, nevertheless, separated in the text satisfied the Israeli prime minister, who was even more anxious to avoid the suggestion that progress in bilateral relations was conditional on any such thing (Quandt: 211, 230).

Summary

The form taken by diplomatic agreements, particularly those giving expression to settlements of great political sensitivity, is often of considerable significance. When creating an international legal obligation is at a premium, the parties to an agreement will want to package it as a treaty; that is, write it out and give a copy to the UN. If they want to draw special attention to it as well, they might go so far as to *call* it a 'treaty'. If the press of business is great and their agreement is not so important, they will readily settle for an informal agreement such as an exchange of notes – which might or might not be published and which, therefore, might or might not be a treaty. If saving face is at a premium, the parties to an agreement can resort to any number of expedients, the tactical purposes of which are to obscure and minimize the most sensitive concessions. This is not disreputable; it is a significant part of the art of negotiation.

Further reading

Cohen, R., *Negotiating across Cultures*, rev. edn (US Institute of Peace Press: Washington, DC, 1997): ch. 9.
Cradock, P., *Experiences of China* (John Murray: London, 1994): chs 19, 20, 23.
Dalton, Robert E., 'International documents of a non-legally binding character', US Department of State, Memorandum, 18 March 1994 [www].
Franck, T. M. and E. Weisband, *Foreign Policy by Congress* (Oxford University Press: New York, 1979).
Garcia, Michael John, 'International law and agreements: their effect upon U.S. Law', *CRS Report*, 23 January 2014 [www].

Glennon, M. J., 'The Senate role in treaty ratification', *American Journal of International Law*, 77, 1983.

Grenville, J. A. S. and B. Wasserstein, *The Major International Treaties since 1945: A history and guide with texts* (Methuen: London, 1987).

Lantis, Jeffrey S., *The Life and Death of International Treaties* (Oxford University Press: Oxford, 2009).

Lisbon Treaty, 'Ratification' [www]. This page of the official EU website on this important constitution-shaping treaty lists the date and manner of ratification of each member state.

Ramsey, Michael, 'Is the agreement with Iran unconstitutional?' *The Originalism Blog*, 25 November 2013 [www].

Roberts, Sir Ivor (ed.), *Satow's Diplomatic Practice*, 6th edn (Oxford University Press: Oxford, 2009): chs 35–9.

Shaw, M. N., *International Law*, 6th edn (Cambridge University Press: Cambridge, 2008).

UN Treaty Collection: *Treaty Reference Guide* [www]. The notes and definitions provided here are extremely valuable.

6
Following up

The great Florentine statesman and historian Francesco Guicciardini wrote:

> In matters of business take this as a maxim, that it is not enough to give things their beginning, direction, or impulse; we must also follow them up, and never slacken our efforts until they are brought to a conclusion. Whoso conducts business on this system contributes in no small measure to its settlement; while he who follows a different plan will often assume things to be ended which in truth are hardly begun. (Guicciardini: 85)

Guicciardini's maxim on the need to prevent agreements unravelling by following them up applies with at least as much force today as when it was written in the early sixteenth century. 'As soon as agreement is reached by the negotiators,' wrote the world-weary George Shultz, US Secretary of State under President Ronald Reagan, 'it usually starts to collapse in the hands of those who implement it' (Shultz 1993: 747).

It is true that, as explained earlier (see p. 69), states have incentives to honour international treaties; from time to time, some also show willingness to submit disputes over their interpretation to judicial procedure. But the jurisdiction of bodies such as the International Court of Justice continues to rest on the consent of states, which is invariably withheld where matters of vital interest are concerned. Furthermore, where consent is given, the means of enforcement are generally inadequate; and there is no settled, general principle that international law should prevail over domestic rules (Shaw: 177–8, 1057–117). Even when international agreements are self-executing or subsequently embodied in domestic legislation, states might seek to

81

evade their responsibilities or fail to act properly by reason of distraction, lack of capacity, or inadvertent error. If, therefore, international agreements – however well constructed, appropriately packaged, and solemnly ratified – are to be properly implemented, they must certainly be followed up; and it is still usually on *diplomacy* that the responsibility for this falls.

In practice, diplomatic follow-up means careful monitoring of implementation so that sticks and carrots might be applied, as and when necessary, to those falling down on their obligations. Monitoring has always been an element in ensuring implementation but, in earlier times, it was by no means so easy, and other methods were usually more prominent. It will be interesting to note these briefly before concentrating on the varieties of the characteristic method of the present.

Early methods

Until about the seventeenth century, rulers sought to make agreements more durable by inviting their gods to bear witness to them in an oath-swearing ceremony. Implementation was a divine responsibility presumed to take the form of smiting down with ferocious blows any backslider, however powerful in the world of ordinary mortals. At oath-swearing ceremonies in western Asia in the second millennium BCE, as no doubt elsewhere in early times, the nature of the divine punishment to be inflicted was symbolized by ritual gestures and sacrifices (Munn-Rankin: 84–92).

Prudently enough, where agreements of special importance were concerned, an additional precaution was usually provided in the form of a tangible guarantee for the performance of promises. A popular surety of this sort was the exchange or unreciprocated surrender of valuable hostages (typically nobles, and even the sons or daughters of ruling families), but this method expired in Europe with the Treaty of Aix-la-Chapelle in 1748. Another form of surety was the pawning or mortgaging of towns or provinces, which – should the promise not be kept – would be lost for good in the first case, and liable to seizure in the second. This method lasted longer but was problematical to execute, struggled in the age of nationalism, and did not survive the first half of the twentieth century – except when employed by victors in war as, for example, in the Treaty of Versailles of 1919.

Another device occasionally employed to ensure treaty observance was to entrust the task to men of stature from both signatory states. Appointed to a standing commission with certain powers of enforcement, these men were known as *conservatores pacis* – preservers of the peace. This device was certainly obsolete by the beginning of the twentieth century, and probably well before.

A final method was the treaty of guarantee, by which powerful states undertook to enforce, if necessary, an international agreement. Such an agreement would invariably deal with a subject of great importance; for example, the position of a dynasty, the possession of specified territory, security against aggression, the independence and territorial integrity of a state, or permanent neutrality. This method continued to be employed until 1960, when it underpinned the treaty regime by which the Republic of Cyprus was established. But this – at least in the grand style – appears to have been its last gasp.

The treaty of guarantee had always been of limited use because of the onerous responsibility it placed on the guarantors. It was only likely to be signed by a state with a strong indirect interest in the observance of an agreement or a special friendship with one or more of the parties – and even then to be so riddled with escape clauses that serious doubt always attended the probability that the guarantor would stand by its promises. That it would do so became even less likely with the enhanced risks of warfare in the twentieth century. For example, in separate treaties signed in December 1994 (the so-called 'Budapest Memorandums'), Russia, the USA, and Britain gave 'security assurances' for the independence, sovereignty and existing borders of Ukraine, Belarus, and Kazakhstan – in return for their accession to the Nuclear Non-Proliferation Treaty (NPT). However, these assurances would only be activated in the event of a threat or act of *nuclear* aggression and then require their protectors only to 'seek' immediate assistance for the victims from the UN Security Council – where, of course, each of the signatories has a veto. The use of the word 'guarantees' in the Budapest Memorandum was deliberately avoided (Pifer).

For one reason or another, then, almost all of the diplomatic devices customarily employed to ensure that agreements were honoured had become obsolete by the middle of the twentieth century. Thus bereft, treaty implementation has, as a general rule, needed to rely more and more on expert and systematic monitoring. However, the form this takes varies with the subject of the agreements concerned, and whether they are multilateral or bilateral. What costs follow any defaulting depend on the reasons for non-compliance but, at a minimum, will usually mean bad publicity and consequent damage to reputations. In some cases, assistance in what is now generally known as 'capacity-building' is more appropriate than sanctions. Diplomats are not always to be found at the sharp end of following-up although, even when not prominent in the activity, they are invariably to be found in its wings. What are the chief methods of monitoring by means of which international agreements are followed up today?

Monitoring by experts

Agreements that are complex, technical, and sensitive always have to be followed up by experts, including scientists, engineers, and lawyers, and sometimes by national intelligence agencies. Arms control agreements and UN Security Council-imposed disarmament regimes, especially those limiting WMD, provide the best-known cases in point. Compliance with these has long been monitored by intelligence agencies employing technical means, including SIGINT and observation via spy satellites. The US Department of State houses an inter-agency organization – the Bureau of Arms Control, Verification and Compliance – with intimate links to the intelligence community, which is dedicated to the analysis of compliance with arms control, non-proliferation, and disarmament agreements. But multilateral bodies also play a major part in this work, as was clearly seen in Iraq.

The IAEA has a whole division – the Department of Safeguards – devoted to verifying compliance with the promise not to obtain nuclear weapons made by signatories of the NPT, of which Iraq was one. After the ejection of the forces of the Iraqi leader Saddam Hussein from Kuwait in 1991, the UN Security Council also established a special commission of weapons inspectors to oversee compliance with the disarmament obligations then imposed on his regime. The first commission, UNSCOM, was dominated by the United States and discredited by well-documented media allegations that it had allowed Western intelligence agencies to piggy-back on its activities in Iraq for purposes of military planning. As a result, it was replaced in 1999 by the UN Monitoring, Verification and Inspection Commission (UNMOVIC), the entire staff of which was on the UN payroll (Blix: 36–40).

Weapons inspectors from both the IAEA and the UN struggled for a long time to establish, in the face of immense difficulties, whether Saddam was concealing WMD. In 1998, he opened the highly sensitive 'presidential sites' only after the United States threatened air strikes and the UN Secretary-General, Kofi Annan, negotiated a short-lived agreement with his foreign minister on special arrangements for the inspections (Box 6.1). The cat-and-mouse game played by Saddam with

Box 6.1 Special Group on visits to presidential sites: Iraq, 26 March–2 April 1998

The memorandum of understanding (MoU) establishing the Special Group provided, among other things, that the IAEA and UNSCOM weapons inspectors should be led by a Commissioner appointed by Kofi Annan and accompanied by foreign observers comprising 'senior diplomats', also to be appointed by the UN Secretary-General. In the event, the group was headed by the Sri Lankan diplomat Jayathan Dhanapala, then UN Under Secretary-General for Disarmament Affairs. Following a canvass by Dhanapala for volunteers from senior diplomats already based in Baghdad or in the region, a group representing 20 different states was selected. This arrangement clearly helped to reconcile the Iraqis to the exercise. The diplomats also helped to smooth relations between the inspectors and lower-level Iraqi officials when misunderstandings occurred as a result of 'cultural differences and miscommunication'. However, as a model arrangement, the need to organize a large and diverse body of diplomats had the drawback of making it more difficult for UNSCOM and the IAEA to make surprise inspections.

Sources: MoU between UN and Republic of Iraq, 23 February 1998, UN Doc. S/1998/166 27 March 1998; Report of the Special Group established for entries into Iraqi presidential sites, UN Doc. S/1998/326, 15 April 1998.

the weapons inspectors certainly contributed to the impression that he was concealing WMD. Nevertheless, the inspectors were highly professional and, having found nothing significant in 1998 or later, became highly sceptical about their existence. Prior to the attacks on the United States on 11 September 2001 ('9/11'), even the Bush administration was content that Saddam was being successfully contained by the 'regime of inspection, eradication and monitoring by the UN, supported by military pressure from the U.S. and the U.K' (Blix: 259, 273). It is a great pity that UNMOVIC, which was wholly concerned with Iraq, was disbanded by the Security Council in 2007 and not given a wider brief. With safeguards agreements in force with over 170 states at the time of writing, the IAEA remains very active, especially in connection with Iran and North Korea; but its remit does not include chemical and biological weapons.

There is also great need for monitoring by experts to try to ensure compliance with multilateral human rights agreements; for example, the Convention against Torture and Other Cruel, Inhuman or Degrading Treatment or Punishment (CAT), which entered into force in 1987. Torture is conducted in secret and can leave no obvious physical marks; furthermore, its victims – through fear for their families, as well as themselves – are understandably reluctant to testify against their tormentors if and when they are eventually released. International NGOs such as Human Rights Watch and Amnesty International are particularly well known for their work in monitoring torture and other abuses, publicizing their findings, and reporting them in detail to governments and such bodies as the UN Human Rights Council. International NGOs have the advantage over states that share their repugnance for torture of not having to pull their punches for fear of harming other interests; but they have the disadvantage that their staff do not enjoy diplomatic immunity and, in consequence, are vulnerable to harassment or worse in the states where they are most needed. National NGOs are often enlisted by states and intergovernmental organizations as partners in monitoring compliance with human rights agreements, although they often work on a shoe-string and their position is usually even more exposed.

A body that has some of the advantages in the human rights field of both an NGO and an intergovernmental organization is the International Committee of the Red Cross (ICRC), which is a hybrid of the two. On the one hand, it is a private body, established under the Swiss Civil Code; on the other, 'its functions and activities – to provide protection and assistance to victims of conflict – are mandated by the international community of states and are founded on international law, specifically the Geneva Conventions' (Rona). As with an intergovernmental organization such as the UN, therefore, its staff enjoy special privileges and immunities that are widely recognized. These include the right to decline to testify before such bodies as the International Criminal Tribunal for the former Yugoslavia. The ICRC also provides its reports in confidence to the state whose activities are being monitored. It helps that Switzerland, where the ICRC is headquartered, has the firm legal status of permanent neutrality. These credentials make it effective in varying degrees in even the most viciously governed states, such as North Korea and Zimbabwe, where other human rights bodies find it difficult if not impossible to operate. It has a network of missions and delegations extending over 80 countries.

Monitoring by embassies

In a number of respects, embassies are ideally placed to follow up agreements, whether bilateral or multilateral ones in which the sending state has a close interest. As well as having the advantages of local knowledge and contacts that come from being on the spot, the larger embassies, at least, are not without their own experts (traditionally known as 'attachés'); for example, in commerce, culture, defence, drugs, and immigration.

A good example of the role played by embassies in encouraging compliance with the terms of multilateral agreements is that of US embassies relative to the numerous conventions outlawing human trafficking. Under the national authority of the Trafficking Victims Protection Act (2000), the State Department's Office to Monitor and Combat Trafficking in Persons publishes an annual Trafficking in Persons Report. This places each country in one of three tiers based on the extent of their government's efforts to comply with the act's minimum standards for the elimination of trafficking. It is one of the responsibilities of US embassies, albeit in partnership with various agencies and NGOs, to supply the information on which this annual report is based.

Embassy staff enjoy special privileges and immunities, and are therefore unlikely to fear the reprisals likely to be suffered in authoritarian states by the representatives of campaigning NGOs, and especially investigative journalists or opposition politicians whose questions prove too awkward. For example, apart from the ICRC, it was only the embassies in Harare that were able to provide any effective monitoring of the extreme and widespread flouting of international humanitarian law by the Zimbabwean authorities during their violent confrontation with the supporters of the opposition leader, Morgan Tsvangirai, in the election year of 2008. At one point, Tsvangirai actually had to take refuge in the Dutch embassy.

On the other hand, resident embassies have the general interests of their own state to protect, and this requires normal – if not good – relations with the government of the receiving state. Pushing too hard for compliance with the terms of an agreement on a sensitive subject like human rights, therefore, might well compromise completely the rest of their work; and apprehension on this score will often render them ill-suited to take the lead in following up. It is clear, nevertheless, that they sometimes play an unobtrusive but important supporting role where other bodies take the lead. In this context, it is instructive to look at the practice of the British government in attempting to secure compliance with bilateral MoUs on torture.

British embassies and 'Deportations with Assurances' agreements

Since the July 2005 bomb attacks in central London, Britain has found itself detaining a growing number of foreign nationals suspected of engaging in or sponsoring terrorism but whom, for one reason or another, it has been unwilling either to subject to criminal trial or release without charge. Anxious, therefore, on grounds of national security to send them back to their countries of origin, which often wish to lay hands on these persons for reasons of their own, it has nevertheless been hindered by its status as a signatory of the European Convention on Human Rights and the CAT. For these instruments not only prohibit torture, but also the deportation or extradition of persons to countries where there are good grounds for believing that they would be in danger of suffering it. Unfortunately, many of the states to which Britain wishes to deport terrorism suspects – chiefly in the Middle East and North Africa – have precisely such reputations. As a result, it has been obliged to negotiate MoUs or other forms of agreement with them under which they give 'diplomatic assurances' that their nationals will not be subjected to unfair or inhumane treatment if returned. These are now officially known as agreements on 'Deportations with Assurances (DWAs)'.

But what provision is made in these DWA agreements for ensuring that the receiving states live up to their assurances? The UK–Jordan agreement, which became the prototype for those negotiated later (Box 6.2), spelled out the arrangement as follows:

> If the returned person is arrested, detained or imprisoned within three years of the date of his return, he will be entitled to contact, and then have prompt and regular visits from the representative of an *independent body nominated jointly by the UK and Jordanian authorities* [emphasis added]. Such visits will be permitted at least once a fortnight, and whether or not the returned person has been convicted, and will include the opportunity for private interviews with the returned person. The nominated body will give a report of its visits to the authorities of the sending state.

Insisting in a published agreement on the need for an 'independent' monitoring body implies lack of trust in the willingness or ability of the receiving state to keep its promises; in a case such as this, it also amounts to interference in its domestic affairs, for the returnees are, after all, its own citizens; and accepting such a body might be construed as an admission that torture has previously taken place. These are among the reasons why the United States does not insist on publication of 'diplomatic assurances' (Deeks: 10).

Non-interference in internal affairs is a basic – if now somewhat embattled – norm of the society of states and is a major theme of the Vienna Convention on Diplomatic Relations (1961). As a result, Algeria – although giving the desired 'assurances' – refused to sign any agreement with Britain that required an independent monitoring body

(SIAC 2007a: para. 39; Metcalfe), and those that did come to fruition provided for reciprocity: Britain had to agree to identical procedures to guarantee its own good behaviour in case one of these countries should wish to deport UK nationals back to Britain. More significantly, the generic MoUs gave the receiving state a veto in the choice of the so-called 'independent monitoring body'; and, in the most recent to be signed, the term employed was changed to the more neutral one of 'follow-up mechanism' (Box 6.2).

Box 6.2 States with which Britain has 'Deportations with Assurances' agreements, and local NGOs appointed as monitoring bodies*

Jordan**	10 August 2005	Adaleh Centre for Human Rights Studies
Lebanon	29 December 2005	Institute of Human Rights
Algeria***	11 July 2006	–
Ethiopia	12 December 2008	Ethiopian Human Rights Commission
Morocco	7 August 2013	('follow-up mechanism' to be agreed)

* An MoU signed with Qadhafi's Libya on 18 October 2005 has ceased to operate.

** In March 2013 the British government agreed a new treaty with Jordan that guaranteed a fair trial for any deportee sent by one party to the other. Shortly afterwards, the radical Muslim cleric Abu Qatada, who had been granted asylum in Britain in 1994, was finally deported to Jordan, where, in absentia, he had been given a 15-year prison term in 2000 for plotting terror attacks. In September 2014, he was acquitted on these charges by a court in Amman on grounds of insufficient evidence and released from prison.

*** This was an exchange of letters rather than an MoU, and contained no mention of a monitoring body.

The British government describes the monitoring bodies appointed as a result of these agreements as 'local NGOs' but, given the fact that they must be acceptable to the receiving government, it is clear that this is a typical official gloss. Some of these bodies are no doubt more independent than others and, in Jordan and Lebanon, the monitoring bodies both have links to the local Bar Associations. But independence and enthusiasm are not enough. The Adaleh Centre in Amman – which at the time of its selection was small, inexperienced, and little known even in Jordan – was not the British government's first choice (SIAC 2007b: paras 186–204). In Libya, the Qadhafi Development Foundation was headed by Seif al-Islam, the second son of the then Libyan dictator, Colonel Muammar al-Qadhafi; in Ethiopia the monitoring body was established by the ruling party under the chairmanship of a former Ethiopian ambassador to Russia.

The nature of these monitoring bodies has led organizations like Human Rights Watch and Amnesty to charge that the MoUs are not worth the paper they were written on. They are not alone. In April 2007, the Special Immigration Appeals Commission (SIAC) in Britain declared unsafe the decision of the Home Office to deport two Libyan terrorism suspects to Libya; monitoring by the Qadhafi Development Foundation, it declared, was unlikely to be effective. SIAC's judgement was subsequently supported by the Court of Appeal. It was against this background that it emerged that the British embassies in the countries concerned were also playing a role in monitoring compliance with the DWA agreements. It was in the interests of the Foreign Office to let this be known, albeit discreetly, in order to meet the charge that Britain intended to wash its hands of these suspects once they had left the country.

Although the importance attached to these agreements had led to the direct involvement in their negotiation of senior officials and ministers in London, the British embassies in the receiving states were also intimately concerned with them from the beginning, having been asked by the Foreign Office, in 2003, to report on the prospects for negotiating a 'generic MoU' (SIAC 2007c: para. 209). Thereafter, they led in the search for suitable monitoring bodies and supported the negotiation of their terms of reference. This positioned them well to assume the role of local coordinator of the 'capacity-building' assistance then provided by Britain to these bodies, as also to prison officers, police officers, judges, and so on. Finally, the embassies not only monitor the monitors but also *directly* monitor the treatment of returnees. In countries such as Algeria, there is no other body allowed to do it (SIAC 2007a: para. 39; and 2007d: passim; FAC 2013: para. 58), but their direct involvement appears to be a normal expectation even in those where there is a local monitoring body. As SIAC said in dismissing the appeal of 'VV' against deportation to Jordan:

> Experience of deportations to Algeria has demonstrated that the British Government takes its obligations to see that diplomatic assurances in relation to deportees are fulfilled seriously. We have no reason whatever to doubt that the embassy in Amman would do the same. (SIAC 2007e: para. 23)

In sum, while the British government maintains that diplomatic assurances are reliable chiefly because it is in the interests of the receiving countries to honour them, it also recognizes the need to follow them up and, in this activity, effectively assigns the major role to embassies. It is, therefore, hardly surprising that a Home Office review of counter-terrorism in early 2011 noted that 'Negotiating and maintaining successful arrangements is complex and requires significant diplomatic resources, sometimes at the cost of other important policy objectives' (Home Office: 33). Despite this, and despite the equally costly process of dealing with appeals against deportation, the review concluded that agreements on DWAs – which it believed had so far worked satisfactorily – should be actively sought with more countries. In this, Britain is not alone. Reliance on 'diplomatic assurances' in order to deport terrorism suspects without flagrantly ignoring international human rights law is widespread among the other states of Europe, which, presumably, also rely on their embassies to secure these assurances and then monitor them.

Review meetings

The value of follow-up procedures is now so well understood that formal 'compliance mechanisms', as they are sometimes known, are often created by, or pursuant to, the provisions of international agreements – and then become institutionalized. The most common sort is a review meeting, sometimes also referred to as a 'conference of the parties', a 'joint commission' (in the case of bilateral agreements), an armistice commission (in connection with an agreement to suspend hostilities) – or simply as a 'follow-up conference'.

With the exception of the one usually known as an international commission (Box 6.3), a review meeting is a gathering of representatives of the parties to the original agreement called for the express purposes of measuring progress on its implementation and securing an understanding of what needs to be done to move matters forward. When matters of exceptional importance are concerned, these meetings can be held at summit level, as in the case of biennial Nuclear Security Summits launched at Washington in 2010 against the background of a growing fear of nuclear terrorism. The original agreement usually stipulates that these meetings are to be held on a regular basis and at a venue rotating among the participant states. (If the venue is fixed, as at IAEA headquarters in the case of the review meetings of the Convention on Nuclear Safety, the president of the meeting might be rotated.) This puts all of the parties – especially the host – under pressure to make progress before the meeting so as to avoid the charge of backsliding, and possible public criticism.

Box 6.3   The international commission

This is an unusual review meeting. Rather than comprising the parties to an agreement, the members of this body consist of friends of each (in equal measure), together with a neutral. International commissions of this sort, as well as military joint commissions comprising representatives of the previously warring parties, were created to supervise the ceasefire agreements for Cambodia, Laos, and Vietnam signed at the Geneva Conference on Indochina in 1954 co-chaired by Britain and the Soviet Union. Each international commission consisted of delegates from states representing the principal groupings in the Cold War: the Free World (Canada), the Communist world (Poland), and the emerging Non-Aligned Movement (India). Furthermore, the Indian representative occupied the chair in each commission and had a casting vote. Among other things, the commissions had the right – indeed the obligation – to refer to the members of the Geneva Conference any refusal on the part of one of the parties to the ceasefires to accept one of their recommendations. A cruder version of the international commission, lacking a neutral element, was the 'International Commission of Control and Supervision' established under the Paris Peace Accords on the Vietnam War of 1973.

Review meetings, although regular, often have large gaps between them, but this does not mean that following up is not being taken seriously. For example, the interval between review meetings of the Convention on Nuclear Safety, which entered into force in 1996, might be as long as three years, but an organizing committee must meet well before this. Moreover, six months prior to the review meeting the parties are required to submit a national report for 'peer review' on the measures they have taken to implement their obligations. If they do not, they are named and shamed in the published summary report of the review meeting (*Summary Report*: paras 4–5). (Just for the record, the culprits named in 2014 were Albania, Bahrain, Bangladesh, Cambodia, Kuwait, Lebanon, Libya, Mali, Nigeria, Saudi Arabia, and Sri Lanka.) Review meetings of the NPT are held only every five years but meetings of a preparatory committee – which all states parties to the treaty are entitled to attend, and which discuss substantive as well as procedural matters – are held in the intervening period. It is also common for agreements to stipulate that review meetings might be held at short notice in an emergency, as when in 2012 there was an extraordinary meeting of the Convention on Nuclear Safety to discuss long-term nuclear safety in light of the Fukushima Daiichi accident in Japan.

When there is no provision for review meetings, as in many bilateral agreements, follow-up might be facilitated by other means. For example, an agreement can list the competent authorities in each signatory state – and, ideally, the named individuals in them – responsible for implementation. Such an agreement might also require the establishment of direct channels of communication between these authorities or named persons. Provision for all of these procedures was made in the India–Russia agreement on cooperation against illicit trafficking in narcotics signed in Moscow on 12 November 2007 and published on the website of the Indian embassy. But such, or similar, procedures need not be substitutes for review meetings, as is clear from the US–Mexico agreement of 14 August 1983 on cooperation for the protection and improvement of the environment in the border area. This provided for nomination by each state of both a 'national coordinator' to be responsible for implementation and an annual review meeting to be held alternately in the border area of the USA and Mexico.

In the case of fragile agreements painfully constructed, such compliance mechanisms might be a necessary condition of implementation, but they are not a sufficient one. This is only too tragically revealed by the 'road map' on the Middle East of 2003, which provides that 'The Quartet will meet regularly at senior levels to evaluate the parties' performance on implementation of the plan'. This particular formulation has been criticized for its vagueness by the International Peace Academy but it is hardly that alone that has prevented the Israelis and Palestinians from reaching the destination marked out on the map.

Review meetings sometimes evolve into international organizations (see Chapter 11), which are, therefore, the ultimate expression of follow-up machinery. A good example is the Organization for Security and Co-operation in Europe (OSCE), which exists to consolidate and build on the Helsinki Final Act of 1975. A permanent structure had been proposed by the Soviet Union at the start but opposed by NATO countries, and it was another 20 years before *ad hoc* follow-up procedures evolved into the OSCE.

Summary

States often sign up to agreements they intend to observe only in limited and belated fashion. As a result, however well constructed, appropriately packaged, and solemnly ratified these agreements might be, it is essential that steps be taken to follow them up. Agreements that are complex, technical, and sensitive always have to be followed up by experts, whether employed by governments, international organizations, or NGOs. Embassies, too, are in some respects ideally placed to follow up agreements, as can be seen in their work in monitoring and encouraging compliance with Deportations With Assurances agreements. Review meetings are also valuable in following up bilateral as well as the better-known multilateral agreements. 'Naming and shaming' and assistance in capacity-building are the main levers in diplomatic follow-up but, if this is insufficient, the implementation of agreements may in some circumstances be sought through international courts and tribunals and – in extreme cases – by economic sanctions, blockade, or military intimidation.

Further reading

Adcock, Sir Frank and D. J. Mosley, *Diplomacy in Ancient Greece* (Thames & Hudson: London, 1975): 216–26.

Beyerlin, U., P. T. Stoll and R. Wolfrum (eds), *Ensuring Compliance with Multilateral Environmental Agreements: A dialogue between practitioners and academia* (Martinus Nijhoff: Leiden, 2006).

Blix, Hans, *Disarming Iraq* (Bloomsbury: London, 2004).

Budapest Memorandum ('Memorandum on security assurances in connection with Ukraine's accession to the Treaty on the Non-Proliferation of Nuclear Weapons', Budapest 5 December 1994), Wikisource [www].

Carlson, John, 'NPT safeguards agreements – defining non-compliance', 31 August 2008 [www].

Deeks, Ashley S., 'Avoiding transfers to torture', *Council on Foreign Relations Special Report*, 35, June 2008 [www].

Dinstein, Yoram, *War, Aggression and Self-Defence*, 4th edn (Cambridge University Press: Cambridge, 2005): 263–7, on treaties of guarantee.

FCO, 'Memoranda of Understanding on Deportations with Assurances', 7 August 2013 [www]. Provides links to the texts of all these agreements.

Flodén, Gunilla, Elisabeth French, Peter Jones, Natalie Pauwels, and Jean Pascal Zanders, 'Iraq: The UNSCOM experience' (Stockholm International Peace Research Institute: October 1998) [www].

Haines, John R., 'Ukraine and the misunderstood Budapest Memorandum', *E-notes* (Foreign Policy Research Institute: March 2014) [www].

Home Office, *Review of Counter-Terrorism and Security Powers. Review Findings and Recommendations*, Cm 8004, January 2011 [www].

Horne, Alexander, Melanie Gower and Joanna Dawson, 'Deportation of individuals who may face a risk of torture', *Standard Note*: SN/HA/4151 (House of Commons Library: 10 February 2014) [www].

Metcalfe, Eric, 'The false promise of assurances against torture', *Justice Journal*, 6(1), June 2009 [www].

Munn-Rankin, J. M., 'Diplomacy in Western Asia in the early second millennium B.C.', *Iraq*, 18, 1956: on oaths.

Pifer, Steven, 'Ukraine crisis impact on nuclear weapons', *CNN*, 4 March 2014 [www]. The author is a former US ambassador to Ukraine and helped negotiate the Budapest Memorandum.

Roberts, Ivor (ed.), *Satow's Diplomatic Practice*, 6th edn (Oxford University Press: Oxford, 2009): ch. 32, on NGOs.

Rona, Gabor, 'The ICRC's status: in a class of its own' (ICRC: 17 February 2004) [www].

UN Environment Programme, *Manual on Compliance with and Enforcement of Multilateral Environmental Agreements* (UNEP: 2006) [www].

UNMOVIC, *Compendium: Observations and lessons learned* (UNMOVIC: 27 June, 2007) [www].

US Department of State, *Trafficking in Persons Report 2013* [www].

Vattel, Emmerich de, *Le droit des gens* [*The Law of Nations*] (first pub. Neuchâtel, 1758) [English trans. www]: Book 2, chs 15 and 16, on hostages, oaths, and treaties of guarantee.

Whitfield, Teresa, *Working with Groups of Friends* (USIP: Washington, DC, 2010) [www]: 63–9.

See also the websites of the following bodies: Canadian Centre for Treaty Compliance (Carleton University, Ottawa), Human Rights Watch, IAEA (Department of Safeguards), OSCE (Who We Are>History), and US Department of State (Bureau of Arms Control, Verification, and Compliance).

Part II
Diplomatic Relations

Introduction to Part II

On 10 February 2004 the Republic of Ireland established diplomatic relations with the oppressive government of Myanmar (Burma). 'In view of Ireland's responsibilities during our EU Presidency,' said the Irish foreign minister, 'this decision...will ensure that, during the Presidency, we can contribute more directly to promoting the process of democratisation and national reconciliation there.' This example illustrates the fact that when states are in diplomatic relations they can, in principle, communicate freely with each other and, therefore, in the most effective manner possible.

To be in diplomatic relations is the normal condition between states enjoying mutual recognition; hence, diplomatic relations is often spoken of as 'normal relations'. This condition might have grown up naturally and be taken for granted, as in the case of states having dealings with each other over centuries. In other instances, the establishment of diplomatic relations – or the 'normalization' of relations – might be the result of a well-advertised written agreement to this effect, today typically taking the form of a joint communiqué signed by their permanent representatives to the United Nations in New York, such as those of Kazakhstan and El Salvador in February 2014 and Fiji and Iraq in the following August. Such communiqués commonly add that the step has been guided by the principles and purposes of the Charter of the UN and the VCDR (1961), and indicate both the date when and the manner in which normalization will commence.

For the conduct of normal relations, resident embassies are frequently established, but diplomatic relations – broadly understood – can also be conducted by other means; for example, via telecommunications, consulates, conferences, and summits. It is the different channels, or modes, of diplomacy that are the subject of Part II of this book.

It has been argued in Part I that the most important function of diplomacy is the negotiation of agreements between states. It has also been noted, however, that this is not always the function to which those professionally involved in the conduct of diplomatic relations devote most of their time, and that diplomacy has other important functions. These include political and economic reporting, lobbying, supporting the activities of businesses from home, assisting distressed nationals, and propaganda. The opportunity will be taken in Part II to examine these functions as well.

7
Telecommunications

From ancient times until comparatively recently, all messages, including diplomatic messages, were carried by hand. In the twenty-first century, diplomatic couriers are still employed for the delivery of certain top-secret packages, together with crates of sensitive equipment and even construction materials. But since the middle of the nineteenth century, diplomatic messages have been increasingly carried by telecommunication: any mode of communication over a long distance (*tele* is Greek for 'far') that requires human agency only in the sending and reception of the message it contains and not, as with a courier, in its conveyance. This chapter will consider the advantages and disadvantages of the different kinds of telecommunication. It will also give some emphasis to crisis diplomacy, because it is in this activity that telecommunication is often held to be of greatest value, and it is certainly here that it has received the greatest attention.

The communication by drums and smoke-signals that originated in ancient times, and the optical telegraph or semaphore systems introduced in Europe in the late eighteenth century, were forms of telecommunication. Nevertheless, it did not make a major impact on diplomacy until the introduction of the electric telegraph towards the middle of the nineteenth century. Soon, using submarine as well as overland cables, written messages sent by telegraph cut delivery times over some routes from weeks to hours, although they were insecure and so needed to be enciphered, and for a long time were also expensive and prone to garbling. The invention of radio telegraphy in the 1890s improved this medium further, although it remained insecure. In the early twentieth century, it became possible to deliver the spoken word over vast distances by telephone (available in the late nineteenth century only over short distances) and short-wave radio. Since World War II, further well-known refinements have been added, among them fax, electronic mail, instant messaging, mobile or cell phones, and multi-media video-conferencing; and other exciting developments in information and communications technologies are no doubt in the pipeline.

Worries over security have traditionally caused foreign ministries to employ the latest form of telecommunication only with great caution – and after considerable hesitation. Nevertheless, eventually the appeal of these various means of communication has generally won the day, and the appeal of none has been greater than that of the telephone, especially in a crisis.

Telephone diplomacy flourishes

Telephone diplomacy has flourished in recent years, as 'secure phones' have become cheaper and safer. However, it has dangers other than vulnerability to eavesdropping, and marked limitations; some of these are common to most forms of telecommunication. It is as well, therefore, to consider these first.

First among the limitations of telephone diplomacy is that it forgoes all forms of non-verbal communication. By means of body language, dress, venue, and setting, diplomats or political leaders at a summit can add nuance or emphasis to a verbal message; or, alternatively, by such means signal their real intentions despite *saying* something quite different – but none of this is possible in telephone diplomacy. Second, compared with a personal visit by a foreign minister, with all its attendant preparations, a telephone call is far less effective in forcing officials to focus on the questions at issue. Third, a phone call reduces the opportunities, should this be advantageous, to generate news coverage for a message. Attention to the last two limitations of telephone diplomacy was drawn by critics of Colin Powell, US Secretary of State from 2001 until 2005, who – always apprehensive of what the White House and Pentagon were doing 'behind his back when he was on the road' (Rice: 291) – undertook relatively few foreign trips and relied instead more on the telephone. Finally, different time zones on top of congested schedules can restrict the opportunities for communication by telephone, especially when the users are heads of state or government: 'preparing a phone call can sometimes take days,' remarked a former senior minister and ambassador of Saudi Arabia (Algosaibi: 238).

As for their dangers, telephone conversations cannot be completely scripted: even when the protocols are well understood, the issues that come up are not entirely predictable and remarks made spontaneously

Spontaneous vxns

might not convey exactly the meaning intended, even if simultaneous translation is not needed. A particular danger that flows from this, as well as from the immediacy of the exchange, is that there is 'no time for reflection or consultation' (Satow: vol. I, 157). As a result, either the receiver of the call is bounced into a hasty decision on what might well be a matter of vital importance; or the receiver refuses to make an immediate decision – thereby creating resentment on the part of the caller because the gambit has failed and on the part of the receiver because it has been attempted (Thatcher 1995: 230).

To make matters worse, things said over the telephone cannot be unsaid, and there is no telling to what use an adversary might put a suitably edited tape-recording of a conversation. Written messages that subsequently prove embarrassing can plausibly be dismissed as forgeries but this is more difficult with taped conversations, as President Nixon found to his cost during the Watergate affair in the early 1970s. While there might be disadvantages to the recording of a telephone conversation, a disadvantage might also attach to its absence, namely a subsequent difference of opinion as to what was actually said (Shultz 1997: 6). In a relationship where there is mistrust, a profound cultural gap, and only a limited understanding of the rival's machinery of government, there can also be no confidence that a promise to pass on a message has been acted upon, or even that the person at the other end of the line is who they say they are. The last risk is not merely hypothetical. President George W. Bush once had an extended telephone conversation with a person purporting to be the Iranian President Hashemi-Rafsanjani that was later traced back to the Iranian Ministry of Intelligence and Security; later, a 16-year old Icelandic high-school student pretending to be the president of Iceland and correctly answering background security questions by consulting Wikipedia got as far as President Bush's secretary. *Wow*

The dangers continue. At the level of head of state or government, there are circumstances in which a decision to communicate by telephone might induce a crisis atmosphere when the opposite was intended. It appears to have been fear of this that, after some debate in the Situation Room, induced President George W. Bush to leave to traditional channels resolution of the dispute provoked by the collision over the South China Sea between an American EP-3 spy plane and a Chinese jet fighter in April 2001, rather than telephone his Chinese opposite number Jiang Zemin. Finally, however nominally secure it might be, telephone diplomacy is vulnerable to eavesdropping by the sophisticated and well-resourced SIGINT agencies of the major powers. Among the many known victims of this are a UN Secretary-General (Boutros-Ghali: 276–7) and the German chancellor Angela Merkel (see p. 161).

In light of this catalogue of limitations and perils, it might be thought amazing that telephones are ever used at all in diplomacy. But such are their compensating advantages that the former are accepted and the latter are courted every day.

Unlike the various forms of written telecommunications, the telephone is easier and quicker to use; it can send signals by means of tone of voice and volume; and it is more *personal*. The last point is particularly important because it means that it is more flattering to the recipient; by contrast, written messages, especially at the highest level, are usually drafted by someone else and recognized as such. The telephone also provides considerable certainty that a message has got through and, because it does not always generate a verbatim transcript, might be deniable if this should prove to be expedient. It also makes possible the *immediate* correction of a misunderstanding or *immediate* adjustment of a statement that has evidently given unintended offence, so that neither is allowed to fester. Finally, the telephone provides the opportunity to extract an *immediate* response from the party at the other end of the line – and many people find it more difficult to say 'no' over the telephone than in a written response. Thus, the possibility of being bounced into a hasty decision may be a danger to one party, but the corollary is that it is an attractive opportunity to the other.

In addition, telephone diplomacy need not be – and usually is not – a careless form of communication. For the benefit of their political leaders, advisers can prepare talking points and take notes or make recordings. Employing the latter, press offices – including that of the UN secretary-general – now sometimes issue 'read-outs' providing summaries of telephone conversations for the benefit of their 'public diplomacy' (see Chapter 13). Internal regulations of government can – and do – expressly forbid the treatment of classified issues on the telephone at the sub-political level. Technical steps can also be taken to assure the security of particularly sensitive conversations, and in any case much of the information contained in telephone calls is out of date before hostile intelligence agencies can track, digest, and circulate them to their customers (although this gap seems to be shortening). It is chiefly for all of the above reasons that political leaders and senior government officials, both in foreign ministries and other government departments, attach such importance to using the telephone in maintaining their overseas communications.

Telephone diplomacy, however, is more appropriate in some circumstances, and in some relationships, than in others. Its advantages are particularly apparent during fast-moving situations and major international crises, although less so for making contact with an adversary than with friends and allies, whether to orchestrate their response to a crisis or sort out a serious problem among them. In either case 'conference calls' – claimed to have been used first by US Secretary of State Madeleine Albright in 1999 – can be employed (Albright: 409, 412).

Examples abound of the use of telephone diplomacy to orchestrate the response of friends and allies to a crisis. For instance, between August 1990 – when the forces of the Iraqi President Saddam Hussein invaded Kuwait – and the end of the year, US President George H. W. Bush exchanged 40 telephone calls with Turgut Özal, President of Turkey, whose support was strategically vital to him in the event that force would be needed to expel Saddam (Stearns: 11). Early in the following year, in the run-up to the Gulf War, President Bush phoned the Malaysian prime minister in a Tokyo restaurant in order to secure his support for a vital Security Council resolution. In 2002, against the background of the next major crisis over Saddam Hussein, British Foreign Secretary Jack Straw had 'endless telephone calls' with the 'the key P5 partners' on the subject of UN Security Council Resolution 1441, which sealed the fate of modern Iraq (Straw: 46). And early in the following March, the British government – which was anxious to get a second Security Council resolution that would *explicitly* authorize the use of force against Iraq – worked the phones again. Chile had a non-permanent seat on the Council at that juncture, and Britain went to the lengths of installing a Brent secure telephone in the presidential palace in Santiago so that Tony Blair could speak privately to the president while the former was in Northern Ireland. In the event, this was to no avail: the president of Mexico, which also had a seat on the Security Council at the time, 'retired to hospital and stopped taking telephone calls and the Chilean made it clear he wouldn't move without the Mexican' (Powell: 81–2).

A good example of the use of the telephone to lower the temperature in a crisis between friendly states is provided by the calls exchanged in October 1983 on the White House–10 Downing Street 'hotline' (Box 7.1). The first was made by British Prime Minister Margaret Thatcher, and was designed to underline the importance of a written message just dispatched imploring American President Ronald Reagan not to invade the Commonwealth state of Grenada. (Only the previous day the British foreign secretary had publicly stated that he had no knowledge of any American intention to intervene in Grenada. A subsequent invasion of a Commonwealth state by Britain's closest ally, without consultation, would make Mrs Thatcher look weak and foolish.) As it turned out, her telephone diplomacy was ineffective – it was already too late. However, the story was different with the call she received back from Ronald Reagan the following day. The president began with some gallant and disarming opening remarks, which was just as well because, on her own admission, the Iron Lady was 'not in the sunniest of moods'. He then apologized for the embarrassment caused and explained the practical considerations that had made full consultation impossible. This clearly had a soothing effect on Mrs Thatcher. 'There was not much I felt able to say,' she records in her memoirs, 'and so I more or less held my peace, but I was glad to have received the telephone call' (Thatcher 1995: 331–3). This exchange over the hotline was the more effective because, despite the closeness of these two leaders, it was at that time still rarely used (Box 7.1).

Box 7.1 The White House –10 Downing Street hotline

This telephone hotline was probably set up in the early 1960s. In an interview enquiry in 1993 Mrs Thatcher, the then prime minister, was asked whether it was used very often. She replied: 'No, I don't think these things ought to be used very often. But I sometimes received a very welcome call at difficult times from Ronald Reagan, who was very, very thoughtful' (Thatcher 1993: 10). This was consistent with the traditional Whitehall view that personal top-level exchanges of this sort should be regarded as 'the diplomatic weapon of last resort'. However, times were already changing. Only five years after this interview, Bill Clinton and Tony Blair were speaking on the phone on average once a week (Patterson: 57).

A more recent example of the same sort, also instructive in other ways, is to be found in the Khobragade affair. In December 2013, Devyani Khobragade, the Indian Deputy Consul-General in New York, was arrested by the US authorities on charges of visa fraud and exploitation of a domestic employee brought from India. Attempting to end the serious dip in US–India relations to which this had led, Secretary of State John Kerry tried to phone his opposite number in Delhi, Salman Khurshid – but the Indian External Affairs Minister declined to take his call, initially giving as his reason the inconvenience of time-zone differences. Sir Ernest Satow would have warmly approved another explanation Khurshid was reported by the *New York Post* to have given (although not necessarily the fact that he gave it in public): 'We will,' he said, 'study the matter and then take a call. Such decisions are not taken in a hurry.' Nevertheless, India's National Security Adviser did respond to Kerry, and the State Department's under-secretary for political affairs was able to follow this with a call of her own to the senior official in India's Ministry of External Affairs. These were seen in New Delhi as 'positive signals' from Washington.

More examples of the use of telephone diplomacy between friends and allies – whether to orchestrate their response to an external crisis or smooth out an internal one – accumulate every day. In these circumstances, the likelihood of fewer language barriers, together with greater confidence that any slips of the tongue or ill-considered statements will be treated charitably, also favour use of the telephone. The last point is particularly important and is one reason why the telephone is only rarely a feature of diplomacy between hostile states. (The White House–Kremlin 'hotline', established following the Cuban missile crisis in October 1962, was not a telephone connection but a direct telegraph link.) Nevertheless, it seems to be growing in popularity even between them, as statesmen get more used to it and their phones get smarter – and, in consequence, are reached for almost reflexively. President Reagan employed telephone diplomacy with his Syrian counterpart in 1985, albeit not with much success (Box 7.2). And the calls exchanged on the Ukraine crisis in the first half of 2014 between US President Barack Obama and Russian President Vladimir Putin – one of which lasted for 90 minutes – were equally cool and no more immediately productive, although they advertised to the world the personal priority the two men were giving to the question and their willingness to talk. But, on another sort of occasion, telephone diplomacy between adversaries can have value beyond this.

Box 7.2 The Reagan–Assad telephone call

In July 1985, President Reagan placed a telephone call to President Assad of Syria, then a Soviet-backed state regarded in Washington as a sponsor of terrorism. He thanked him for his role in ending the crisis provoked by the hijacking to Beirut of a TWA airliner, and urged him to use his influence to secure the release of the remaining American kidnap victims being held in Lebanon. The president added, however, that he wanted Assad to end his support for terrorism. Not surprisingly, the conversation was 'stiff and cold' (Shultz 1993: 668). 'He got a little feisty,' the president subsequently recorded in his memoirs, 'and suggested I was threatening to attack Lebanon' (Reagan: 497).

This is the occasion that follows a reduction in tension between unfriendly states, typically caused by a change of leadership on one side or a catastrophic event affecting one or both of them, whether natural or man-made. Such a juncture provides a diplomatic moment that must be seized swiftly, and the telephone is the ideal means. It is interesting that such moments have been a feature of the relationship between the United States and Iran, seriously fractured for decades following the Islamic revolution and subsequent embassy hostages crisis at the end of the 1970s. Thus, a phone conversation between British Prime Minister Tony Blair and Iranian President Mohammed Khatami in the immediate aftermath of the 9/11 attacks in 2001 – while Blair was en route to New York – helped temporarily to break the ice; calls exchanged between US Deputy Secretary of State Richard Armitage and Iran's UN ambassador, Mohammad Javad Zarif, helped in the same way by facilitating acceptance by Tehran of the offer of American aid at the time of the earthquake in Bam in December 2003; and the amiable 15-minute phone conversation between Barack Obama and the new, moderate Iranian President Hassan Rouhani, while the latter was on a visit to the UN in New York in September 2013, was rightly regarded as a major breakthrough by both sides. Obama had wanted a personal meeting with Rouhani while he was in New York but the latter's advisers had judged this domestically still too dangerous for him; instead, the phone call was taken while he was on his way to the airport to catch a plane home.

Video-conferencing stutters

Video-conferencing, in principle, allows any number of persons at remote locations, provided they have compatible facilities, to see and hear each other in real time and, as a result, conduct a 'meeting' without having to go to the trouble and expense of travelling to a distant venue for a personal encounter. It represents a significant advance on a telephone conference call, and has for some time been a mouth-watering prospect to the prophets of virtual diplomacy. Its great advantages are that the visual images it produces enable documents and maps, for example, to be seen simultaneously and, above all, for body language to be expressed. Smiles – forced or genuine – and nods of agreement can clearly be witnessed, as can frowns, glares, yawns, bored expressions, rolling eyes, slumped shoulders, fingers drumming on table tops, shaking heads, and lips curling with contempt. As at real conferences, it is also possible to look for clues to the health of other parties in their appearance, movement, and mannerisms: facial tics indicating high levels of stress are, no doubt, readily discerned on high-definition screens. Something of the influence of particular individuals might also be read into their physical proximity to a lead negotiator and the gestures as well as comments exchanged between them.

Video-conferencing is also becoming cheaper and increasingly sophisticated. There is now a large range of screen sizes; high-definition images are available; 'mobile collaboration' – in addition to point-to-point and multi-point conferencing – can now be employed by means of hand-held devices; and there are strong indications that technological advances and software developments are at last making it possible, inexpensively, to produce eye contact via video screens. Nevertheless, the equipment remains often insecure, and it will clearly be some years before Internet speeds in many parts of the world are sufficient to make video-conferencing widespread. But, even when these obstacles are overcome, it will manifestly still lack the diplomatic advantages of the personal encounter:

- The participants in a video-conference will always miss the physical dimension of body language – for example, the handshake or embrace ('greeting tells') – and, in some cultures, physical touch and bodily closeness are particularly important (Cohen 1987: ch. 5; Collett: ch. 6).
- Video-conferences are also known to be intimidating because of the awareness of being 'on camera'. Politicians are used to this (and, in democracies, relish it) but most officials are not, and whether they might get used to it or not must be a moot point.
- Furthermore, unlike a real conference, video-conferences provide no opportunity to relieve the tension inevitably associated with some diplomatic encounters by gracious social ritual and acts of hospitality.
- Video conferences also provide no opportunities for corridor diplomacy; that is, for informal personal contacts, where the real breakthroughs in negotiations are sometimes made and useful information gleaned.
- Finally, by leaving delegations at home, these so-called conferences also leave them under the *immediate influence of their constituencies* and, therefore, in the position in which they are least likely to adopt an accommodating outlook; to this extent video-conferences are actually anti-diplomatic.

In the light of these drawbacks, it is not surprising that there has been little shift from the view expressed – at the height of optimism about video-conferencing – by Gordon Smith, the former Canadian Deputy Foreign Minister. Negotiations, wrote Smith, who was more open-minded on the question than most diplomats, 'are best done face to face ... video does not work very well unless the parties know each other and the stakes are relatively minor' (Smith 1999: 21).

There is, in fact, little evidence at all that video-conferencing has so far made any significant contribution to serious inter-state negotiation. It is true that, during one of the rotating EU presidencies held by the UK while Tony Blair was prime minister, an EU–Canada 'summit' was held by video-conference on 24 November 2005, with participants located in London, Brussels, and Ottawa. But this was little more than a publicity exercise and appears not to have been repeated. Blair evidently did not regard it as in any sense a milestone because it finds no mention in his memoirs.

From the glimpses of video-conferencing obtainable from foreign ministry websites and a few other sources, then, the position is this: its role in negotiations is limited to those between friendly states, and even in these is limited further; namely, to *supplementing* face-to-face negotiations, especially in the follow-up stage (see Chapter 6). At this stage, there is often an emphasis on information exchange, technicalities, the coordination of agreed actions, and the need for mutual reassurance. It is no doubt for this sort of reason that, after the invasion of Iraq in March 2003, Tony Blair and George W. Bush had confidential video-conferences lasting half an hour to an hour, on average once a fortnight (Sheinwald: 19). And in the immediate aftermath of the same event, Sir Michael Wood, chief legal adviser to the Foreign Office, has revealed that there was 'useful coordination' on the question of the rights and duties of occupying powers with the American and Australian lawyers, in Washington and Canberra respectively, through 'ten or so tripartite video conferences' (Wood 2010: 5).

None of this is to deny that video-conferencing now serves other useful diplomatic purposes, while simultaneously allowing foreign ministries to cut travelling time and costs, and advertise their contribution to reducing carbon emissions. Some use it to engage with groups at home in order to garner their support, as well as to provide more intimate contact with – and among – their embassies abroad. Some embassies use it to assist their public diplomacy. And, like embassies, some international organizations, including the UN, also use it for internal meetings. But all of this is quite different from using video-conferencing to conduct negotiations between governments.

Other means multiply

Extraordinary progress has taken place in other areas of telecommunication, and not only in the mobile-phone technology and text messaging that is now so cheap and ubiquitous. Radio and television broadcasters (with 24-hour news channels at their disposal) now reach wider audiences, not least by streaming over the Internet. So do foreign ministry websites, which are now more informative, available in more languages, easier to use, and more numerous. These media – together with so-called social media – can be used for direct communication between states, as well as for communication with their peoples (see Chapter 13).

In a crisis, radio and television channels, social media, and foreign ministry websites are particularly valuable if, for example, an urgent 'no change in policy' message needs to be sent to a large number of allied states simultaneously. The fact that the commitment has been made publicly also gives added reassurance. If all other channels of communication with a rival state or alliance have collapsed, broadcast communications might be indispensable. With its capacity to present visual images of political leaders, ministerial spokespersons, and ambassadors, television broadcasts and webcasts are particularly useful because – as with video-conferencing – they can send non-verbal, as well as verbal, messages. Also, there is little risk that these messages will be missed. This is because the official monitoring services of a number of countries select and record foreign broadcasts, together with the content of social media and other open source media; they then translate (when necessary) and summarize them. All of this is done with an eye to the special interests of customers in the governments that support them, and those abroad who are friends or are willing to pay. The best known are the US intelligence community's Open Source Center (formerly Foreign Broadcast Information Service) and BBC Monitoring, which have a long-established 'burden-sharing agreement' (BBC: 4); as it happens, both traditionally relied heavily on embassies and consulates as bases for their overseas operations.

Finally, it is necessary to emphasize the impact of electronic mail and text messaging (SMS). This has now more or less replaced the telegram or cable in communications between foreign ministries and missions, and – via smartphones – has the capacity to maintain contact with diplomats via these modes in most locations. There is also sufficient confidence in the security of smartphones – with enhanced encryption – to permit their use at head of state and government level, although it was not always so. Bill Clinton was the first American president to use email (Patterson: 59), but there were reports that Israeli intelligence had tapped into his messages; partly for this reason, George W. Bush never used it at all. This changed with the inauguration in January 2009 of Barack Obama, who was already addicted to his BlackBerry, as was Secretary of State Hillary Clinton to hers. In 2014, this device was still popular with other leaders, despite the Canadian company's declining fortunes.

Electronic mail and text messaging have brought their own perils, some of which – for example, the risk of impulsive decision-making – are identical to those of telephone diplomacy. However, email probably presents a more serious threat to security. Messages can be accidentally forwarded to unintended recipients too easily, and the 'reply to all' facility is a special hazard. The latter is not only a particularly clear security threat but can also create a perfect email storm, with the capacity to capsize a whole service. In January 2009, just such an event caused the US Department of State to threaten employees worldwide with disciplinary action in the event of its careless use. (This threat was issued by means of a cable.) The temptation to diplomats of some countries with poor government email services to use instead free, web-based services like Gmail, Yahoo and Hotmail for official business on ministry computers can also be difficult to resist. This is a security threat because of the risk of importing viruses and spyware, and led the Indian external affairs ministry to ban it in February 2009. And then there are weak passwords and poorly understood encryption systems, which can easily render email accounts public knowledge. In 2007 such failings were responsible for embarrassing numerous governments – including those of Russia, India, China, and Iran – when the login credentials of many email accounts at embassies were published on the Internet by a Swedish hacker (the password for the Iranian embassy in Tunisia was, you guessed it, 'Tunisia'). Because it makes it so easy for everyone to have their say, this kind of communications technology also weakens or (depending on your point of view) makes more democratic the authority structure in foreign ministries and embassies.

Despite its risks, email – probably more so than video-conferencing – is a valuable *supplement* to negotiating between states by means of face-to-face meetings and telephone conversations. It is fast, cheap, and rarely goes astray; it makes very easy the exchange of documents, reference to relevant Internet sites via provision of URLs, copying messages to interested parties, and keeping an accurate record of a negotiation. A crude means of helping to avoid misunderstanding in email messages is also now well understood: the use of 'emoticons' – symbols expressing emotions.

Summary

Direct telecommunication between governments is now a very important channel for the conduct of diplomacy, both in crises and more normal times, despite its risks and limitations. In crises, the telephone is especially valued by allied and friendly states, not least at head of state and government level. Here it seems to be used chiefly as a vehicle for providing reassurance and intelligence, urging support, explaining attitudes, and agreeing joint responses to fast-moving events. Adversaries in a crisis are more likely to use written telecommunication, although use of the telephone might be essential when an opportunity to improve relations is a fleeting one. Video-conferencing has had little impact on the world of serious international negotiations, while in routine diplomacy email is now the written mode of telecommunication of choice.

Further reading

Berend, Dennis, 'The last days of the FBIS Mediterranean Bureau', 18, Winter 1974 (CIA Historical Review Progam) [www.]. A declassified document providing a dramatic account of what happened to the Cyprus bureau after the Turkish army landed.

Callaghan, James, *Time and Chance* (Collins: London, 1987): 344–6.

Cohen, Raymond, *Theatre of Power: The art of diplomatic signalling* (Longman: London, 1987): ch. 5.

Collett, Peter, *The Book of Tells: How to read people's minds from their actions* (Transworld: London, 2003): on body language.

Dobrynin, Anatoly, *In Confidence: Moscow's ambassador to America's six Cold War presidents (1962–86)* (University of Washington Press: Seattle, 2001): 96–8.

International Telecommunication Union, 'History' and 'Landmarks' [www].

Johnson, Joe, 'Wiring State: A progress report', *Foreign Service Journal*, December 2005 [www].

Jones, R. A., *The British Diplomatic Service 1815–1914* (Smythe: London, 1983): ch. 7.

Kennedy, P. M., 'Imperial cable communications and strategy, 1870–1914', *English Historical Review*, 86, October 1971.

Kissinger, Henry A., *Years of Upheaval* (Weidenfeld & Nicolson and Michael Joseph: London, 1982): chs 11–12.

McNamara, Robert, *Blundering into Disaster: Surviving the first century of the nuclear age* (Pantheon: New York, 1986): 10–13.

National Security Archive, 'The Kissinger Telcons: The Dobrynin files' (2004) [www].

'Negotiation Training Workshop: Negotiating via e-mail?' Negotiation Training Institute [www].

Nickles, David Paull, *Under the Wire: How the telegraph changed diplomacy* (Harvard University Press: Cambridge, MA, 2003).

Patterson, Jr., Bradley H., *The White House Staff: Inside the West Wing and beyond* (Brookings: Washington, DC, 2000): 57–9.

Rana, Kishan S., *21st Century Diplomacy: A practitioner's guide* (Continuum: London, 2011): ch. 10.

Smith, Gerard C., *Disarming Diplomat: The memoirs of Gerard C. Smith, arms control negotiator* (Madison: New York, 1996): 107–9, 174–5.

US Department of State, 'US diplomacy and the telegraph, 1866' [www].

United States Institute of Peace, *Virtual Diplomacy Initiative* [www].

8
Embassies

Resident embassies are the normal means of conducting diplomacy between any two states. The British scholar-diplomat Harold Nicolson called such bilateral diplomacy the 'French system of diplomacy' because of the dominant influence of France on its evolution and the gradual replacement of Latin by French as its working language. This chapter will begin by glimpsing the evolution of this system and follow with an outline of today's normal embassy – and thus of what most embassies have in common. It will conclude with a lengthy examination of the most significant variations from this norm: the fortress embassy, the mini-embassy, and the militarized embassy. *Middle Ages & Start of Embassies*

In the Middle Ages, responsibility for diplomacy was given chiefly either to a *nuncius* or a plenipotentiary, both temporary envoys with narrowly defined tasks. The former was no more than a 'living letter', whereas the latter had 'full powers' – *plena potestas*, hence the later 'plenipotentiary' – to negotiate on behalf of and bind his principal (Queller: chs 1 and 2). But envoys of the last sort were expensive to dispatch, vulnerable on the road, and always likely to cause trouble over precedence and ceremonial because of the high status required of them. And it was chiefly for these reasons, when diplomatic activity in Europe – especially on the Italian peninsula – intensified in the late fifteenth century, that the most visited courts saw them replaced by resident embassies with broad responsibilities. It may well be, too, that the example of permanent consular posts, long employed by trading peoples, encouraged this development (Queller: 82; also Satow: vol. I, 240–1).

Resident embassies in a foreign country not only minimized the risks and expense of constant journeying by rough roads and unpredictable seas; they also aided political reporting and the more discreet preparation, conduct, and following up of negotiations. At first most states were reluctant to tolerate such missions because of fear that they would house spies and give support to traitors, while some disdained to send them out because of complacency about their own omnipotence (the Ottomans did not establish them until 1793 and the Chinese not for almost another century). Nevertheless, by the sixteenth-century resident missions were an established institution of major significance. This was reflected in the customary law of nations and the slow but sure professionalization of the diplomatic craft.

It was gradually accepted by jurists that diplomats – together with their domestic families, official staffs, communications, means of transport, and buildings – needed special 'privileges and immunities' under local criminal and civil law. There were, however, different views as to why this should be so. Some said that embassies were an extension of the territory of the sending state; but this mistook a metaphor for a justification. Others maintained that special treatment rested on the ambassador's character as a '*full* representative' of a sovereign; but this left the rest of his staff in the cold. Accordingly, the functional theory gradually gained ground. This held that diplomats need special legal protection simply because without it they might be subjected to so much local harassment that they would be unable to discharge effectively their essential functions.

In 1961, with the assistance of the UN's International Law Commission (ILC), the corpus of diplomatic law was codified in the Vienna Convention on Diplomatic Relations (VCDR). This clarified the customary rules and adjusted them to modern conditions. In the process, it sought not only to provide more protection to diplomats but also to reconcile to their privileges those most apprehensive of their abuse: states such as Yugoslavia, anxious about the uses to which the superpowers were putting their embassies in the Cold War; the new, ex-colonial states, fearful that the missions of the rich capitalist states were an instrument of neo-colonialism; and the citizens of major capital cities in the West, apprehensive at the prospect of a rip current of unpunished 'diplomatic crime' as the numbers of their diplomatic residents swelled with arrivals from the Third World.

Basing itself squarely on the functional theory of the special legal position of diplomatic agents, among other things, the VCDR strengthened privileges important to the proper functions of embassies, notably by asserting flatly that agents of the receiving state could not enter a mission's premises without the consent of its chief, and by placing a special duty on the receiving state to protect them. On the other hand, the Convention tightened the categories of those by whom privileges could be invoked; and it repeatedly referred to the embassy duty of non-interference in domestic affairs, making a number of practical stipulations to ensure its observance. Among the latter were the provisions that *agrément* might be required for service attachés (always suspected of being spies) as well as new heads of mission, and that receiving states could insist on the slimming down of missions they thought too large. At the time of writing, 190 of the 193 states members of the UN are parties to the VCDR.

The professionalization of embassy work had developed much more slowly than diplomatic law, although the interest of all diplomats in defending its rules had long encouraged a sense of professional identity among them. This was seen in the emergence of the *corps diplomatique* (diplomatic body) not long after the invention of the resident embassy itself. The 'diplomatic corps', as the term was corrupted in English, is the community of diplomats representing different states resident in the same capital, and is headed by the longest-serving ambassador among their number (the dean); until the early twentieth century it was strengthened by aristocratic class solidarity and the fact that many diplomats had foreign wives. (The diplomatic *corps* is not be confused with the diplomatic *service* of individual states, although it usually is.) In most cases, it was not until well into the nineteenth century that the members of the diplomatic service began to enjoy the advantages of a profession: controlled entry, some form of training, a code of conduct, regular payment, clear ranks through which upward progression might be made, and a pension on retirement.

Conducting diplomacy principally by means of resident embassies had always suffered certain drawbacks. Prior to the great improvements in the means of connecting them with home witnessed in the later nineteenth century, one in particular was the diplomats' tendency to 'go native'. This occupational hazard meant at best losing touch with sentiments at home and at worst becoming the mouthpiece for the government to which they were accredited rather than the one they were supposed to represent. The causes of 'localitis', which is not unknown today, are not difficult to understand: it might come via the kind of immersion in the local culture necessary to effective diplomacy, from gratitude for gifts and decorations from local rulers and other influential figures, or from the need to show sympathy for the local point of view in order to gain official access. Awareness of this occupational hazard eventually led to the rotation of diplomats between postings, typically after three or four years, which did not necessarily mean the waste of hard-won area expertise because diplomats could be returned to early postings later in their careers or placed on the desks of the foreign ministry dealing with the same country or region.

[handwritten margin note: During & after WWI]

During and immediately after World War I, attacks on the 'old diplomacy' conducted by resident missions had barely a whiff of concern about localitis. Instead, its drawbacks were alleged to be the resistance to democratic control of its aristocratic members, its excessive secrecy, and the snail's pace at which it proceeded. Hence the popular view that a more 'open' multilateral system was needed, and the consequent creation of the League of Nations in 1919.

Despite much rhetoric about a 'new diplomacy', embassies remained numerous and important in the inter-war years. However, a few decades after World War II they were once more on the defensive, with almost the whole emphasis this time on their alleged obsolescence. This case was supported by three chief arguments:

[handwritten note: After WWII]

- Direct contact between the political leaders and home-based experts of different states had been made much easier by the combined effects of dramatic improvements in travel and communications and the multiplication of multilateral meeting points – not least at the new United Nations.
- Embassy political reporting had been overtaken by the huge growth in the international mass media.
- Ideological tensions and deepening cultural divisions across the world meant that the exchange of embassies by hostile states provided – quite literally – dangerous hostages to fortune, as illustrated by the fate of the US Embassy in Tehran, the seizure of which by revolutionary students in late 1979 was condoned by the new Iranian government and its staff held hostage for 444 days.

In short, embassies were a worthless liability and should be abolished.

Nevertheless, although the networks of resident embassies of some states have shrunk, those of others have expanded. China now has almost as many as the United States – over 160 – and the national embassies of EU member states have recently been supplemented by roughly 140 missions under the direction of the European External Action Service, which are called 'delegations' only to avoid trampling on the sensitivities of those EU member states anxious about the implication of sovereignty carried by the term 'embassy'. Many embassies are also larger than ever. For example, the staff of the British Embassy in Turkey is now four times the size that it was during the heyday of Lord Stratford de Redcliffe in the Crimean War, and twice the size it was in 1878, despite the fact that, in that year, it was temporarily inflated by the first cohort of student interpreters from the newly created Levant Consular Service and a flood of military attachés caused by the outbreak of the Russo-Turkish war (Berridge 2009: 274).

Permanent diplomatic missions vary not only in their size but also in many other respects. This has always been true, but in recent years their differences have become more marked owing to dramatic changes in their operating conditions in some regions and a more difficult climate at home. Which are the most important variations from a public policy point of view? All things considered, these are perhaps the fortress embassy, the mini-embassy, and the militarized embassy. First, however, we must consider the norm from which these are the most significant deviations.

The normal embassy

The normal embassy is that assumed by the provisions of the VCDR. This gives it the functions, among others, of representing the sending state and protecting its interests in the receiving state, while gathering information about the latter state, and negotiating and promoting friendly relations with it – all within the limits of international law (Article 3). The Convention adds that receiving states can insist that missions be kept to a size they regard as 'reasonable and normal, having regard to circumstances and conditions in the receiving State and to the needs of the particular mission' (Article 11). How is the normal embassy organized, could its organization be improved, and how valuable is its contribution to diplomacy?

The normal embassy is led by an ambassador, who is supported by a deputy chief of mission (DCM) of sufficient experience and rank – usually minister, minister-counsellor, or counsellor – to be able to take charge of the mission when necessary (chargé d'affaires). In diplomatic law, the embassy's premises include the residence of the chief of mission as well as the business part or 'chancery', even though they are often physically separate. The chancery is divided into sections, traditionally administration, political, economic-commercial (see Chapter 14), defence, public diplomacy, cultural, and consular; in safer cities some of these might also be dispersed to different addresses. Where other sections exist, their functions reflect the peculiarities of national diplomatic services and the priorities of a particular relationship. Thus the French Embassy in Delhi has a nuclear energy section and the numerous sections of the US Embassy in Mexico City include two dealing with narcotics and another handling customs and border protection.

The rank held by section heads varies with the size and importance of the embassy but is rarely below first secretary. The more specialized sections are often staffed by personnel employed by agencies and ministries other than the foreign ministry, including one or more intelligence officers under 'diplomatic cover' (see Chapter 10) – but such personnel (often 'attachés') all constitute theoretically what in the US Foreign Service is called a 'country team' under the authority of the ambassador.

However, embassy sections can become silos, in which staff become unresponsive to each other and to the ambassador. In order to create instead a 'one-team mentality', with the added advantage that the chief of mission is the 'boss' rather than just the 'host', it has been suggested that the traditional organization of embassies into sections should be more or less abandoned, and 'project-based working' employed instead (Advisory Committee: 65–6). This seems a good idea in principle, but its over-enthusiastic introduction would probably produce furious arguments over priorities, cause important but temporarily unfashionable projects to be lost sight of, and lead to permanent administrative turmoil. On the other hand, larger embassies could – and evidently do – benefit from a compromise between these two administrative models: traditional sections with broad remits, plus some themed on current projects of particular importance. This is seen in the examples of the French and American embassies given in the preceding paragraph.

The normal embassy is supported by administrative and technical staff and by domestic staff. In recent years, chiefly because they are much cheaper and have local knowledge and language skills, the numbers of locally engaged (LE) as opposed to home-based staff employed in embassies have greatly increased, even in more sensitive roles. However, they have no diplomatic protection and often live at some distance from the embassy. In times of serious unrest in the receiving state, especially if this is accompanied by a deterioration in relations with the sending state, this can present acute problems to the embassy: LE staff might find it impossible to get into work and even be arrested. This was the fate of the Iranian employees of the political and economic section of the British Embassy in Tehran in June 2009.

As to the work of the embassy, what, first of all, of representation? As representative of a state, the embassy has value even if the ambassador never gets out of bed. This is because the existence of the mission highlights the sending state's recognition of the receiving state and the value it attaches to normal relations with it. If designed and built by the sending state, it might also symbolize values or aspirations to which this state attaches high importance. For example, the new Turkish Embassy opened in Berlin in October 2012 consists of two halves separated by a high, copper-covered archway meant to represent Turkey's position as a bridge between Europe and Asia.

But the chief of mission, on whose shoulders the representative function principally falls, can do much more to advance it – hosting social occasions, giving public lectures, appearing on television and radio shows, attending state ceremonies, and so on. The embassy's contribution in this area is also important when it is expedient for senior government figures to go abroad on similar duties, for they are highly dependent on its support; this applies as much to the forward planning and aftermath as to the period of the visit itself (Berridge 2009: 234–6). The existence of a resident embassy also broadens a state's representative options and thus its repertoire of non-verbal signals. For example, at the funeral of Soviet leader Leonid Brezhnev in Moscow in 1982, most foreign delegations were headed by dignitaries flown in for the occasion. Nevertheless, a few countries found it expedient to be represented merely by their resident ambassadors; in their absence, it might have been difficult to avoid showing either too much or too little respect (Berridge 1994: 142). For representational purposes, resident missions are generally of special importance to new states and established ones in declining circumstances.

A further duty of the normal embassy, according to the VCDR, is to promote 'friendly' relations with the receiving state, although it might have been better had it said 'civil' relations, for an embassy seeking the emotional embrace of a hostile government would obviously be in a false position (Barder: 93–4). The real point is, then, that – in any country – the normal embassy seeks simply to be as well networked as possible: to cultivate extensive social contacts, especially in influential quarters; to honour local customs and mark important local events, in so far as these are compatible with its own values; and, in the process, avoid giving gratuitous offence if some unpleasant message has to be delivered to the host government, a newspaper editor, or anyone else. By these means it is easier to gain influence and gather information, and the embassy is better placed to handle a crisis in relations should one subsequently develop. Diplomats who are courteous, agreeable without being ingratiating, familiar with the understatement of their profession, fluent in the local language, fully acquainted with protocol, and sensitive to local prejudice – in short, professionals – are more likely to pull all this off than anyone else.

In negotiations, the normal embassy also continues to have more than a walk-on part, acting under instructions which are now so easy to issue and update electronically. Subjects that might still be left largely or even entirely to it include those of relatively minor importance, a few of greater significance (such as status of forces agreements or the rescheduling of loan repayments), and kidnappings – which usually take a long time and great secrecy to resolve. And when busy home-based experts or, more rarely, government ministers take the lead in the 'around-the-table' stage of a bilateral negotiation, embassies are still needed to nurse them through it and to take a more prominent role in the prenegotiations and follow-up stages (see Part I). Sometimes, too, ambassadors particularly respected for their local knowledge are brought back to reinforce a negotiation being conducted at home, as when the US ambassadors to Egypt and Israel were included in the 11-man US negotiating team at the Camp David summit in September 1978 (Carter: 327).

Closely related to negotiating is lobbying by the embassy: encouraging those with influence in the receiving state to take a favourable attitude to its country's interests on particular issues. The character of embassy lobbying varies with the receiving state's constitution and political culture. In general, personal contact is essential and typical targets are government departments and opinion leaders in business and the media. Only where elected assemblies have real influence, as in the United States in consequence of its constitutional doctrine of the separation of powers, do legislators also attract embassy attention. All former ambassadors at Washington report their heavy involvement in lobbying; Allan Gotlieb, Canadian Ambassador in the US capital during the 1980s, gives the impression that he had time for little else (Gotlieb: 44, 56, 76). However, such is the institutional maze of US official decision-making and so great the appreciation of the need for lobbying that many embassies in Washington hire American public relations companies, law firms, and others for this purpose (Newhouse: 74). This tendency has increased despite the fact that since at least the mid-1930s the employment of US citizens as 'nondiplomatic representatives of foreign principals' has periodically attracted hostile attention in Congress and legislation designed to expose them. This is not least because, as Senator Fulbright pointed out in 1963, their acceptability is not subject to the same degree of official approval as that of bona fide diplomats (*Hearings*: 3); that is, they cannot, if necessary, be declared *persona non grata* (PNG).

Clarifying intentions is another task where the embassy's contribution remains important. This is chiefly because foreign ministers, and especially presidents and prime ministers – who, it is only fair to acknowledge, have much wider briefs to master – too often indulge in vague public posturing and out and out waffling. A foreign government might need to be reassured ('relax – we're only invading your neighbour'), alarmed ('these sanctions are just the first step'), encouraged ('we like what you're doing'), or deterred ('do that and you'll regret it'). And an ambassador can supplement a written expression of intent with an oral explanation; the resident diplomat can also convey it without the speculation likely to be aroused by the arrival of a special envoy on the same mission. If reassurance is the import of a message, a statement by a trusted ambassador will be as good a medium as many and better than most. In time of war, the ambassadors of allies play a particularly important role in this regard.

Reporting home on present conditions and probable developments in the receiving state also remains a valuable role of the normal embassy, immersed as it is in the local scene. What is particularly impressive is the extent of reliance on embassies for knowledge of the *mind* of the local leadership. For example, during the American-mediated negotiations between Israel and Egypt in the 1977–9 period – in which accurately sensing the mood of Egyptian President Anwar Sadat was of vital importance to the Carter administration – great reliance was placed on the reports of the US Ambassador in Cairo, Herman Eilts, who, by 28 November 1978, had enjoyed more than 250 meetings with the Egyptian leader (Carter: 320–1; Quandt: 166, 284). Carter also paid close attention to the on-the-spot reports of the US Ambassador in Tel Aviv, Samuel Lewis (Carter: 321). By contrast, a mission at the UN can usually do no more than pick up clues about another country from the latter's own mission, while the quality of information obtained by special envoys tends to be impaired by the brevity of their visits. As for spies – except for that rare specimen, the agent in place – they do not enjoy regular, high-level access. Neither do journalists, who, in any case, do not always ask the questions to which governments attach special interest, or give the same priority to the *accuracy* of their information. And, while a journalist's dispatch might be censored, a diplomat's might not. In closed societies, the information gathered by a diplomatic mission is particularly important.

It follows naturally from the respect still generally accorded to the local knowledge of the competent embassy that its advice on policy is usually welcomed as well. Even in 1969, at a time when resident missions were often said to be out of date, the Duncan Report in Britain picked this out for special emphasis (HCPP 1969: 18, 91), as did the Murphy Commission Report in the United States six years later. Advice on policy is particularly valued if ambassadors have acquired a high professional reputation. Moreover, dramatic advances in telecommunications, previously believed to have weakened their office, now enable heads of mission to communicate their views to their own governments with great rapidity: as already noted, embassies have become more completely integrated into foreign ministry policy formulation than ever before (see p. 10). An ambassador might also be recalled for consultation, and in some countries there is a tradition of discussing policy at periodic or *ad hoc* conferences of chiefs of diplomatic and consular missions from a particular region.

The normal embassy can also fulfil any number of subsidiary functions, some less defensible than others. Those of donor states are valuable in the administration of foreign aid in the developing world. One reason for this is that the bigger powers commonly have a variety of agencies involved in aid work and the embassy is the natural vehicle for the coordination, as well as the protection, of their efforts; another is that the political relationship between givers and receivers is notoriously fragile and thus needs delicate handling (Trevelyan: 106). Embassies can also provide diplomatic cover for drugs liaison officers and immigration liaison officers, as well as for the traditional intelligence officer. These agents, whose work is equally sensitive and sometimes dangerous, are now quite strongly represented in European and American embassies in countries along the transit routes of illegal narcotics and people trafficking (Berridge 2009: 255–61).

An illegal subsidiary function sometimes imposed on the normal embassy is intervention in the political affairs of the receiving state. The major powers in particular find their embassies to be excellent forward bases from which to conduct political operations. Such activities might be aimed at propping up a friendly regime or undermining a hostile one, and involve anything from the secret channelling to the friendly faction of funds, arms, and medical supplies, to organizing a military coup against the opposition. Zbigniew Brzezinski, who saw no use for embassies *before* he became National Security Advisor to President Jimmy Carter in 1977, wanted the US ambassador in Tehran to persuade the Iranian military to seize power. The ambassador had no objection to this in principle, opposing it only on the grounds that it would not work.

The normal embassy might well be useful, too, in conducting relations between hostile states on the territory of a third. If the United States and the PRC had not both had resident missions in such places as Geneva, Warsaw, and Paris, a channel of communication that played an important role in limiting their conflict and ultimately in facilitating their *rapprochement* in the 1970s would have been unavailable. Later, communication between the United States and the Socialist Republic of Vietnam was facilitated by their missions in Bangkok and between the United States and North Korea by their missions in Beijing. To take a final example, in 2013 there was for a brief period a hope that American and Afghan Taliban missions in Qatar would serve a similar purpose.

As a 'full-service' mission, the normal embassy now often serves as a 'hub' to much smaller, limited-service ones at the ends of the communication 'spokes' in its regional wheel (see the section on mini-embassies below). The hub-and-spoke model is hardly new because this was always the nature of the relationship between an embassy and its (subordinate) consular outposts, the more important instances of which were embassies by another name – and at least in emergencies had the right to report directly to the foreign ministry at home. Nevertheless, it is a relatively novel development that missions with embassy status should be formally dependent on a bigger embassy in their region. In the case of the Dutch diplomatic service, this 'regionalization' has started in the Baltic and Central America (Advisory Committee: 20).

The fortress embassy

The fortress embassy is the most spectacular and controversial deviation from the normal embassy. Harbingers of this can be found in the 'compounds' of early Western embassies in the East and in the re-designed defences of the legation quarter in Peking following the attacks it suffered during the Boxer uprising in 1900. But the genuine fortress embassy is very much a development of recent years.

Traditionally, embassies usually occupied existing residential properties that were either bought or – more often – rented by their governments. This suited the ebb and flow of diplomatic relations and also enabled states to maintain their embassies close to government offices, where vacant building land was not always easy to obtain. Such buildings were not positioned or designed for defence, and the renting or purchasing of office or residential properties by embassies remains common today.

In the nineteenth century some richer states began to build their own embassies in states with which they had stable and important relationships, but these were not built for defence either. Instead, they were constructed to be comfortable, serviceable, and fire-proof, and to provide an outward appearance that showed off national characteristics – including wealth. After World War II, the United States, awash with holdings of soft local currencies, lavished money on embassies featuring glass walls, visual openness, and easy access to the public.

Whether rented, bought or purpose-built, embassies were thus exposed to popular unrest both by their physical characteristics and locations – central, and usually close to the street. For their safety, they relied chiefly on token guards, the advice of a service attaché if they had one, and – above all – on the principle of reciprocity and the fact that under diplomatic law 'a special duty' was placed on receiving states 'to take all appropriate steps' to protect them (VCDR: Art. 22.2).

Unfortunately, receiving states have too often proved unable – and occasionally unwilling – to discharge this duty. As the battle involving the Legation Quarter in Peking following the Boxer uprising in 1900 reminds us, this is not a new development. But until the late 1950s, attacks on diplomatic and consular missions were comparatively rare. At that point, however, noisy demonstrations outside embassies escalating to their invasion began to become a recurrent fact of international life. Where US missions were concerned, this trend culminated in the suicide bomb attack on the American Embassy compound in Beirut on 18 April 1983, which killed approximately 60 people, injured 120, and completely destroyed the central consular section of the building. The missions of other states have also had to accept that they are at permanent risk of bomb attacks from hostile groups. For example, Israeli embassies have suffered at the hands of pro-Palestinian factions, notably in Buenos Aires in 1992; and those of Turkey have for many years attracted the violent attention of Armenian organizations. The missions of close allies of America in its recent military adventures have also experienced deadly assaults, as in the case of the Australian Embassy in Jakarta in 2004.

In consequence of this development, new security-driven design and building standards for its diplomatic properties were devised by the United States and copied – or partially copied – by others. Introduced in the late 1980s, following an investigation led by Admiral Bobby R. Inman, and elaborated further following more devastating attacks on US embassies in East Africa in 1998, among the most important of the new standards called for were:

- spacious sites set back at least 100 feet from any surrounding streets;
- concentration on the 'compound' of all non-military personnel;
- blast-proof construction;
- high perimeter walls;
- vehicle arrest barriers; and (should all else fail)
- strengthened safe rooms resembling the 'keep' in a Norman castle to which all personnel might retreat.

In practice, the first two of these standards combined to demand remote locations, and hill-top sites in the case of a few missions thought to be especially vulnerable; for example, the US Consulate-General in Istanbul and the Israeli Embassy in Amman. All have been given more security guards (some supplied by private companies), and in a few imploding states embassy military contingents have even been supplied with heavy armaments, including anti-tank weapons. Thus the fortress embassy, the ultimate expression of which is the vast US Embassy in Baghdad, officially opened in early 2009. Near copies of this are still being planned or in process of being built by other states in volatile countries important to them – thus Australia's designs for new embassies in Jakarta and Bangkok (Australian Government 2009 and 2011).   *Opponents*

The fortress embassy divides opinion among diplomats. Opponents claim that it badly impedes their work because their buildings no longer symbolize attractive values; instead, advertising lack of trust in the local authorities. Their forbidding aspect is also said to discourage local visitors, and their costliness to reduce the amount of money available for the foreign ministry to spend on other projects. It is a sad irony, add the opponents of this deviant embassy, that, while it might reduce the threat to its staff in some ways, it actually increases it in others. Thus, by putting off local visitors, it requires the holding of more meetings on the outside if any business is to be done (Pope: 69), while remote locations mean that car journeys to and from it take longer and those who come and go are more readily identified.   *Supporters*

Supporters of the fortress embassy, on the other hand, while conceding that it hinders diplomatic business (especially when remotely located), insist on the overriding duty of care for the safety of mission staff, the majority of whom are usually not diplomatic officers anyway. They also claim that there is no firm evidence that the unwelcoming appearance of the fortress embassy puts off local visitors (Pietrowicz), and argue that it would show even less trust in the ability of the local authorities to provide embassy protection if, instead of fortifying their premises, sending states were to shut up shop and leave the country altogether. Finally, supporters point out that, if the fortress embassy is a 'hub' embassy that provides back-up to smaller missions in the region, it is essential to *regional* diplomacy even if not well suited to *local* diplomacy.

In practice the popularity of the complete fortress embassy has dropped off markedly in the last few years, partly because of the criticism and partly because of the difficulty of finding sites that meet its standards. Some new American embassies – those in Berlin and Beijing, for example – have already been erected in *central* locations and architectural innovation is once more being valued. Sensibly enough, risk management rather than risk avoidance has become the watchword.

The mini-embassy

The mini-embassy is usually defined as a diplomatic mission with no more than four home-based staff, principally diplomatic. (Foreign ministries tend not to distinguish between diplomatic officers and administrative and technical staff in reporting on these posts.) Such embassies might even have only one home-based diplomat, as until recently did two British high commissions in the Caribbean. They will, however, usually be strengthened greatly by a larger number of LE staff, so the term 'mini-embassy' (or 'micro-mission') is sometimes misleading.

This kind of embassy is relatively cheap and has been made a more practical proposition by the extraordinary advances in diplomatic communications of recent years. As a result, it is attractive not only to poor countries but also to richer ones in Europe accustomed to widespread representation but now suffering from hard-pressed foreign affairs budgets. It is seen by the latter as a device to maintain a presence in regions such as Central Asia and sub-Saharan Africa, where the rising powers of China and Turkey are extending their diplomatic reach. The mini-embassy can also be set up quickly in response to rapidly changing circumstances (even physically assembled Ikea-style from flat-packs, as in Baghdad in 2003) and, by the same token, be swiftly evacuated. It is also a good diplomatic training ground, for it provides a more varied experience and earlier responsibility to junior officers.

On the other hand, this very small embassy has many disadvantages, and some regard it as never advisable (Jazbec: 182). It provides no scope for specialization, and what it can actually do is also severely limited. As a result, it is likely to produce discontent among expatriates dissatisfied with its services, and invite invidious comparisons among locals with the larger embassies of rival states. It also risks deluding politicians at home into announcing grandiose ambitions for a region on the grounds that it has a 'presence' there. Clearly, too, the mini-embassy is not viable in countries where security is a major issue; and over-reliance on LE staff has its own drawbacks (see p. 120). The impact on this dwarf-like embassy of failings on the part of just one individual – particularly at isolated posts in periods of sustained tension – is proportionately higher and often remarked on (FAC 1998–9: 157; FAC 1999: 217). When there are failings on the part of two it can be disastrous: at the US mini-embassy in the quixotic and barbarous dictatorship of Equatorial Guinea in 1971, the chargé d'affaires murdered the only other American at the post, whom he regarded as incompetent (Erdos; Hoffacker; Shurtleff). Fortunately, steps can be taken to minimize at least some of the risks attending the tiny embassy. Regular inspections should provide early warning of staffing problems. Its security problems, as well as its financial overheads, are eased if it is housed in the same building as the missions of like-minded states; for example, in 2010 Sweden established a mini-embassy in Astana, Kazakhstan, co-located with similar Norwegian and Finnish missions. And the mini-embassy can be supported by a regional hub embassy like the British Embassy in Stockholm, which backs up five much smaller embassies in the FCO's 'Nordic-Baltic network'. A variation on this theme is the rapid deployment team, on standby either at home or in regional bases. Headed by a senior diplomat, composed of staff with a variety of skills, and complete with its own communications and security, this is designed to reinforce speedily *any* mission in a consular crisis, but is particularly valuable in sustaining the viability of the mini-embassy.

The militarized embassy

The militarized embassy is a wartime embassy that, to a significant extent, displays a military outlook and style without necessarily also being a fortress embassy. Such embassies might be found among those of belligerents to important neutrals, neutrals to belligerents engaged in a conflict that touches the neutrals' own vital interests, or belligerents finding themselves in enemy states after the outbreak of fighting, with little to do but work out how to get home – unless diplomatic relations remain formally intact. But the paradigm case of the militarized embassy, in which the supremacy of the ambassador is regularly under more or less subtle challenge from the mission's large military component, is usually to be found among the embassies of belligerents accredited to the governments of frontline allies.

The experience of the militarized embassy depends chiefly on the nature of the military conflict in which its country's frontline ally is engaged. In a conventional war, some routine embassy functions are relegated to the sidelines or fall away altogether, and non-essential staff and dependants are usually sent home, especially if the mission needs to up sticks and follow a retreating government: the embassy is stripped for action and focussed almost completely on supporting the war effort. A first priority is to preserve close, high-level personal contact with the allied host government in order to concert policy and preserve its morale. When belligerent embassies have major military forces of their own on their ally's territory, as was the case with the embassies in Saudi Arabia of the United States and its 'Coalition' partners at the time of the war to rescue Kuwait from Iraq in 1991, they also have to assist in the negotiation of such sensitive matters as status of forces agreements and serve as political adviser to the commander-in-chief. Whether the belligerent embassy is accompanied by a major military force or not, it has numerous other duties to perform once fighting has started. These include advancing plans for the evacuation of any remaining expatriates and, in the meantime, offering advice on how they might protect themselves; handling hordes of VIP visitors and journalists; and, if they have any time left, offering advice on post-war affairs, including a war-termination strategy.

In a low-intensity conflict, the role of the belligerent embassy to an allied frontline state is normally similar but usually includes attention to at least some routine tasks in order to pretend that things are going on much as normal. When large forces of the embassy's country are committed to fighting a domestic insurgency against a new, weak client regime, as recently in Iraq and Afghanistan, what is also different is the intense and sometimes open involvement of the embassy in politics and, indeed, in government; as also in promoting reconstruction. When, however, the situation deteriorates into a Hobbesian state of nature, as in post-Qadhafi Libya, the temptation is to establish only a mission staffed by 'expeditionary diplomats' (Cordesman) – the foreign ministry's equivalent of the military's special forces, a brave but risky concept (Berridge 2013b).

Whether the background is a conventional war or a low-intensity conflict, the consequences of embassy militarization can be serious. Insensitive behaviour is more likely to occur and might cause local alienation; strong local suspicions about the mission's intentions might also be aroused, even if they are in fact benign. Worst of all, if the fighting is going badly, the embassy will be more likely to attach priority to the demand for more troops and equipment than to the search for a political solution.

Summary

The resident embassy has survived the communications and transport revolutions chiefly because it remains an excellent means by which to support if not lead in the execution of key diplomatic functions. However, due to dramatic changes in operating conditions in some regions and public spending cutbacks at home, variations from the full-service normal embassy have become more marked. Notable among these are the fortress embassy, which strongly divides diplomatic opinion and seems to be on the wane; the mini-embassy, which elicits respect only from xenophobes and finance ministries; and the militarized embassy, the paradigm case of which is usually the embassy of a belligerent to a frontline ally, and tends to be more widely accepted as a regrettable necessity. This variety is, nevertheless, eloquent evidence of the resilience of the resident embassy: the death of this institution, so confidently predicted in the 1970s and early 1980s, has been indefinitely postponed.

Further reading

Accountability Review Board for Benghazi, *Report* (2012) [www].

Advisory Committee on Modernising the Diplomatic Service, *Modernising Dutch Diplomacy: Progress Report, Final Report* (May 2014) [www].

Argyros, George L., Mark Grossman, and Felix Rohatyn, *The Embassy of the Future* (Center for Strategic and International Studies: Washington, DC, 2007) [www].

Austermann, Frauke, 'Towards embassies for Europe? EU Delegations in the Union's diplomatic system', *Policy Paper*, 8, January 2012 [www].

Berridge, G. R., *British Diplomacy in Turkey, 1583 to the Present: A study in the evolution of the resident embassy* (Martinus Nijhoff: Leiden, 2009): ch. 10.

Berridge, G. R., *Embassies in Armed Conflict* (Continuum: New York, 2012).

Berridge, G. R., 'A weak diplomatic hybrid: U.S. Special Mission Benghazi, 2011–12', January 2013 [www].

Berridge, G. R., *A Diplomatic Whistleblower in the Victorian Era: The life and writings of E. C. Grenville-Murray* (December 2013) [www].

British Diplomatic Oral History Programme [www]. Use the Search facility for individual diplomats or places.

Cargill, Tom, 'More with less: Trends in UK diplomatic engagement in Sub-Saharan Africa', *Africa Programme Paper* AFP PP 2011/3 (Chatham House: London, 2011) [www].

Cleverley, J. Michael, 'How to measure an ambassador', *Foreign Service Journal*, March 2007 [www].

Cowper-Coles, Sherard, *Cables from Kabul: The inside story of the West's Afghanistan campaign* (HarperPress: London, 2011).

Cowper-Coles, Sherard, *Ever the Diplomat: Confessions of a Foreign Office mandarin* (HarperPress: London, 2012): ch. 3.

Denza, E., *Diplomatic Law: A commentary on the Vienna Convention on Diplomatic Relations*, 3rd edn (Oxford University Press: Oxford, 2009).

Filler, Martin, 'The New Tower of London', *New York Review of Books*, 8 March 2010 [www].

Foreign Service Journal, 'Embassies as command posts in the war on terror', March 2007 [www].

'Frontline Diplomacy': The Foreign Affairs Oral History Collection of the Association for Diplomatic Studies and Training [www]. A massive and invaluable collection of often frank reflections by former US diplomats. Use Search.

Giraldi, Philip, 'The myth of embassy security', *The American Conservative*, 2 October 2012 [www].

Grabar, Henry, 'Fortress America: How the U.S. designs its embassies', *The Atlantic Cities*, 17 September 2012 [www].

Hoffacker, Lewis, 'Murder in an embassy', Parts 1 and 2, *Moments in U.S. Diplomatic History*, ADST [www].

Jazbec, Milan, *The Diplomacies of New Small States: The case of Slovenia with some comparison from the Baltics* (Ashgate: Aldershot, 2001).

Lloyd, Lorna, *Diplomacy with a Difference: The Commonwealth office of high commissioner, 1880–2006* (Martinus Nijhoff: Leiden, 2007).

Loeffler, J. C., *The Architecture of Diplomacy: Building America's embassies*, 2nd edn (Princeton Architectural Press: New York, 2011).

Loeffler, J. C., 'Beyond the fortress embassy', *Foreign Service Journal*, December 2012 [www].

Meyer, Christopher, *DC Confidential* (Weidenfeld & Nicolson: London, 2005).

Newhouse, John, 'Diplomacy, Inc.: The influence of lobbies on US foreign policy', *Foreign Affairs*, May/June 2009.

OIG, *Semiannual Reports to the Congress* [www]. Very instructive.

Pietrowicz, Nick, 'The value of fortress embassies', *Foreign Service Journal*, February 2013 [www].

Rana, Kishan S., *21st Century Diplomacy: A practitioner's guide* (Continuum: London, 2011).

Sunlight Foundation, 'Foreign Influence Explorer' [www]. A highly respected site identifying lobbyists acting for foreign governments in Washington and the sums of money involved.

US Government Accountability Office (GAO), 'Diplomatic Security', June 2014 [www].

Young, John W., *Twentieth Century Diplomacy: A case study of British practice, 1963–1976* (Cambridge University Press: Cambridge, 2008): ch. 4.

9
Consulates

A 'consulate', technically, is only one kind of consular post, but in common usage is the term used to describe them all. Only pedants, protocol departments, and lexicologists wince at this and hasten to point out that consulates are distinct because there are vice-consulates on which they look *down* as well as consulates-general to which they must look *up*. This chapter therefore discusses all of them – as, indeed, also the consular sections of embassies, even though international law is unclear as to whether the latter should be treated as consulates.

Consulates today are attracting unprecedented attention. What are their origins? Why do those who work in them no longer inhabit what D. C. M. Platt, the historian of British consuls, called a 'Cinderella Service'? Why are they now so important? How is their work organized?

The consulates of European states, which were first established chiefly around the Mediterranean and its adjacent seas, had their origins in international trade. When cargo vessels from distant lands arrived in a port, the scope for misunderstanding and trouble was obvious. Sailors speaking strange tongues, displaying unusual habits, and – having been cooped up at sea, sometimes for months – soon drunk, were rarely impressive advertisements for their homelands. Attitudes to commercial dealings and the civil and criminal law generally were also often at serious odds, especially when religions were different. To make matters worse, there was usually intense competition between ship-owners from different states; and, where foreign merchants settled and formed a community at an important port, they needed to be internally regulated as well as defended against rivals and rapacious local officials. If trade between distant lands was to flourish, therefore, there had to be some representative of the merchants in the ports who had the authority and ability to sort out these problems. Enter the consul: spokesman for the merchants and, where this suited the local authorities – as in the Ottoman Empire – magistrate over them.

Consuls appointed by Italian merchant colonies in the Levant pre-dated the emergence of the resident embassy in the late 1400s by at least three centuries, and probably encouraged it.

The first consuls, then, were part-timers: merchants chosen from the ranks of a local trading settlement by the merchants themselves. They were supported financially by the small tax they were permitted to charge on the goods moving through their settlements ('consulage'), as well as by what they earned from their private trading; their duties concerned exclusively the affairs of their fellow merchants. In short, although home government authorization might sometimes be given to them and minor political duties performed in return, the first consuls were, in general, neither appointed nor paid by the state, and had nothing to do with advancing its interests, except indirectly.

In Britain, it was only in the middle of the seventeenth century that the state began to assert its control over the consuls and require them both to take on additional responsibilities (notably the organization of naval supplies) and place the national interest first: at this point only did private sector spokesmen become public servants. But even after a partial reorganization in the early nineteenth century, many consuls – especially at minor posts – still survived on the basis of fees and private trading for some time. These 'trading consuls', as they were known, were unpopular at home but cheap. It was to be the beginning of the twentieth century before the general consular service in Britain was put on a modern footing, although the French service had for long been much better organized, as had certain specialized services in Britain itself, among them the Levant Service.

Until well into the twentieth century, there was an entrenched view among diplomats not only that consular work and diplomacy were quite different, which up to a point was defensible; but also that a person suited to the one was not suited to the other, which was less so. Diplomats, who busied themselves at royal courts and foreign ministries, were thought to need the refined manners, self-assurance, and skill at field sports that came from an aristocratic lineage or roots in the landed gentry; whereas consuls, whose habitat was a grubby seaport or smoky industrial city in the provinces, were firmly believed to require little more than certain attributes of a solid middle-class background – some knowledge of business, a general if rudimentary command of the law, and 'common sense'. Clearly, so the argument went, the humble consul did not need and did not have either the money to live in the style of a diplomat or the personal qualities necessary to deal with foreign leaders as equals.

From this perspective, therefore, it was entirely appropriate that there should be completely separate diplomatic and consular services. This also had the effect of making it still more unlikely that even the most outstanding consul-general would be able to obtain promotion to a diplomatic post, although in some states – such as Austria-Hungary – this was easier than in others. This state of affairs was deeply resented by the consuls.

By the late nineteenth century they were engaged in a much broader range of duties – in the Ottoman Empire there were even many 'political consuls' – and they were shaking off their seaport image. Conversely, diplomats were being forced more and more to support the commerce of their nationals (see Chapter 14). In other words, the differences between diplomatic and consular work were eroding. The result was that a consul or consul-general at an important post was usually doing more or less the same kind of work in relation to a regional authority that a diplomat was doing in relation to the central government. Furthermore, by this time some embassies had a consular section, while in the European embassy in the East members of specialized consular services had usually come to take the senior positions in the 'oriental secretariat' or 'dragomanate'. In the latter circumstance, the consuls might even find themselves doing most of the work of the diplomats, while the latter spent much of their time riding, picnicking, bathing in local waters, and entertaining important visitors. For their troubles, the consuls were paid far less and often treated with breathtaking condescension. An easing of transfers between the services was not the solution to this situation: such concessions were seen by the consuls as acts of grace by the high and mighty aristocratic establishment that tended to monopolize the diplomatic career. What the consuls began to push for instead was *amalgamation*: the creation of a unified foreign service in which, at least in principle, there was no such thing as 'a consul for life'.

Fortunately, in the late nineteenth century, political and social attitudes were slowly changing. It was beginning to be felt, even by some diplomats, that it was not only unfair but also imprudent to deny diplomatic appointments to persons who were perfectly qualified for them in every way except for the fact that they had previously been a consul and came from the wrong social class. In a situation where the best person could not be placed in a vacant diplomatic post, and where there was contempt on the one hand and envy on the other, the first casualty was efficiency. Eventually, therefore, the consuls got their way. In the United States, the separate diplomatic and consular services were amalgamated by the Rogers Act of 1924, although it was not until 1943, as part of the general reform of the 'foreign service', that the same step was taken in Britain. The white paper announcing the change in Britain said:

What is aimed at is wider training and equality of opportunity for all. Every officer of the combined Service will be called upon to serve in consular and commercial diplomatic as well as in diplomatic posts and in the Foreign Office and will have the opportunity of rising to the highest posts. Interchange between the different branches, and between posts at home and those abroad, will be facilitated with the object of giving every man as wide an experience as possible and of enabling the best man to be sent to any vacant post. (HCPP 1943: para. 6)

In the course of the twentieth century, the diplomatic and consular services of most other states were also amalgamated: for example, Germany in 1918, Norway in 1922, Spain in 1928, and Italy in 1952.

A strong trend towards the administrative fusion of their previously separate services, and a growing overlap between what consuls and diplomats actually did there might have been. Nevertheless, it is still true, as the quotation from the British white paper of 1943 unmistakably implied, that there remained – and remains – a great deal of difference between *typical* consular work and *typical* diplomatic work. The former deals chiefly with the problems of individuals and corporate bodies; the latter is concerned mainly with issues of general policy in intergovernmental relations, especially those of a political nature. Besides, a sending state can only establish one embassy in a receiving state; if it needs representation in provincial ports and inland cities, it must have posts of a different kind where the mission premises and staff, lacking the full representative character of the embassy and usually handling matters of less political sensitivity, will not be justified in claiming the same privileges and immunities. Traditionally, such posts have been called consulates and, until recently, no one appears to have seen any reason to change the designation. So, while separate consular *services* might have been abandoned, consuls and consulates remain.

Reflecting this understanding that consular work remains a distinct activity, the separate consular corps remains alive and well. Analogous to the diplomatic corps, it is often better organized and more collegial. This is probably because of its relatively non-political interests and its strong leaven of honorary consuls (see p. 144); some also admit local government and corporate members. The consular corps of New York City, organized in 1925 into the Society of Foreign Consuls, claims to be the largest in the world, although Los Angeles protests that it has the largest among 'normal' cities. Consuls are numerous and particularly well organized in the United States, where they even have their own professional association – the National Association of Foreign Consuls, alternatively known as the 'Consular Corps College'. In Britain, the

Manchester Consular Association, founded in 1882, claims to be one of the oldest in the world – as does that of Liverpool.

Box 9.1 The main differences between diplomatic and consular privileges and immunities

Immunity from jurisdiction

Consular officers and employees are immune from the jurisdiction of the receiving state's courts and administrative authorities only in respect of their official acts. By contrast, diplomats generally enjoy this immunity in respect of their private acts as well; as, indeed, where criminal jurisdiction is concerned, do members of the administrative and technical staff of embassies. For entirely political reasons, this distinction was glossed over by Indian opinion in the affair – clumsily handled by the US authorities – of Devyani Khobragarde (see p. 106 above).

Liability to give evidence

Consular officers might be called upon to give evidence at judicial or administrative proceedings (except in matters connected with the exercise of their functions), although not under threat of coercive measure or penalty. By contrast, diplomatic agents are under no such obligation.

Personal inviolability

In the case of a grave crime, a consular officer might be liable to arrest or detention pending trial; required to appear in court in person, if facing a criminal charge; and be imprisoned in execution of a final judgement. By contrast, the personal inviolability of a diplomatic agent is unqualified.

Inviolability of premises

Consular premises may be entered by the authorities of the receiving state without the express consent of the head of the post 'in case of fire or other disaster requiring prompt protective action', and may also be expropriated with compensation. By contrast, inviolability in the case of embassies is unqualified.

The private residence of a career consular officer (including the head of a consular post) is not part of 'consular premises', and so does not enjoy its inviolability or protection. By contrast, the private residence of a diplomatic agent shares these rights in equal measure with the premises of the diplomatic mission.

Freedom of communication: the consular bag

A suspect consular bag may – if a request to open it is refused – be sent back. By contrast, no diplomatic bag may be detained, let alone opened.

Recognition that consular work was a separate activity was acknowledged when the customary and treaty law on consuls was codified and amended in a separate multilateral convention in 1963: the Vienna Convention on Consular Relations (VCCR). This convention neither

overrode existing bilateral consular treaties nor precluded the negotiation of new ones. Nevertheless, it became 'an accepted guide to international practice' (Gore-Booth 1979: 212) and, in so doing, brought
the privileges and immunities of consuls closer to those of diplomats,
although differences remain (Box 9.1). In insisting on these differences,
the conference held at Vienna in 1963 that produced the final convention played a more significant role than the ILC, the final draft of which
had gone much further to assimilate consular to diplomatic law, notably
by assigning complete inviolability to consular premises (ILC, 'Consular
Intercourse and Immunities'). What is the burden of consular work
today?

Consular functions

The work of consuls is famously rich in variety. This is a fact easily
appreciated by looking at the list of consular functions in Article
5 of the VCCR, the European Convention on Consular Functions
(Box 9.2), or the consular services page of the website of any large
embassy or consulate-general. Despite the length of these lists, they
do not provide a complete picture of what many consulates actually
do. This can be broken down into five broad categories: commercial
work; assistance to nationals; entry clearance; diplomacy; and secret
intelligence.

Box 9.2   European Convention on Consular Functions

This contains a particularly long list of consular functions. It is the handiwork
of a committee of experts appointed in 1960 by the Council of Europe (not to
be confused with the European Council), and was signed on 11 December 1967.
However, it did not enter into force as between member states of the Council
until 9 June 2011, most European states seeming to prefer the greater flexibility
afforded by the VCCR's more summary treatment of the subject. Nevertheless,
the European Convention's influence should not be discounted, for Europe
has great political and economic weight and West European consular practice
remains a model in the world beyond (Lee and Quigley: 113).

Reflecting their origins, many consuls are still much preoccupied with
commercial work, except in the case of those in the consular sections of
embassies, since the large embassies, at least, now tend to have separate
commercial sections. But this need not detain us here because commercial diplomacy is discussed at length in Chapter 14. More characteristic
of the daily diet of consuls today is providing help to their nationals,

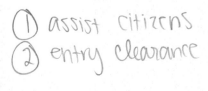

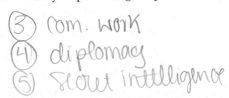

particularly those finding themselves in distress. This priority is to be expected because the modern media coverage of this aspect of consular work makes it probably the most important activity by which the diplomatic services of many countries are judged.

As foreign travel has become easier and cheaper, there has been an enormous increase in population movements across national frontiers by holiday-makers, students, business people, and those seeking better paid employment. For example, hundreds of thousands of skilled and semi-skilled workers have flooded out of India to the oil-rich states of the Gulf and north Africa (Rana 2000: 198); while the number of British nationals travelling abroad (1.8 million at any one time) has tripled since the 1980s, and there are approximately 13.6 million (many elderly) resident abroad (FCO: 1).

Whatever their reasons for being abroad, individuals might find they need the services of one of their consuls. It might be for a relatively routine matter, such as the issue or renewal of a passport, the registration of a birth or death, or the issue or witnessing of a certificate of life – a document verifying that a retired person living abroad is still alive and entitled to continue receiving a pension from home. However, individuals might also need a consul when in difficulty or acute distress, typically because they have suffered from an accident (including loss of a passport), illness, crime, or arrest; or been caught up in a natural disaster or civil emergency. Among the services consuls are expected to perform in situations such as these are providing new travel documents, advising on local lawyers, visiting in prisons, trying to trace the missing, and arranging evacuations – and, all the while, keeping family at home in the picture. In the worst cases, consuls help to identify the dead and make arrangements for funerals or (if necessary) the transport home of bodies or ashes. In *True Brits*, there is a grim photograph of a British vice-consul in Bangkok overseeing the cremation of a British national who died in the city, one of an average of six a month with whose deaths he was dealing; he was known as the 'Death Man' (Edwards: 172). The stresses of this kind of consular work are not made easier by the public's unreasonably high expectations of what consuls can do for them. The modern enthusiasm for zombies notwithstanding, they are not usually expected to revive the dead; but many of those thrown into foreign prisons are more confident that their consul will be able to secure their immediate release. Others behave so badly abroad that the occasional consul, weary of having to clear up after them and ashamed of their behaviour, resigns in disgust (Box 9.3).

Box 9.3   Disgusted in Ibiza

In August 1998, after only 18 months at his post, the British Vice-Consul on the Spanish holiday island of Ibiza, Michael Birkett, resigned. He was disgusted at the way too many young Brits behaved when they turned up in their hundreds of thousands for sun, sex, booze, and drugs. 'I have always been proud to be British,' he told the *Mail on Sunday*, 'but these degenerates are dragging us through the mud.' The officer who stepped into this particular breach, Helen Watson, was subsequently made a Member of the Order of the British Empire (MBE), an honour granted for 'a significant achievement or outstanding service to the community'; she was also given more office assistance. In 2008, the consulate was renovated and expanded, and opened in the presence of a Foreign Office junior minister, the British ambassador to Spain, and the President of the Island Council. Not a bad repair job.

Many travellers find themselves in distress overseas because they are ignorant of the conditions they will find and careless in their preparations. It is not surprising, therefore, that consular posts are now commonly required to provide constantly updated reports on foreign destinations and advice on suitable precautions: prevention is better than cure. 'Know Before You Go' campaigns and 'Foreign Travel Advice', which are prominent features of foreign ministry websites, depend heavily on information supplied by their consular networks. The US State Department, for example, has a 'Consular Information Program' consisting of country specific information, with travel alerts and warnings.

A third task that falls to the lot of some consuls, especially those of the richer states in the West, is that of entry clearance: deciding to whom, among the many applicants for travel to their countries, they should issue visas. In light of the spread of poverty, insecurity and disease in many areas of the world, the numbers of those seeking visas for travel to the safer and more prosperous countries has grown enormously; and people-smuggling by organized crime gangs has increased with them. This has produced a mounting concern in the West about a floodtide of immigrants. The outbreak of the so-called 'War on Terror' also produced a much greater anxiety about the sort of people trying to cross borders (including 'jihadists' returning to Europe from fighting in Syria and Iraq), as well as about their numbers.

There is great variation in the emphasis given to the work of sifting travellers not only between consulates of the same diplomatic service located in different countries (not all are in 'migration hotspots'), but also between diplomatic services themselves. In Britain, for example, much of the burden of processing potential immigrants is placed on consular posts, whereas in others, such as France, most of this is done at home. The British view, which is similar to that of the United States, is that, although expensive, offshore migration control reduces delays at ports of entry, facilitates investigation of the applicants' circumstances, and minimizes their inconvenience – especially if they are refused. Another probable reason is the avoidance of heartrending scenes at ports and airports, and fear of what the media would do with them. In migration hotspots in Africa and the Asian sub-continent, consular posts are increasingly outsourcing the more routine aspects of visa work to private sector companies, thereby allowing more time for consular visa staff to concentrate on difficult cases.

A special instance of what is effectively a consulate's entry clearance work (it is unlikely to be called that) is the handling of non-nationals in distress: refugees rushing their gates, banging on their doors, or clambering over their walls. This is now an important task for some missions because the numbers of those fleeing across national frontiers in search of temporary or permanent refuge from war or persecution is rising even more dramatically than the statistics of 'normal' cross-border movements. In 2013, the global total of refugees – magnified greatly by tragedies in Africa and the Middle East – exceeded 50 million for the first time since World War II. Consulates close to the frontiers of particularly troubled countries and representing states expected by escaping refugees to be sympathetic tend to be in the front line. This is a complex question, often fraught with political difficulties, as the recent history of the increasing numbers of North Korean refugees turning up at the consulates of Japan, South Korea, and the United States in the north-eastern Chinese industrial city of Shenyang (not much more 100 miles from the North Korean border), only too well testifies.

The fourth important consular responsibility is that of diplomacy. Under the VCCR (art. 17.1), a consular post in a state where a sending state has no diplomatic mission might – subject to the approval of the receiving state – be formally permitted 'to perform diplomatic acts' (this is discussed more fully in Chapter 15) but, in practice, 'consular diplomacy' is more common than this suggests. In fact, the encouragement of good relations is a normal consular function. So, too, is political reporting. Indeed, consulates have long been regarded by larger states as their eyes and ears in the provinces of receiving states. In the Balkan and Asiatic provinces of the Ottoman Empire in the nineteenth century, for example, many were established for this reason alone (Berridge 2009: 86–90). And it is reasonable to assume that anxiety to know as much as possible about the nightmare in North Korea helps to explain the presence in Shenyang of so many large consular missions – refugees might be a problem for them, but they are a valuable source of political intelligence.

The fifth and least advertised role of consular posts, as with embassies, is providing cover for intelligence officers and serving as instruments of political warfare. In World War II, Britain's consulates in neutral Turkey were even used as dumps for explosives against the possibility of the country falling to Nazi Germany and the need arising for agents of the Special Operations Executive to blow up key installations (Berridge 2009: ch. 8). It is not just the consulates of major powers that might be used for political purposes, as was vividly demonstrated by the activities in 2001 of the consulate of the Afghan Taliban regime in the Pakistani port city of Karachi. The head of this mission had supported Islamic movements in the country and addressed rallies in protest at Pakistan's pro-NATO policy. This, however, was obviously going too far, and the consulate was subsequently closed down by order of the government in Islamabad.

So much for consular functions. What now of the two categories of consular officer – career consuls and honorary consuls – who carry them out?

Career consuls

Career consular officers are so called in order to distinguish them from honorary ones, not to suggest that they are consuls for life, as would have been the case prior to the early twentieth century. They are members of a foreign service who happen to have a consular posting at the time but might have come from – and, in future, be destined for – a diplomatic posting. They are found in the consular sections of embassies (discussed separately later in the chapter), but chiefly at posts in the provinces of the receiving state, typically in major ports and inland cities. In descending rank order, these posts can be consulates-general, consulates, or vice-consulates, depending on the size of their staff or district, their importance, or the personal standing of their head of post. Vice-consuls might be found in consulates (strictly defined), and both vice-consuls and consuls might be found in consulates-general, although the last is always *headed* by a consul-general.

In theory, this traditional hierarchy suggests a pyramidal structure, with a broad base of numerous vice-consulates tapering upwards to just a few consulates-general at the top. However, in practice this was only ever seen, as a rule, with the consular networks of major or medium powers in receiving states of particular importance to them – as when, in 1879, Britain had 30 vice-consulates, 9 consulates, and 4 consulates-general in the Ottoman Empire. Today, a pyramidal structure of career consular posts is difficult to discern even in situations similar to this. In fact, the picture is often turned upside down: vice-consulates (as opposed to vice-consuls) have virtually disappeared, while consulates and especially consulates-general have multiplied. A number of European states still use a few vice-consulates; and the American 'presence post' – with its single Foreign Service officer – looks very much like a vice-consulate by another name. But most states appear to have consigned them, along with legations (headed not by ambassadors but ministers), to the past, and for the same reason – their lowly status makes them unflattering to both the receiving local authorities and to those who have to run them. Nevertheless, it must not be concluded that the disappearance of the pyramidal structure of career consular posts means the disappearance altogether of the pyramidal structure of consular representation as a whole, as we shall see in a moment.

Many states have a number of consular posts staffed by career officers in countries where they have important interests and where many of their citizens are regular visitors and permanent residents, each post having its own consular 'district' (Box 9.4). In France, for example, Britain has consulates at Bordeaux and Marseilles, and a Trade and Investment Office at Lyons. Such posts are usually supplemented by numerous honorary consulates and consular correspondents (explained later in the chapter).

Box 9.4 Consular districts

A consular district is the area over which a consular post is permitted to exercise consular functions. Under Article 4.2 of the VCCR, these must be agreed between the sending state and the receiving state, and vary considerably. For example, the consular district of the US consulate-general based in Sydney covers New South Wales, Queensland, and the Australian Pacific Ocean territory of Norfolk Island. (According to the mission's website, in 2014 there were an estimated 25,000 Americans living in New South Wales and 12,000 in Queensland.) By contrast, the district over which the German consulate-general in the same city has responsibility includes the states of Western Australia and Victoria in addition to New South Wales and Queensland – but, according to the mission's website, does not include Norfolk Island.

All consular posts are formally subordinate to their 'sovereign' embassy in the state in which they are established. This no longer extends to hiring and firing consular staff, as it often did in earlier centuries, but it still gives an ambassador a considerable degree of authority over the general lines of their conduct. As subordinate posts, therefore, and except in emergencies, consulates usually take their orders from the embassy and report to it. (By the same token, those vice-consulates that remain are superintended by consulates.) Nevertheless, a consul-general in a major provincial city sometimes accepts this subordination only with reluctance and, in practice, acts in some respects as if it did not exist. It can well be imagined that this is more likely to be so if these cities are physically remote from the capital, as are Perth in Western Australia and those on the west coast of the United States, or if a consular post in a city much closer to the embassy is nevertheless exceptionally large and important for special reasons, as in the case of the US consulate-general in Dubai (see p. 229), which is bigger than many embassies and in 2013 was a platform for 11 US government agencies (OIG 2014a: 4, 19). A disinclination to accept embassy rule is even greater if the consul-general has previously been an ambassador elsewhere, which is no longer rare. It is not necessary to look far to find such cases (Barder: 193–6; Berridge 2009: ch. 10).

Consulates have always placed great reliance on LE staff, and this has increased even more in recent years; some posts are run entirely by nationals of the receiving state or permanent residents who are nationals of the sending state. Another trend – prompted by security as well as financial worries – has been the creation of 'virtual consulates'. These are interactive websites that provide information and also facilitate electronic access to limited consular services in an area where there is no actual consular post. They are locally branded and customized, although ideally supplemented by cultural and commercial initiatives, telephone links, and video-conferencing facilities, and by periodic visits to the region in question by staff from the nearest 'real' consular post or embassy. In 2014, the US State Department, which calls them 'virtual presence posts', had approximately 40 of these sites, including one for the Welsh capital, Cardiff.

Honorary consuls

Honorary consuls – and their close cousins, consular agents and consular correspondents – have to some extent rescued the pyramidal structure of consular representation as a whole. At the ILC in 1960, they were reckoned to be in charge of half of all of the consulates in the world (ILC 1960: vol. 1, 171). But they were thought by some of the jurists – and hoped by others – to be on the way out (Lee and Quigley: 515–516). The Soviet Union and its client states, together with the PRC, refused either to appoint or accept these 'bourgeois spies' and, with little tourism in either direction, had little use for them anyway. As for the United States, even today it still does not appoint its own honorary consuls; and, although it has admitted them since 1895, it now shares the attitude of those European countries that refuse to acknowledge those appointed for purely political or honorific reasons (Dunham; Rana 2004: 239, n. 35). Other states have become less squeamish and more in need of their services.

Honorary consuls are usually nationals of the receiving state with close connections to the sending state, or nationals of the sending state permanently resident in the receiving state; in either case, they usually know their way around both. They are frequently self-employed business people, shipping agents, or the sort of professionals who have some control over their own time. They undertake the role on a part-time basis, and are thus usually unable to offer the full range of consular services. They are paid at most a small salary, fees for certain services, and their expenses. Under the VCCR, they enjoy more limited privileges and immunities than career consular officers, largely because of their more limited functions and the suspicion they have tended to attract of not being entirely respectable. The sad, whisky-drenched character of Charley Fortnum in Graham Greene's novel *The Honorary Consul* has probably done nothing for the reputation of the institution either. Every two years, Fortnum supplemented his income as an honorary consul in Argentina by selling a new Cadillac he had imported duty free.

While some honorary consuls simply like helping people in difficulties, it is usually assumed that most of them undertake the responsibility chiefly for the social, commercial, and other advantages offered by its prestige. Honorary consuls can at least fly the national flag, display the national coat-of-arms, and have freedom of official communication; they have the same immunity from jurisdiction in respect of their official acts as career consular officers; and, among other things, are entitled to uncommonly respectful treatment in the event that criminal proceedings are instigated against them.

Despite the arrival of virtual consulates, flesh and blood honorary consuls are not in retreat; on the contrary, since the 1960s resort to them has been steadily growing. They found vigorous support in the ILC and subsequently at the Vienna Conference in 1963, particularly from the Scandinavian countries; and the separate chapter on them in the VCCR both stabilized and legitimized their role. The Soviet Bloc began to relent on its hard line against them in the 1970s and the later collapse of the Soviet Union itself merely accelerated the process. The Russian Federation now embraces honorary consuls, as do the numerous states formerly in the Soviet orbit (Lee and Quigley: vii, 518). The PRC still holds out against them altogether (except in the 'special administrative region' of Hong Kong), but is now alone among major states in this regard.

Wealthy states such as Sweden that have traditionally had large merchant shipping fleets, as well as the many poor countries in the modern world, depend heavily on honorary consuls. But many other states also find them immensely useful. For example, in 2014, in the United States alone, Germany had almost 40 honorary consuls, in addition to its eight consulates-general and its Washington embassy; it had approximately 350 honorary consuls worldwide.

The base of the pyramid of consular representation is broadened further by consular agencies, although this venerable institution is more problematic. The VCCR identifies consular agents as a class of the category of *career* consular officer – the lowliest, ranking below vice-consuls – but not all states accept this or even recognize the term, and practice varies among those that do. In the British and French services, the terms 'honorary consul' and 'consular agent' are virtually synonymous. By contrast, the United States employs consular agents (particularly in Mexico) and pays them according to how much work they do. American practice, however, is exceptional (Lee and Quigley: 35). Consular agents, then, are either a component of, or identical to, the *category* of honorary consuls, rather than being a fourth *class* of the category of career consuls.

The final addition to the pyramidal base to be noted is the consular correspondent, an individual employed by states such as Italy and the Netherlands. Such persons are voluntary representatives who serve as contact points between a consular post and a particular section of the community of their nationals resident in the receiving state. Their liaison role is valuable when such a group finds itself in a hostile environment. It is a moot point whether consular correspondents are 'consular officers' in the meaning of the VCCR. They are now more commonly known as 'wardens'.

Consular sections

Finally, it is necessary to say a few words about the consular sections of embassies, which are staffed chiefly by career consular officers. Most embassies had been concerned with consular affairs in their immediate vicinity long before the twentieth century, particularly when the capital city in which they were located was also a major port, as in the case of Constantinople. In these circumstances, consular matters might be dealt with in a separate building, closer to the dockside – but still close enough to the embassy to be regarded as a part of it. Sometimes, the head of a diplomatic mission, whether the capital was a port or not, even doubled as consul-general, as at the British missions in Tokyo, Tehran, Cairo, and elsewhere. Nevertheless, encouraged by the merging of the two services and the need to reduce expenses, following World War I consular staff began to be re-housed within the embassy proper (Strang: 124; ILC 1961: vol. 1, 271). But numerous anomalies remain. For example, while the British Embassy in Paris is located at 35 rue du Faubourg Saint-Honoré, its consular 'section' is still to be found some distance away in the rue d'Anjou; it is also described officially as the 'British Consulate-General'.

Only larger embassies tend to have a whole section devoted to consular affairs. In mini-embassies, one officer will usually have to combine functions of both a consular and diplomatic character. But, whether in a full section or not, the discharge of consular functions by the embassy has another great advantage to the sending state: the consular staff have full diplomatic privileges and immunities, awkward though this is for the functional theory of these immunities (see p. 116). This was useful to the representation of Western states in Moscow during the Cold War (ILC 1961: vol. 1, 7), and it remains useful to many states today. In this connection, it is a striking fact that in recent years over half of the states with embassies in London have had no consular representation – honorary or career – outside the capital: their embassies have handled all consular affairs themselves. Whether this is to the advantage of their citizens visiting or resident in the UK is another matter.

Summary

Consulates have a longer history than the resident embassy. In the twentieth century, consular services merged with diplomatic services and the differences between their respective privileges and immunities narrowed. But typical consular work remains, in many respects, different from typical diplomatic work, and is often more stressful; this is one reason why it tends to be less popular. This is a pity because consulates are the foreign service's shop window to both foreigners and its own nationals abroad. To the latter, this should represent protection; to the former, a warm welcome if entry can be permitted and a polite and regretful farewell if it cannot. As international trade – with some ups and downs – has expanded and population movements have increased dramatically, the demand for consular services has grown commensurately. This is why the consular representation of larger states still tends to have a pyramidal structure, even though, chiefly for reasons of economy, honorary consuls now play an even more important role in supporting it. Nevertheless, many smaller states rely entirely on the consular sections of their embassies. In Chapter 15, we shall see how consular posts also play an important role when diplomatic relations are severed.

Further reading

Berridge, G. R., *Gerald Fitzmaurice (1865–1939), Chief Dragoman of the British Embassy in Turkey* (Martinus Nijhoff: Leiden, 2007).

Berridge, G. R., *British Diplomacy in Turkey, 1583 to the Present: A study in the evolution of the resident embassy* (Martinus Nijhoff: Leiden, 2009): ch. 4.

Coates, P. D., *The China Consuls: British consular officers, 1843–1943* (Oxford University Press: Oxford, 1988).

Edwards, R. D., *True Brits: Inside the Foreign Office* (BBC Books: London, 1994): ch. 11.

European Convention on Consular Relations (1967) [www].

FCO, *Consular Strategy 2010–13*, 4 August 2011 [www].

Godsey, William D., Jr., *Aristocratic Redoubt: The Austro-Hungarian Foreign Office on the Eve of the First World War* (Purdue University Press: West Lafayette, IN, 1999): 76–81.

Hertz, Martin F. (ed.), *The Consular Dimension of Diplomacy* (University Press of America: Lanham, MD, 1983).

ILC, 'Consular intercourse and immunities' [ch. 2], in *Report... to the General Assembly on its work, 1 May–7 July 1961* [www].

Jazbec, Milan, 'The creation of the Slovenian state and its diplomatic service', February 2012 [www].

Lee, Luke T. and John Quigley, *Consular Law and Practice*, 3rd edn (Oxford University Press: Oxford, 2008).

Mattingly, Garrett, *Renaissance Diplomacy* (Penguin Books: Harmondsworth, 1965): 63–4.

Platt, D. C. M., *The Cinderella Service: British consuls since 1825* (Longman: London, 1971).

Rana, Kishan, *The 21st Century Ambassador* (DiploFoundation: Malta, 2004): 154–6.

Rana, Kishan S., *21st Century Diplomacy: A practitioner's guide* (Continuum: London, 2011): ch. 11.

Roberts, Sir Ivor (ed.), *Satow's Diplomatic Practice*, 6th edn (Oxford University Press: Oxford, 2009): Book V.

Shaw, L. M. E., *The Anglo-Portuguese Alliance and the English Merchants in Portugal, 1654–1810* (Ashgate: Aldershot, 1998): chs 4 and 5.

UN Conference on Consular Relations, Vienna 4 March–22 April 1963. *Official Records*. Vols. I and 2 [www].

US Department of State, *Digest of United States Practice in International Law* [www]. All volumes since that for 1989–90 online. This is a mine of information for the intrepid – search 'consular'.

Vienna Convention on Consular Relations (1963) [www].

10
Secret Intelligence

The two chief purposes of secret intelligence activity abroad are to provide governments with valuable information unobtainable from open sources and covertly to weaken or eliminate their foreign enemies – be they shipping-lane pirates, serious organized criminal gangs, dissidents living abroad, terrorist organizations, or even hostile governments. However, as the consequences of military and terrorist surprise have become more deadly, secret intelligence has also increased the attention it pays to the allies on which particular reliance is placed – for governments feel the need to be *sure* of their friends. These objectives have some overlap with those of diplomacy, while intelligence officers have also come to rely more and more on the shelter provided by diplomatic missions and consulates. But diplomacy itself rests on the maintenance of normal relations between even unfriendly governments and operates under a legal regime proscribing espionage, let alone active interference in the internal affairs of other states. In such circumstances, how do the spies and the diplomats coexist? With difficulty, as we shall see – but coexist they do.

The association of secret intelligence with diplomacy is as old as diplomacy itself. This is because diplomats – planted at the heart of foreign power centres and whether by religious injunction or codes of hospitality afforded some protection in their work – were usually the best placed of all agents of any political entity to obtain sensitive information. Furthermore, until comparatively recently they were largely on their own because the only dedicated spies or 'intelligencers' tended to be occasional freelancers who sold information to the highest bidder. Separate, state-funded intelligence agencies as we know them today did not begin to emerge until the end of the nineteenth century.

The risks of espionage were, however, only rarely taken directly by an ambassador himself, whose efficient discharge of his other duties depended on the maintenance of good relations with the receiving government. His personal pursuit of information tended to consist instead chiefly of quizzing all those with whom he came into official contact (including other members of the diplomatic corps), while encouraging them to open up by offering some titbits in exchange, together with copious quantities of food and wine. But at some posts he routinely bribed ministers or court officials for information, even keeping important ones on a regular 'pension', and he was not above paying for the theft of documents and codes (Andrew: 1–3); in some diplomatic services he was able to submit claims for these as 'extraordinary' expenses. Consular officers, familiar figures in a dockyard, were also routinely instructed to keep a weather eye open for developments of military significance, as in the case of the British consuls in southern Russia in the late 1850s, when fears began to grow in London that St Petersburg was seeking to evade the humiliating clauses of the Treaty of Paris of 1856 – imposed on it following the Crimean War – that prohibited it from rebuilding its Black Sea fleet (Berridge 2013a: 61–2). Heads of mission had their own codes and were usually adept at getting home intelligence reports as swiftly and securely as possible, if necessary by an official messenger or other 'safe hand'. working together

It was during the late nineteenth century that diplomats – with a collective sigh of relief – began to seek and sometimes secure more of an arm's length relationship with the 'dirty' world of secret intelligence. This was a result of two developments: first, the appearance in the embassy of the military attaché (with the later arrival of naval and air attachés, these came to be known collectively as service or defence attachés); and second, the emergence of the separate foreign intelligence agency. How did the relationship between diplomacy and secret intelligence evolve following these developments? What are the main problems caused by the inability of diplomacy to shake off its intimacy with the 'spooks'?

Service attachés

In the late seventeenth century, the great scholar-diplomat Abraham de Wicquefort – as it happens, also himself an intelligencer – had advised the appointment of military officers to embassies where the ambassador was at constant risk of being invited by the local ruler to join him on a military expedition. Such an officer, he pointed out, if available as a substitute, would not only be more 'capable of judging of martial actions' on a foreign campaign, but also – lacking the full representative character of the ambassador – avoid implying its political endorsement by his master (Berridge 2004: 131).

This idea seems not to have been lost on some governments of early modern Europe. It was not, however, until the second half of the nineteenth century that it became a reflex of the major states formally to appoint military attachés to diplomatic missions; sometimes to consulates as well, in particular those close to a major naval base such as Kronstadt, the Russian base at the head of the Gulf of Finland. And it was well into the twentieth century before service attachés became almost as common in peacetime as in war (Berridge 2012b: 4–5). By then, however, it was well understood that the exchange of these officers, by reducing mutual suspicions, contributed to the stability of the balance of power. Even during tense passages of the Cold War they were tolerated by both sides.

The minimum duties of service attachés include obtaining intelligence on the armed forces of the country or countries to which they are accredited: their numbers, morale, equipment, training, geographical disposition, tactical and strategic doctrines, defensive fortifications, capacity for swift mobilization, and so on. The former British ambassador and editor of the latest edition of *Satow's Diplomatic Practice* has recorded that: 'They could dress down, disappear into the night and pick up information that it was not possible for me to pick up, so I found their role very important in several posts where I went' (FAC 2007: 170).

One reason why service attachés are well placed to gather military intelligence is that it is customary for them to be closely involved in defence collaboration when relations are friendly, and – whether they are or not – to enjoy the hard-drinking intimacy of their 'comrades in arms' at the post to which they are accredited. For these tend to form a well-organized and often convivial sub-division of the diplomatic corps, with its own *doyen*.

It remains true that service attachés are sometimes thought to take too many liberties; besides, there are always states, notably those reckless of international stability or not attracted by appeals to reciprocity since unable to field competent service attachés of their own, that are extremely apprehensive of what these officers get up to. It is for this reason that the VCDR stipulated (art. 7) that, apart from the head of mission (for whom *agrément* is mandatory), the service attaché is the only member of the staff of a diplomatic mission whose name *might*, if the receiving state so requires, need to be submitted for approval prior to appointment. In practice, this is something on which receiving states usually insist.

The introduction of service attachés might have relieved diplomats of responsibility for the gathering of military intelligence, while their careful selection by sending states and vetting by receiving states tends to reduce fears that they will stir up a hornets' nest. But they can still create problems for diplomats. For one thing, it is inevitable that their primary allegiance will continue to be given to the military establishment on which they depend for their promotion, and it is to armed forces intelligence headquarters at home or to a defence ministry, or both, that they report. For another, armed forces personnel who are any good sometimes tend to fit uneasily into the atmosphere and routines of an embassy, and when the mission's defence section is large it is not unusual to find it housed separately from the building containing the chancery; this was the case with the Soviet mission in London during the Cold War. For these reasons, service attachés are 'inclined to regard themselves as in, but not of the Embassy' (Hoare: 130). This can make for uncomfortable relations in a peacetime mission, especially if the military establishment and the foreign ministry are tugging in different directions on policy regarding the bilateral relationship in question. Service attachés can also be required by their own military masters to engage occasionally in illegal activities, which if exposed or simply suspected can jeopardize a head of mission's own good relations with the local foreign ministry.

In short, while the introduction of service attachés and their acknowledgement by the VCDR has institutionalized and regulated the gathering of military intelligence by embassies, it has by no means eliminated the diplomatic incidents caused by them. Fortunately, such events tend soon to be forgotten. For example, improving relations between Israel and Russia suffered nothing more than a temporary hiccup following the expulsion from Moscow in May 2011 of the Israeli military attaché on grounds of espionage. Such expulsions are also as often as not a symptom rather than a cause of bad relations, as when Venezuela gave two US defence attachés 24 hours to get out of Caracas in March 2013.

Intelligence officers

Intelligence officers are employees of civilian foreign intelligence agencies or one or other of the branches of armed forces intelligence, which in most countries originated before the former – in the late nineteenth century. The development of both was given great impetus by World War I.

Some foreign intelligence agencies are actually supervised by foreign ministries, as is the case with the British Secret Intelligence Service (SIS, also known as MI6, the cover name given to it in World War II), which began life as the Secret Service Bureau in 1909. Others, among them the French Direction Générale de la Sécurité Extérieure, come under a defence ministry. And yet others function as in effect ministries in their own right, answering only to the head of government. Notable among these are the American Central Intelligence Agency (CIA), which evolved in 1947 from the wartime Office of Strategic Services; the German Bundesnachrichtendienst; the Russian External Intelligence Service – Sluzhba Vneshney Razvedki (SVR), formerly the first chief (foreign intelligence) directorate of the KGB, which had its origins in the Cheka of the first years of the Bolshevik Revolution in 1917; and the Chinese Ministry of State Security, with its own antecedents in the Chinese Communist Party's Social Affairs Department. The military intelligence agency most often remarked on for its size and reach is that of the former Soviet Union, the Glavnoye Razvedyvatelnoye Upravleniye (GRU).

As we shall see, intelligence officers are to be found alongside service attachés in embassies but some are 'illegals' or 'NOCs' (operatives with non-official cover). Illegals work under such natural or 'deep' cover as that of businessman, freelance journalist, press photographer, tourist, or exchange student – in fact, in any role in which it is normal to travel around in foreign countries, mix widely, and ask questions, provided it is not one in an organization likely to make background inquiries prior to employing them. In the popular TV series *The Americans*, a Cold War spy thriller set in the 1980s created and produced by a former CIA officer, the Soviet illegals on whose family life the drama is based run a travel agency. In the case of eavesdroppers, good natural cover is that of a communications engineer.

Training illegals and constructing for them the kind of 'legend' that will withstand scrutiny takes a great deal of time and trouble. Nevertheless, when a state has few diplomatic missions abroad and none in a target country, or does so but fears war with it and the consequent need for their withdrawal, it has little alternative but to employ them. The first of these situations was experienced by Soviet Russia in its early years and the second during the long period when it was apprehensive that its Cold War with the United States, 'the Main Adversary', would turn hot (Andrew and Mitrokhin: 36–7, 214–216). But a state might still use illegals even when it has a secure diplomatic presence in a country, as Russia has in Britain, since embassy and consular back-up can significantly enhance their viability. Thus the murder of the Russian dissident Alexander Litvinenko in London in November 2006 prompted the British Security Service to remind its masters that 'Since the end of the Cold War we have seen no decrease in the numbers of undeclared Russian intelligence officers in the UK...conducting covert activity in this country' (ISC 2009: 18).

Nevertheless, since World War II there appears to have been a trend to install a greater proportion of intelligence officers in embassies and consulates (including missions to international organizations such as the United Nations) under official or 'diplomatic' cover (Bower: 213; Jeffery: 603–4). Hence the legendary embassy 'stations' of the CIA and SIS, and the diplomatic 'residencies' of the KGB. How are they constituted and how do they operate?

In the case of SIS, at first its officers were typically disguised in a variety of lowly positions, among them assistant commercial secretary, press attaché, and vice-consul. Outside recruitment to such posts was in any case quite common and new arrivals without career pedigrees in the diplomatic or consular service were therefore unlikely to arouse suspicion. Nevertheless, there is no reason to doubt the assertion of the SIS officer Kim Philby – although, as a successful KGB double agent, an accomplished liar – that after World War II not only were 'the great majority' of SIS officers serving abroad to be found installed in British embassies but also that, especially at important missions, senior ones were sometimes given high diplomatic rank (Philby: 124). (They appear, however, never to have been heads of mission and only rarely headed important embassy sections.) Philby himself had cover as a first secretary at the British Embassy in Turkey while head of the SIS station in that country in the late 1940s; the same rank was customarily held by the chief of the important SIS station in the Beirut embassy, at least in the 1950s and 1960s; while at Paris and Washington the chief of station was usually a counsellor. Junior intelligence officers had lower ranks: for example, David Cornwell, better known as the master of the spy novel John le Carré, had cover as a second secretary in the British Embassy in Bonn in the early 1960s and then briefly as a consul in Hamburg.

As to today's operational style of SIS officers under diplomatic cover compared to that of genuine diplomats, little is known, but an authoritative source (confirming a KGB report) provides an interesting note on matters in the 1960s, which probably produces the qualified grumble among contemporary officers that 'nothing has changed':

> SIS personnel did not keep to the daily diplomatic routine, spent more time outside the embassy, lived in worse accommodation, drove older cars and gave fewer large receptions at their homes than [genuine] British diplomats, but had higher expense allowances and arranged

more meetings in restaurants and other public places. (Andrew and Mitrokhin: 445)

A veil naturally continues to be drawn over the identities of SIS officers posted at British embassies in more recent times, but that they are certainly still there was officially confirmed in 2011 in a report published by the prime minister. This revealed that the chief of SIS (the legendary 'C') had boasted that in the last year – a change to a more accurate costing system having been achieved – he had persuaded the Foreign Office to accept a lower payment in return for 'hosting SIS stations overseas' (ISC 2011: 32). And that these stations have if anything increased in number is strongly suggested by the repeated emphasis in officially sanctioned reports that SIS needs to maintain 'coverage in as wide a range of countries as possible, given that threats are very fleet-footed at the moment, and they need to be able to turn on intelligence coverage in places like Somalia or Yemen or the Sahel or the Maghreb as the threat moves' (ISC 2011: 32; also Cowper-Coles 2012: 46–7, 92).

The need for 'global coverage' was demonstrated by the 'Arab Spring', beginning in Tunisia in December 2010, which saw the British intelligence agencies with some catching up to do because they had allowed their presence in the Middle East and north Africa to atrophy (ISC 2012: 13–19). And it is perhaps because of the routine dependence on embassy platforms of SIS and the eavesdropping agency Government Communications Headquarters (GCHQ) that, following the assault on and consequent closure of the British Embassy in Tehran in November 2011, the parliamentary Intelligence and Security Committee (ISC) recorded sympathetically its recognition that they were having to become 'more creative' in how they collected intelligence on Iran's nuclear programme – a high priority (ISC 2013: 23).

What are the advantages of diplomatic cover to intelligence officers? The chief one – which is 'vital' in the early career stage (Cowper-Coles 2012: 143) – is that it gives them considerable security: domestic security because of the protected compounds in which embassy staff accommodation is commonly located in turbulent regions; and, above all, legal security when they move outside the compound's walls because of the privileges and immunities from local jurisdiction that come with diplomatic status. By contrast, illegals have no such protection, and if caught – the fate of hundreds on both sides of the Cold War betrayed by disaffected or simply mercenary colleagues – face torture and long-term prison sentences, or worse. The security advantage of diplomatic cover has probably increased further in recent years as the multiplication of threats has led many states to expand hurriedly their intelligence agencies and send many untested officers to particularly dangerous operational environments; high staff turnover is reported by the British agencies (ISC 2009: 25; 2010a: 18; 2010b: 14; 2012: 63, 67).

Since mission premises are inviolable, they also provide great security as well as ideal locations for the technical kit of those working for separate SIGINT agencies like the American National Security Agency (NSA) and GCHQ, or the SIGINT wings of general agencies. This includes the expensive and sometimes cumbersome equipment needed for wireless and satellite communications, and for intercepting mobile-phone calls. It is true that diplomatic and consular premises do not provide the greatest security for intercept stations, particularly when located in states with advanced counter-intelligence capabilities. (The best security is provided by military and naval bases situated in friendly states adjacent to targets, which is why Cuba was so valued by the Soviet Union.) Nevertheless, in such states there is often no alternative to the relative security of mission premises – except for completely different methods of collection, such as the relatively recent tapping of telephone and Internet traffic by the attachment of intercept probes to fibre-optic cables under secret agreements with private companies.

During the Cold War, the GRU and the KGB both developed massive SIGINT networks based largely in Soviet embassies and consulates and targeted chiefly at the United States. The GRU led, starting in the 1950s, and in 1963 the KGB established what seems to have been its own first embassy radio intercept post, at the Soviet Embassy in Mexico City; more valuable ones swiftly followed – on the top floor of the Washington embassy in 1966 and in the New York consulate in the year after. By the 1970s, the KGB had five separate intercept posts at different diplomatic facilities in the Washington area and four in the greater New York City region, including one at the 'diplomatic *dacha*' in Glen Cove, Long Island. Since the KGB lacked high-level penetration agents in Washington during these years, these SIGINT posts were then its chief sources of intelligence on US foreign and defence policy, and in general their activities were 'probably benign' because they made it difficult for Moscow to sustain its previously long-held belief that America was planning a nuclear first strike (Andrew and Mitrokhin: 453). There was another important intercept post at the tall building occupied by the Soviet consulate-general in San Francisco.

By the early 1980s, Moscow Centre had SIGINT stations in 34 diplomatic or consular posts in 27 states. Astonishingly enough, the GRU's network of diplomatic listening posts (which included Soviet trade missions) was by then even bigger than this. The expansion continued remorselessly, so that by 1989 between them the KGB and the GRU were operating – often competitively – covert listening posts in 62 countries (Aid: 509–18; Andrew and Mitrokhin: 447–52).

The revelations made in 2013 by NSA whistle-blower Edward Snowden, supplemented by aerial photography, have therefore merely highlighted what has long been known; namely, that the attics and roofs of embassy and large consular buildings provide ideal platforms for the staff and equipment of SIGINT agencies – and not just those of the former Soviet Union and its Russian successor (Herman, 1996: 185–6; Berridge 2009: 223; Andrew and Mitrokhin: 452; Campbell). This is not only because these buildings are inviolable. The visible, rooftop paraphernalia of the radio equipment which – subject to the consent of the receiving state – is lawful for their own communications is itself a mask for interception work; and they tend to be located very close to the government offices (and sometimes to high-tech industrial zones) which are their targets. In the last regard, the US Embassy in Berlin, on which so much attention was focused in 2013, is not alone.

There are additional advantages to diplomatic cover:

- It makes it easy for intelligence officers to have routine social as well as official contact with well-placed persons who might prove useful, either as sources themselves (traditional 'spies') or as scouts to identify them ('access agents'); in this connection it is interesting that it was early decided to give training to KGB officers in 'bourgeois manners, diplomatic etiquette, fashionable dressing and "good taste"' (Andrew and Mitrokhin: 118).
- The privileges of diplomatic status together with the vagueness of some embassy job descriptions probably provide the intelligence officer with as much legitimate mobility from day to day as the most agile illegal.
- The availability of intelligence officers to an embassy, together with the prospect of asylum it provides, both attracts and expedites the handling of defectors and others with secrets to divulge ('walk-ins'). These are sometimes the most valuable of sources, although usually difficult to distinguish from deliberate fakes ('dangles').
- Embassies of both sides during the Cold War received numerous genuine defectors, among them the KGB archivist Vasili Mitrokhin, who walked into the British embassy in Latvia in early 1992 and, after several return journeys to Moscow, was successfully exfiltrated by SIS – together with the massive archive on which this chapter draws heavily – later in the year.

- The 'legal' status of an intelligence officer in an embassy to a friendly government reassures and facilitates liaison with local security agencies, and should ensure that the genuine diplomats in the mission are always in the picture and on hand if needed.
- Finally, the task of preserving diplomatic cover – even if they are worried about this – need not distract intelligence officers very much from their real work since a great deal of what, say, a political or economic-commercial officer in an embassy would do is also what some intelligence officers would have to do anyway.

It is true that diplomatic cover is usually transparent to the local authorities; indeed, in the case of friendly and particularly of allied countries it is normal for 'legals' to be announced. Liaison between friendly intelligence agencies in the struggle against common enemies has long been valued, no more so than at the moment; and the assistance provided by established intelligence agencies to fledgling ones is also a useful negotiating point for obtaining information in return. But intelligence officers with diplomatic cover in unfriendly states are also usually well known or strongly suspected by the local authorities. This is because embassies tend to be the object of careful surveillance and diplomatic lists sometimes make it relatively easy to form a shrewd idea of the officers' identities (Berridge 2012b: 19). However, while this cramps their style (Radsan: 622), their exposure (at least in official circles) is normally less serious than might at first be thought since they are handlers or case officers, rather than field agents. It is, therefore, unlikely that they will be caught 'red-handed', a risk further reduced by the expedient – popular with the former KGB – of deliberately swelling their number to make it difficult for an under-resourced counter-intelligence agency to keep track of them all. Moreover, as a rule, 'legals' are tolerated on the basis of reciprocity, unless they are indeed detected in criminal activity themselves or are present in thoroughly alarming numbers; even then, their fate is only to be PNGed and sent home.

Cuckoos in the nest?

The invention and growth of intelligence agencies in the twentieth century might have relieved diplomats of direct responsibility for espionage, but – as we have seen – only at the cost of harbouring the thinly disguised personnel of these agencies in their missions, sometimes in large numbers. This often causes tension – sometimes acute – between diplomats and intelligence officers. Why should this be so – why are the latter sometimes described by the former as 'cuckoos in the nest'?

After all, they are both on the same side, and the intelligence officers do work regarded by their governments as vital to their security and which – despite their diplomatic protection – sometimes courts personal danger.

The most common source of tension between intelligence officers and diplomats (particularly the chief of a mission) is the customary difference in the importance they attach to good relations with the local government: intelligence personnel are usually willing to take more risks with this than their diplomatic colleagues. And these risks might be considerable because all states dislike being spied on and object even more to foreign agents meddling in their internal affairs. Moreover, receiving states usually have the law on their side.

It is true that in peacetime there is no general prohibition on espionage in public international law (Talmon), but intelligence officers do not operate in a vacuum of international law, and certainly not in one of national law. Treason and espionage are crimes in most states, as are many activities regularly associated with them, most of which are also contrary to international law. These include crimes such as the breaking by SIGINT eavesdroppers of laws on privacy, intellectual property rights, and data protection; the breaking by a case officer's agents of similar laws in the theft of classified material, including scientific and technical secrets, as well as the use of bribery and blackmail; and then there are the small matters of the illegal possession of weapons, and the kidnap, torture, or killing of such persons as dissidents, suspected terrorists, and scientists engaged in military work, in which the intelligence officers of some states have always engaged from time to time and those of others have done so indirectly. Not surprisingly, therefore, the use of embassy and consular premises for purposes of espionage (as opposed to the 'lawful' collecting of information and liaison or capacity building by intelligence officers) is contrary both to diplomatic law (VCDR: arts 3(1)d and 41(1), (3)) and consular law (VCCR: arts 5(c), 55(1), (2)), even though there is ambiguity about what are 'lawful means' for information-gathering (Kish: 55–6).

When, therefore, an embassy's association with espionage is exposed, particularly if the victim is an important ally, trouble for an ambassador's own agenda is bound to ensue. This was no more eloquently demonstrated than by events in Pakistan in the first half of 2011 and Germany in October 2013.

In the first case, a private security contractor employed by the CIA station in Lahore called Raymond Davis shot to death on a busy street two young (armed) Pakistanis shadowing him on motorbikes; and a third (wholly innocent) Pakistani was accidentally run down and killed by a CIA vehicle speeding to the scene to provide back-up. Davis was arrested by the Lahore police, charged with double murder, and imprisoned for almost ten weeks while awaiting trial. Meanwhile, Washington insisted that he had diplomatic immunity on the grounds that he was a member of the administrative and technical staff of the fortress embassy in Islamabad, which was not altogether convincing since he had already been videoed telling the police that he was a 'consultant' with the Lahore consulate-general. Anti-American sentiment – already inflamed by errant drone strikes against Al-Qaeda and Taliban militants in the tribal areas near the frontier with Afghanistan – rose further, and US–Pakistani relations, as the US Ambassador Cameron Munter was later reported as saying, went 'straight to hell'. Neither were they rescued from its fires by the CIA-managed mission that killed Osama bin Laden at Abbottabad, not far north of Islamabad, only a few months later. Munter, who had serious misgivings about the drone campaign and was at loggerheads with the CIA station chief, resigned only half way through his posting (Mazzetti).

The second case was prompted by the revelation in the German press, confirmed by German intelligence and not denied by the US government, that the Americans had been tapping the mobile-phone calls of German Chancellor Angela Merkel, almost certainly by means of a SIGINT post in their Berlin embassy. (Not long before this there had been similar revelations in connection with the presidents of Brazil and Mexico.) The unusual step was taken of summoning the American ambassador John B. Emerson to the German foreign ministry to provide an explanation, and the German Chancellor herself expressed her anger about the matter in a 20-minute phone call with President Obama. The subject also upstaged the formal agenda of the EU summit that took place in Brussels only a few days later, which ended with the issue of a statement saying the lack of trust between allies demonstrated by the recent revelations jeopardized the cooperation between their intelligence agencies essential in the fight against terrorism.

Another reason for the possible discomfort caused to heads of mission by in-house intelligence officers is that they attract unwelcome attention to their posts by the security agencies of receiving states, particularly those of unfriendly ones. This might well happen anyway, but the presence of the spies tends to make it more aggressive. The bugging of diplomatic premises, tapping of phone calls, following and minor harassment of diplomats, active discouragement of their contacts with local citizens, and the expulsion of genuine diplomats (particularly those with local language skills and special country expertise) in 'tit-for-tat' exchanges with intelligence officers charged with espionage all became routine in states locked directly in the Cold War – and remain a regular feature of some international relationships today. The known or simply suspected presence of intelligence officers can even stimulate or at least provide a ready pretext for popular hostility and mob attacks on embassies. This was the notorious fate of the US Embassy in Tehran (which housed a major CIA station) in late 1979.

Matters might not be much better for an embassy in friendly territory if the sending state is sensitive to human rights and the local security service with which the in-house intelligence officers are 'liaising' has a well-earned reputation for brutality. In these circumstances, the main trouble for the embassy will come from home, but it is also likely that intelligence liaison will complicate the efforts of the genuine diplomats to maintain discreet contact with local opposition elements.

Whether in unfriendly states or friendly ones with quite different attitudes to human rights, the net effect of giving diplomatic cover to intelligence officers is sometimes seriously to impair – and in extreme cases terminate – pursuit of the legitimate functions of embassies.

When intelligence officers are numerous, their funds lavish, their agency's lines to their own head of government direct, and – as sometimes happens – their control of an embassy's communications virtually complete, heads of mission might also easily be manipulated by them. Indeed, in such circumstances, chiefs of station might be the 'real ambassador', and be so treated both by the local head of state and their own governments. This was often the case with the KGB resident in Soviet embassies (Andrew and Mitrokhin: 274), but appears to be just as common in those of the United States, and no doubt those of many other countries as well (Stockwell: 63; Church Committee: ch. 14; National Commission: 94; Mazzetti). Hence the completeness of the 'cuckoo' metaphor – for a common variety of this species is a brood parasite, laying eggs in the nest of another species that incubate faster than those of the host bird and produce beefy chicks that frequently eject the unfortunate host's own eggs.

Why, then, do foreign ministries tolerate the practice? Under many regimes, particularly those of such states as Pakistan in which the security and intelligence services have great political influence, they have no choice. It is also reasonable to assume that even the dullest foreign ministry will not be slow to grasp the vital importance of secret intelligence in a world in which technology has made the results of tactical surprise by small terrorist groups potentially devastating – and the consequences of strategic surprise by hostile states threatening to national survival itself; and the spectacular failures of secret intelligence show that its agencies need all the help they can get (Smith 2009: 837). But even in the absence of crude pressure or patriotic sensitivity to the needs of a vital service, there are additional reasons why the diplomats are disposed to give shelter to intelligence officers, together with kindred spirits such as 'drugs liaison officers' and the 'immigration liaison officers' who tackle people trafficking.

First and foremost, the information supplied to diplomats by intelligence officers – whether via well-placed source agents or decrypts of top secret, intercepted diplomatic messages – can greatly assist the success of their negotiations. This is particularly true if it reveals the fall-back position of the other side and what cards it has in its hand. As the former senior GCHQ officer Michael Herman writes, 'peeping at others' hands has always been part of diplomacy' (1996: 51). States have always taken great trouble to conceal what intelligence agencies call 'diplomatic support' or 'policy support', whether in order to protect sources and avoid angering foreign negotiators when they have benefited from it, or to cover their embarrassment if they have suffered from it. As a result, confirmed examples are not easy to find, although some seem beyond doubt.

For instance, vastly superior intelligence gave the Soviet leader Joseph Stalin a great edge in his negotiations with his American and British counterparts at the Word War II conferences at Tehran and Yalta (Andrew and Mitrokhin: 146–8, 175–6). In 1972, intercepts of telephone conversations between dealers by Soviet eavesdroppers in the United States and Cuba enabled the Soviet Union surreptitiously to purchase 25 per cent of the US grain harvest at very favourable prices (Aid: 514; Daugherty: 83). And, later in the same decade, a KGB operation mounted at a Moscow hotel enabled the Soviet Ministry of Foreign Trade to negotiate a major reduction in the price of two large British methane production plants (Andrew and Mitrokhin: 553). Lest it be thought that the gains from diplomatic support were wholly one-sided during the Cold War, the vague but authoritative claim must be noted that revenge of a sort on Moscow was obtained when a source agent provided the Americans with valuable information on Soviet negotiating positions in the mid-1970s (Herman 2011: 894). In 2004, in the Butler Review of intelligence on WMD, attention was also drawn to the diplomatic support provided to counter-proliferation policy by secret intelligence (Butler Review: 38). And since then, the top-secret information released by Edward Snowden has amply confirmed that successful attacks on the computers and smartphones of delegates attending G7/G8 and G20 summits by the SIGINT agencies of the conference hosts, as well as the NSA, has in recent years provided welcome real-time information to their 'customers' in the negotiations at these important events.

Second, intelligence officers – generally skilled at operating in the shadows – can be useful to diplomats by serving as intermediaries in a variety of sensitive relationships, particularly those in which their political masters are busily denying any intention to negotiate with 'terrorists' or hostage-takers. Among other *now* well-known examples, SIS is authoritatively reported to have opened channels to the Provisional Irish Republican Army ('Provos') in the early 1970s (Cowper-Coles 2011: 257; Scott: 335–7) and to have attempted similar manoeuvres with the Taliban (ISC 2013: 28; Scott: 331). 'Clandestine diplomacy' of this sort carries high risks for the intelligence officers themselves – the least of which is exposure of their identities – and for this reason might actually be concealed from the diplomats at the time.

Intelligence officers can also play a valuable diplomatic role to the extent that an entrenched alliance between foreign intelligence agencies remains firm amidst the wreckage of a badly damaged political relationship between their states (Chesterman: 1094). The best known in addition to being the most significant of these is the 'Five Eyes' club, which evolved from Anglo-American SIGINT collaboration during World War II and during the 1950s came to include Australia, Canada, and New Zealand as well. This alliance helped to minimize the harm caused to Anglo-American relations by the Suez crisis in 1956 (Bower: 197). Intelligence officers might also have a soothing effect when a foreign government believes that the diplomats of the sending state have a prejudice against it. Thus the British Foreign Office for long had the reputation of being pro-Arab and it was for this reason that, after Suez, Prime Minister Harold Macmillan employed SIS to communicate with the Israelis (Bower: 240). For similar reasons, service attachés can prove to be of diplomatic value in relations with military regimes.

Third, intelligence officers always have the potential to provide valuable practical assistance to embassies. For example, while their presence might encourage attacks on their premises, they can also help in their defence, as when planned Al-Qaeda attacks on US embassies in Albania and Uganda in 1998 were probably forestalled by the CIA (National Commission: 127). In critical situations, when ordinary channels of rapid, secure communication are disrupted, the intelligence agencies are sometimes able to help in this regard as well (ISC 1999: 6).

Last but not least, the 'platform' provided by embassies and consulates for the conduct of secret intelligence operations helps greatly to justify their continued existence: no cuckoos, then fewer, smaller, and less well-feathered nests.

Diplomats and intelligence officers, therefore, both have interests in living in harmony. Moreover, in the liberal democracies a *modus vivendi* between them has been stiffened both by greater openness in regard to the financing and administration (as opposed to operations) of the intelligence agencies and by improvements in the coordination of their work. Limits on the numbers of intelligence officers might also be part of tacit understandings between unfriendly states based on reciprocity. And at least in the United States, agreements appear to have been negotiated between the intelligence community and the State Department about the percentage of intelligence officers able to enjoy cover at any given post; while the norm that the chief of mission should be given the detailed guidance and political support needed for effective supervision of all CIA officers was strongly reinforced by the Church Committee's final report in 1976 (Church Committee: 308–15, 466–9) – although, as Cameron Munter found in Islamabad, this has not always survived the post-9/11 'War on Terror'.

Summary

The association of secret intelligence with diplomacy is as old as diplomacy itself, but diplomats did not begin to distance themselves from this 'dirty' activity until the late nineteenth century, when military attachés and afterwards separate foreign intelligence agencies appeared. The separation was, however, far from complete because after World War II a trend to give diplomatic cover to intelligence officers – as well as to military officers – gathered pace, chiefly because embassies and consulates give them diplomatic immunity, good security and the best vantage points.

Because of a difference in priorities and attitudes to risk-taking, there is often tension in their relations with the diplomats. That this is usually manageable is due in part to the assistance secret intelligence can give to the diplomats in their own work.

Further reading

Andrew, Christopher and David Dilks (eds), *The Missing Dimension: Governments and intelligence communities in the twentieth century* (Macmillan: Basingstoke,

1984): especially the Introduction. This is the book that launched secret intelligence as a serious object of scholarly research and is still worth reading.

Aid, M., 'Eavesdroppers of the Kremlin: KGB SIGINT during the Cold War', in Karl de Leeuw and Jan Bergstra (eds), *The History of Information Security: A comprehensive handbook* (Elsevier: Amsterdam, 2007).

Andrew, Christopher, 'Vasili Mitrokhin', *Guardian*, 4 February 2004 [www]. An obituary by the British scholar who assisted him with the publication of his archive of KGB records.

Andrew, Christopher and Vasili Mitrokhin, *The Mitrokhin Archive: The KGB in Europe and the West* (Penguin: London, 1999). A work of exceptional interest; extremely long and detailed; a book to be dipped into.

Berridge, G. R., *British Diplomacy in Turkey, 1583 to the Present: A study in the evolution of the resident embassy* (Martinus Nijhoff: Leiden, 2009).

Berridge, G. R., *The Counter-Revolution in Diplomacy and other essays* (Palgrave Macmillan: Basingstoke, 2011): essay 5 ('Specific reciprocity and the 105 Soviet spies').

Berridge, G. R., *Embassies in Armed Conflict* (Continuum: New York, 2012).

Berridge, G. R. and Lorna Lloyd, *The Palgrave Macmillan Dictionary of Diplomacy* (Palgrave Macmillan: Basingstoke, 2012): on the numerous variations on the term 'military attaché'.

Bower, Tom, *The Perfect English Spy: Sir Dick White and the secret war, 1935–90* (Heinemann: London, 1995).

Campbell, Duncan, 'How embassy eavesdropping works' (n.d.) [www].

Chesterman, Simon, 'The spy who came in from the Cold War: Intelligence and international law', *Michigan Journal of International Law*, 27, 2005–6.

Church Committee, *Foreign and Military Intelligence. Book I. Final Report of the Select Committee to Study Governmental Operations with respect to Intelligence Activities. United States Senate* (U.S. Government Printing Office: Washington, DC, 1976) [www]. A very important source.

Corera, Gordon, 'Spying scandal: Will the 'five eyes' club open up? *BBC News*, 29 October 2013 [www].

Farrell, Paul, 'History of 5-eyes – explainer', *Guardian*, 2 December 2013 [www].

Guardian, 'GCHQ intercepted foreign politicians' communications at G20 summits', 17 June 2013 [www].

Guardian, 'The NSA files' [www].

Herman, Michael, *Intelligence Power in Peace and War* (Cambridge University Press: Cambridge, 1996). Written by a former senior member of the staff of GCHQ, so to some extent a primary source.

Höne, Katharina, 'Blurred lines and lost trust? Diplomacy and intelligence gathering. Eavesdropping on G20 delegates in 2009', *Diplo blog*, 18 June 2013 [www].

[ISC] Intelligence and Security Committee, *The Mitrokhin Inquiry Report*, June 2000, Cm 4764 [www].

[ISC] Intelligence and Security Committee of Parliament, *Annual Report 2012–2013*, 10 July 2013, HC 547 [www].

Jeffery, Keith, *MI6: The history of the Secret Intelligence Service, 1909–1949* (Bloomsbury: London, 2010). The official history. Long on detail.

Kish, John, ed. David Turns, *International Law and Espionage* (Martinus Nijhoff: The Hague, 1995): ch. 2 ('Diplomacy and espionage').

LSE Media Policy Project, 'Online surveillance' [www]. An excellent portal to online resources.

Mazzetti, Mark, 'How a single spy helped turn Pakistan against the United States', *The New York Times Magazine*, 9 April 2013 [www].

National Commission on Terrorist Attacks Upon the United States, *The 9/11 Commission Report: Final Report of the National Commission on Terrorist Attacks Upon the United States (9/11 Report)* (US Government Printing Office: Washington, DC, 2004) [www].

Radsan, A. John, 'The unresolved equation of espionage and international law', *Michigan Journal of International Law*, 28, 2006–7. A shrewd and very readable account by a former CIA lawyer of the different views on the possibility of bringing espionage under international law.

Schaller, Christian, 'Spies', in Rüdiger Wolfrum (ed.), *Max Planck Encyclopedia of Public International Law* (Oxford University Press: Oxford, 2013).

Spiegel Online International, 'Embassy Espionage: The NSA's Secret Spy Hub in Berlin', 27 October, 2013 [www].

Talmon, Stefan, 'Tapping the German chancellor's cell phone and public international law', *Cambridge Journal of International and Comparative Law*, 6 November 2013 [www].

11
Conferences

If the role of the resident ambassador was modified in the course of the twentieth century, this is partly because of the explosion in the number of conferences attended by three or more states – multilateral diplomacy. These conferences vary hugely in subject, scope, size, level of attendance, longevity, and extent of bureaucratization. At one extreme is an *ad hoc* conference on a mundane topic lasting perhaps for a week, and attended at the level of officials and experts; in between will be found an 'informal forum' like the two-day meetings of the Group of 20's finance ministers and central bank governors; and, at the other extreme, a major permanent conference, or international organization, such as the United Nations, grappling with many topics of great importance. This chapter will consider why the enormous expansion in multilateral diplomacy has occurred, and examine its characteristic procedures.

It is common to assume that this form of diplomacy is essentially a twentieth-century phenomenon, but its origins lie much earlier. It was known in the ancient world, and somewhat chaotic multilateral conferences devoted to peace settlements became a feature of the European system of states in the seventeenth century. However, it was not until the early nineteenth century that multilateral diplomacy began to take on modern form, and a further century before its growth began to accelerate.

A conference concentrates minds on one issue or series of related issues; ideally brings together all the parties whose agreement is necessary; and advertises their anxiety to see something done about it, even if, privately, they are sceptics. A conference also encourages informality; its members might even develop a certain *esprit de corps*. It has a president with a vested interest in its success, and – at least if it is an *ad hoc* conference – will provide a deadline to concentrate minds because it cannot go on for ever. As a result, when the international agenda is lengthening and matters are urgent, when the number of states is increasing and the means of assembling their representatives in one place are improving, the appeal of international conferences is irresistible. This was the situation in the first decades of the twentieth century. Sir Maurice Hankey, the British civil servant who played such an important role in the development of multilateral diplomacy, laid great stress on the impetus given to this device by 'the perils and the overwhelming press of war business' during the great conflict of 1914–1918 (Hankey: 14).

Other factors also encouraged its acceleration. Among these was the growing strength of the idea that popular consent is the foundation of political authority, which in international relations argued for parliamentary-style 'assemblies' including small as well as larger states, as in the League of Nations. Another was the consolation nevertheless provided to the great powers by the potential of conference diplomacy to advertise their status – and justify their special rights to dispose of the fate of the world, as more recently in the Security Council of the United Nations. Conference diplomacy also prospered because of the impetus it can give to other forms of diplomacy: bilateral diplomacy in its wings, particularly that of states not enjoying diplomatic relations; and the diplomacy of powerful mediators, who can hold a multilateral conference in order to kick-start, and then discreetly shroud, a series of essentially bilateral negotiations taking place elsewhere, as in the case of the Six-Party Talks in Beijing in March 2007 that launched direct US–North Korea negotiations on the latter's nuclear programme. Finally, multilateral conferences hold out the promise of making agreements stick – partly by signing ceremonies displaying in the most visible manner the wide consensus achieved, and partly by their reflexive disposition to provide monitoring or follow-up machinery (see Chapter 6).

International organizations

The advantages of multilateral conferences do not explain why some have become permanent: that is to say, international organizations, of which there are now well over 200. No doubt important ones have achieved this transformation partly because it suits the powers with the greatest influence in them to have the world permanently reminded of their claims to high status. After all, the alternative – the periodic calling of *ad hoc* conferences – would cause much justified anxiety to those whose real international weight had been called into question in the interval between one meeting and the next. Other multilateral conferences that have become fixtures have done so under the additional impact of the enduring functionalist notion that it is out of such structures that regional – and perhaps even, ultimately, global integration – will grow. Nevertheless, it seems clear that the conferences that become permanent on the international scene do so *principally* because the issue with which they were established to grapple is itself seen as a permanent problem. The paradigm case is the unceasing problem of preserving international peace and security that led the peace conferences following the general wars of the twentieth century to give birth first to the League of Nations, and then to the UN.

An international organization has a constitution or charter in which its aims, structure, and rules of procedure are laid out. Most important is provision for a governing body and a permanent secretariat housed in permanent headquarters. In important cases such as the UN, the governing body – in this instance, the Security Council – is in virtually continuous session. The international organization will also have periodic meetings of the full membership. In normal circumstances these meetings do not have much influence, but this might be greater in emergencies, when special meetings can be held. In the interests of avoiding an excessive concentration of power or serious resentment at unequal burden-sharing, it is also important that substantial contributions to the budget of the international organization should come from more than a small handful of countries. Another good example of an international organization, and a very significant one, is the IAEA.

None of the assemblies, councils, committees, or working groups of international organizations would find it possible to operate without temporary delegations and diplomatic missions permanently accredited to them by the member states. As a result, their members have special legal status under 'headquarters agreements' between individual host states and the international organization concerned. In 1975, an effort was made to strengthen these by giving them the same privileges and immunities as the regular embassies treated in the VCDR (1961) (see Chapter 8). However, this foundered on the opposition of the wealthy Western states that host most international organizations, whose delegates were appalled at the extent to which the numbers of specially privileged diplomats in their capitals would be swollen were this proposal to go through (Fennessy).

A multilateral conference that settles down to permanent status has obvious advantages. It permits the initial breakthrough to be consolidated, keeps the problem under constant surveillance (see 'Review meetings' in Chapter 6), encourages the accumulation of specialized knowledge, signals serious commitment, creates a lobby for the cause in question, often provides technical assistance to states requiring it – and does all this without raising the excessive expectations often generated by *ad hoc* conferences. There is a price to be paid for this, it is true: permanently constituted conferences tend to freeze the power struc-ture in existence at the time of their creation, together with the culture convenient to it. This is good for some, but bad for others – and usually bad for the respect in which the international organization is generally held.

Procedure

Whether multilateral conferences are *ad hoc* or permanent, they tend to share similar procedural problems, among them those of venue, partici-pation, agenda, style of proceedings, and decision-making. The solu-tions they produce, however, are by no means identical.

Venue

This question of sometimes symbolic, and always practical, signifi-cance in prenegotiations has already been discussed at some length in Chapter 2. Nevertheless, it must also be mentioned here, since venue is of special importance when the creation of an international organi-zation is contemplated; and the more important the organization the greater the excitement this issue tends to generate.

A case in point is the controversy surrounding the site for a perma-nent home for the United Nations, a question that fell into the lap of its Preparatory Commission in late 1945. Although many different sites were suggested, the argument – inspired in the main by concerns over prestige, but rationalized in a different language – resolved into one over whether it should be located in Europe or America. The argument for Europe was that this had always been the major cockpit of international conflict and, therefore, where the UN was likely to have most of its work to do. Besides, the pro-Europe camp maintained, the old buildings of the League of Nations remained available in Geneva, itself in a neutral country and within easy reach of the Middle East and the east coast of the Americas, as well as from Europe. As for the case for the United States, this rested on the view that a US headquarters was essential to sustain American interest and prevent a return to isolationism, while many Latin Americans preferred it for practical and political reasons of their own. In the end, a decision was made for the United States – but where in that country exactly? New York was finally chosen, despite the opposition of the Arabs, who disliked its strongly Jewish character and favoured San Francisco instead (Gore-Booth 1974: 151–2; Nicholas: 44). For sound political reasons, the UN's other major agencies were distributed among important cities elsewhere – notably Paris, Vienna, Geneva, Washington, and Rome.

Venue might be of special importance for permanent conferences, but it is also significant for those of an *ad hoc* nature. Today, this is principally because only a limited number of cities have the communications systems, hotel space, and pools of qualified interpreters to cope with the huge size of many of these conferences. Venues are also sometimes chosen, however, because it is believed they will assist the publicity of the conference, which is why small island developing states are always the venues for international conferences on this subject – in 2014, at Apia, the capital of the Pacific island state of Samoa. Finally, an old and enduring reason why the venue of *ad hoc* conferences is important is that it is customary for their presidents to be the foreign minister or principal delegate of the host country. Conference presidents have important duties: stating the background and purposes of the conference, and setting its tone in an opening speech; directing administrative arrangements; orchestrating any 'diversions' (which often includes showing off local achievements); and, above all, chairing plenary sessions and perhaps drawing up any final report. It is true that the host country will generally have a special interest in the success of the conference and that this may put it under pressure to make concessions of its own to ensure this is achieved (Putnam: 61). But its possession of the conference presidency is a position of influence, as it was in the Concert of Europe in the nineteenth century. 'The question of president never raised any difficulty,' noted Sir Charles Webster. 'It belonged to the state in whose territory the meeting took place, an advantage,' he added, 'of which both Palmerston and Metternich were very conscious' (Webster: 63).

For largely political reasons, the presidents of plenary sessions of permanent conferences tend to be less influential than those of *ad hoc* conferences. They are commonly chosen from smaller states, and also lack the ability of a senior politician operating on home territory to determine the ambience of a conference. Furthermore, UN Security Council presidents, for example, rotate every month in the English alphabetical order of the names of the Council's members.

Participation

The sponsors of conferences dealing with matters of peace and security are traditionally major powers with worldwide interests. In other matters, they are those with a strong interest in the subject and anxiety to get something done about it, willing to shoulder the administrative and financial burden, and prepared to risk the possible political complications of staging the event.

But who should the sponsors invite? This is usually a sensitive question, since an invitation acknowledges the importance of the invitee to the outcome of the conference, and might even amount to de facto recognition of a government or state of unsettled status. An invitation also acknowledges legitimacy of interest, which might have far-reaching consequences.

Except for the 'open-to-all' conferences spawned by the UN system, the rule of thumb has generally been that invitees to *ad hoc* conferences should be limited to important states with a direct interest in their subject matter. Those with an important indirect interest, or whom it is hoped might be encouraged to take a future interest, can be accorded observer status. For example, the Geneva Conference on Indo-China in 1954 was limited to the USA, the Soviet Union, France, Britain, the PRC, Vietnam, Cambodia, Laos, and the Vietminh. And a determined effort was made by the UN to limit the participants in the Geneva conference on Syria in January 2014 ('Geneva II') to three chief categories: the internal parties (the Assad government and the opposition 'coalition'), the outside states and international organizations with significant influence over them (which, for the UN and Russia, included Iran, a powerful backer of President Assad), and the states in the region suffering most from the massive exodus of refugees and most at risk from a spread of the increasingly sectarian nature of the conflict (Brahimi).

But employment of the criterion of interest in determining the membership of a conference is not sufficient to remove all problems. For one thing, there is ample room for disagreement on whether a particular state has a *legitimate* interest in attendance – and there is no mechanism for resolving this point other than diplomacy itself. There is even more room for doubt where the interests of non-state bodies are concerned. In fact, there was for a long time strong resistance in principle to the idea that such entities had any right to attend international conferences at all, particularly those dealing with the termination of military hostilities and territorial settlements. For example, representatives of the Communist guerrilla movement, the Vietminh, were not admitted to the Indo-Chinese phase of the Geneva Conference in 1954 until the last minute (Randle: 159–60); and none of southern Africa's large and well-known guerrilla movements was a formal participant in any round of the decisive Angola/Namibia talks in 1988.

However, the need is being increasingly recognized to include in international conferences *any* party with a strong interest in its subject and – if granted a seat – the power to assist a workable settlement. A good example of such 'multi-stakeholder diplomacy' is the conference hosted by the South African government at Kimberley in 2000 that made a significant contribution to curbing the trade in 'conflict diamonds'. This was attended not only by delegations from the major diamond-producing states of southern Africa, but also from the international diamond industry and various NGOs, among them Global Witness and Partnership Africa Canada.

Growing acceptance of and familiarity with multi-stakeholder diplomacy might have eased the problem of conference participation, but borderline cases of invitee entitlement will always remain. Besides, even when this is admitted in the case of one party, a second might object to their participation so strenuously on other grounds that it makes its own attendance conditional on the absence of the first; this is why UN Secretary-General Ban Ki-moon's last-minute invitation to Iran to join Geneva II had to be swiftly withdrawn following the objection to this of the Syrian opposition. Furthermore, conference sponsors are sometimes influenced by considerations of political rivalry when deciding whom to invite, which presents them with a classic dilemma: *exclusion* of an interested rival has the advantage of denting their prestige and making the deliberations of the conference easier, but *inclusion* provides an opportunity to carry them along and forestall the subsequent sabotage of any agreement reached. This was the uncomfortable position occupied by US Secretary of State John Foster Dulles, apropos the British agitation to invite the PRC to the Geneva Conference on Indo-China in 1954. It was also in a similar fix that US President Jimmy Carter found himself in 1977 in considering whether to keep the Soviet Union involved in the multilateral diplomacy over the Arab–Israeli conflict. In view of their quite different reputations, it is ironical that it was Dulles who agreed to open the door to his rival and Carter who decided to keep it closed.

Finally, it is important to note that states or other agencies widely acknowledged to have a legitimate interest in a particular subject, and sometimes prepared to engage in confidential bilateral discussions, might be reluctant to be observed on the same conference platform. This was a constant problem for the multilateral diplomacy in Africa sponsored by the South African government in the 1950s, and – until the early 1990s – for all attempts to involve the Israeli government in multilateral talks including the PLO.

Box 11.1 The UN Security Council

A special case of problematical conference participation is the question of membership of the UN Security Council. Presently consisting of five permanent, veto-wielding members (the United States, Russia, France, Britain, and the PRC – the 'P5'), plus ten members appointed for non-renewable two-year terms, there has for many years been a growing belief that this membership is no longer appropriate. Reformists claim that the Council fails to reflect the distribution of either world power or diversity and, therefore, lacks authority. Britain and France, it is claimed, are no longer great powers, while Russia is a pale reflection of the former Soviet Union: although still a nuclear power, its assessed net contribution to the UN's regular budget for 2014 was little more than one-fifth of that assessed for Japan (UN Secretariat: 7–10). Besides, the less developed countries have no permanent representation at all. Features common to most of the more radical reform proposals include a substantial net increase in the size of the Security Council; no granting of the veto to any new permanent members for a long probationary period, if ever; and more restricted use of the veto, particularly in cases of mass atrocities. There is less agreement on the character of the additional members. According to one view with strong support, permanent membership should be given to the 'G4': Japan and Germany (the second- and third-largest contributors to the UN's regular budget after the United States), plus India and Brazil. Against the reformers, it is argued that it is a mistake to tamper with the Security Council when, since the end of the Cold War, it has at long last started to work – 'if it ain't broke, don't mend it' sums up their position; that steps have been taken to ensure greater transparency; that powerful members such as Japan are virtually permanent members anyway – since they are re-elected so often to a non-permanent seat, and are carefully consulted by the P5 even when they are not sitting; that reform entailing enlargement would make the Council unwieldy; and that there is no consensus either on how the membership should be restructured or on which states should be given the great prizes – permanent seats – and, therefore, little chance of obtaining the two-thirds majority in the UN General Assembly for the Charter amendment that changes of this sort would require. The defence of the status quo on the Security Council pays insufficient attention to the question of legitimacy. It also fudges the question as to whether it is working because of, or in spite of, its present composition – if it is, in fact, working that well anyway (the improvements of recent decades started from a very low base). Nevertheless, the conservative rearguard is a sophisticated one, and in May 2013 intergovernmental negotiations authorized by the General Assembly in 2008 ground to a halt (Lehmann). Security Council reform is urgently needed, but it generally takes a cataclysmic upheaval to alter the composition of the councils of the major powers.

In many international organizations, the problem of participation is in principle solved, as already noted, by admitting all states. These are the so-called universal membership organizations, which have the added advantage of permitting discreet contact between states lacking

diplomatic relations. However, the UN itself was not a universal organization at the start of its life or for many years after, during which period
participation was confined to the founding members and 'all other
peace-loving states which accept the obligations' of the Charter and 'are
able and willing to carry out these obligations.' This permitted the black-
balling of many important states for long periods, most signally in the
case of the PRC, which was not admitted to membership until October
1971. Unpopular countries such as South Africa were also forced out of
some international organizations.

Universal or near universal membership of an international conference also brings problems of its own. The most important of these
returns us to the concept of interest. This is because throwing the doors
of a conference wide open permits, and might even encourage, each
participant to have a say in the affairs of all of the others, whether they
have a direct interest in them or not. 'Mind your own business!' is the
natural reaction to this of the others. This problem will be exacerbated
if discussion is conducted in public and decision-making proceeds, as it
did for a long time in the UN General Assembly, by means of majority-
voting (discussed later in this chapter). In short, universal membership
might well be anti-diplomatic, gratuitously worsening relations between
states that, in an earlier era, would either have had little contact at all
or been in touch only on issues where both had a direct interest. It is,
for example, unlikely that relations between Britain and Ireland (so
important to resolving the problems in Ulster) would have suffered as a
result of the Falklands crisis in 1982 had they not at the time both been
members (the one permanent, and the other temporary) of the Security
Council of the United Nations.

Agenda

Problems concerning the agenda of a multilateral conference vary
between *ad hoc* and permanent conferences. If a party is invited to an
ad hoc conference, whether it will attend or not is likely to depend on
the draft agenda. This might contain items that are embarrassing or,
in themselves, innocuous, although prejudgement is obvious from
the manner in which they are worded: for example, 'Chinese aggression against Vietnam', rather than 'the situation concerning China and
Vietnam' (Nicol: 41; Bailey and Daws: 83–4). As in any kind of negotiation, the draft agenda might even be so framed as to amount to a
proposed deal (see Chapter 2), although this is less likely to be true of
the increasing number in recent years inspired by the reports of independent global commissions (Evans).

One agenda problem is peculiar to permanent multilateral conferences, because their founding charters or statutes impose on them 'functions' or 'purposes' that are translated into a working agenda by the most influential members before each session. And those who do not like it can only refuse to attend with difficulty, since they have already accepted permanent membership. Even one of the P5 on the Security Council cannot veto the inscription of an item or veto its inclusion at a particular point on the agenda. This is because the customary law of the Security Council states that these are procedural rather than substantive matters (Bailey and Daws: 84–5).

On the other hand, devices exist to ensure that the sessional agendas of permanent multilateral conference are broadly acceptable, typically the requirement that they should be approved by two-thirds of the members present and voting; in any case, broad consultation usually ensures that a vote on the agenda does not need to be taken. If some states remain hostile to the inclusion of a particular item, it is always possible to mollify them by a vague, general, or altogether obscure formulation of it, which is the practice increasingly adopted by the UN Security Council (Bailey and Daws: 83–4). If all else fails, they can temporarily absent themselves from meetings or maintain only a token presence, as South Africa did at the UN General Assembly for several years after November 1956 in protest at its insistence on discussing the policy of apartheid. However, states in a minority tend to stay for the discussion of items on which they would prefer silence to prevail. This is partly because they want their reply to any charges to be heard, and partly because they have other reasons for wishing to remain a part of the organization.

Public debate and private discussion

It is the character of public debate in the plenary sessions of international conferences that has caused multilateral diplomacy to gain a poor name. When discussion takes place between numerous delegations in a public setting, the political necessity of playing to the audience outside is inescapable, and the give and take of genuine negotiation dissolves. The style of proceedings is self-consciously point-scoring or 'parliamentary', and the result is that diplomacy is replaced by propaganda. Until recent decades, this was typically the case with both the UN General Assembly and the formal meetings of the Security Council. Even closed plenary sessions of conferences are hardly likely to encourage real negotiation when, as is often the case, well over 150 states are represented and the corridors outside are crawling with journalists and lobbyists from NGOs.

Widespread recognition of the drawbacks of over-reliance on public debate in multilateral diplomacy has led to increased employment of subcommittees, private sessions, and informal consultations. Since the 1970s, the UN Security Council itself has regularly met informally in private, and the P5 have caucused in secret since the mid-1980s. Conferences within the broader UN system are now preceded by preparatory committees and, once launched, employ an elaborate mix of different kinds of session – private and public, plenary and small group. For example, in the Arab–Israeli multilaterals, overseen by a largely ceremonial steering group, the real business was conducted in five functionally defined and informally conducted working groups, and in their 'inter-sessional activities' (Peters: ch. 3). Where there is a constitutional tradition of public meetings, however, these are difficult if not impossible to avoid. In any case, while public sessions of conferences that effectively rubber-stamp agreements thrashed out in private might induce cynicism, they are valuable in demonstrating unity on important international problems.

The number of participants and the technicality of the issues in most multilateral conferences held today make them extremely complex. Despite the procedural advances just noted, therefore, it might be imagined that this alone would vitiate the advantages of conducting diplomacy by this method. Complexity is, indeed, a problem – but not normally fatal. This is because, in most large conferences, the order of battle is simplified by the formation of coalitions. In the UN Conference on the Law of the Sea, for instance, 150 states participated but, in reality, this boiled down to the West Europeans, the East Europeans, and the Group of 77 (Touval 1989: 164). Furthermore, there is invariably a small number of states both willing and able to make the running, while their need to carry the rest usually inclines them to make their own demands with moderation. In this connection, Michael Alexander's inside account praised the 'informal directorate' in the NATO Council, consisting of the USA, Britain, Germany, and France (Alexander: 199–200). The opportunities for package deals are also far more numerous than in bilateral diplomacy.

Decision-making

The method by which decisions are finalized in bilateral talks has never been an issue: when there are only two parties, there can be no agreement unless both concur. By contrast, multilateral conferences provide the opportunity to make decisions by voting. As a result, the strength of the democratic idea, together with the fear that a rule of unanimity might induce paralysis when numerous states are involved, has produced widespread support for this method. Indeed, despite important exceptions such as the North Atlantic Council and the Council of the Organization for Economic Co-operation and Development (OECD), this has been a formal feature of decision-making in all major international organizations, notably the UN, since the end of World War II.

Where majority voting is employed, it is usual to find differences in the treatment of procedural and substantive issues. Furthermore, some international organizations employ weighted voting, and some require special rather than simple majorities. In the UN Security Council, for example, an affirmative vote of only 9 of the 15 members is required for a decision on a procedural question. But decisions on 'all other matters', says Article 27 of the Charter, require 'an affirmative vote of nine members *including the concurring votes of the permanent members*' (emphasis added) – the great power veto. (It was subsequently accepted that an abstention did not amount to a veto.) For its part, the UN General Assembly was authorized to pass resolutions on a simple majority of members present and voting – except in the case of 'important questions', which require a two-thirds majority.

In practice, however, decision-making by voting has not been as significant across the whole spectrum of multilateral diplomacy as this picture might suggest. *Ad hoc* conferences, especially those with few participants and not constituted under UN auspices, have rarely employed voting, while those that have – including the permanent, large-membership ones within the UN system – have generally found it necessary to qualify their voting arrangements. This has been observed at least since the mid-1960s.

The problem for the UN system is that its 'one state, one vote' rhetoric has collided head-on with political reality as a result of the admission (particularly since the late 1950s) of a huge number of small, weak states. In these circumstances, even the requirement for a two-thirds majority can fail to block the 'wrong' decision. This has rendered 'majority voting increasingly useless for law-making decisions because of the danger of powerful alienated minorities' (Buzan: 326). Having lost its own majority following in the UN in the 1960s, the United States emerged as the most powerful member of just such a minority. Increasingly expected to provide the lion's share of the money for programmes it found objectionable, it drastically scaled back its funding of the organization in the 1980s. The result was that the UN, together with particularly anathematized satellites such as UNESCO, was threatened with collapse.

Could this dangerous position not have been prevented by giving more votes to the bigger battalions by using a system of weighted voting? Although perhaps attractive in principle, this idea has three main problems: it is politically sensitive, because it draws attention to massive inequalities between states when all are supposed to be equal; it might avoid the risk of alienating powerful minorities, but only at the price of antagonizing weak majorities; and it raises complex political issues concerning the criteria to be employed in establishing the appropriate differences between states and practical issues over their measurement. As a result, weighted voting has only proved acceptable in specialized economic organizations such as the International Monetary Fund (IMF) and the World Bank, where the size of readily calculable financial contributions provides a strong claim on the size of votes.

Rather than weighted voting being generally adopted, then, multilateral diplomacy has witnessed a growing acceptance of decision-making by consensus, especially following its successful employment at the Third UN Conference on the Law of the Sea (Buzan: 325–7; Peters: 7–8). In practice, most decisions are taken by consensus, even in the IMF and the World Bank. It is also this procedure that has saved the UN: the General Assembly itself has, for many years, been passing its own resolutions and decisions largely on the basis of consensus.

Consensus decision-making is the attempt to achieve the agreement of all the participants in a multilateral conference without the need for a vote and its inevitable divisiveness. A consensus exists when all parties are in agreement – which, on the face of it, is another way of saying that they are unanimous. However, a consensus might include some members whose support has been given only grudgingly and who have simply registered no *formal* objection; whereas unanimity implies broader enthusiasm – hence the view that, in fact, they are not the same. It might be more accurate to say that a weak consensus is not the same as unanimity, but that a strong one is.

But is decision-making by consensus simply negotiation by another name? After all, if the reluctant agreement of all participants is to be obtained, those most in favour of a proposal must either water it down, make concessions to the unenthusiastic in some other area, or alarm them with the prospect of isolation. In short, they must negotiate with them. Nevertheless, it is now common to find even a strong consensus fostered by special procedural devices.

One of these methods is to give a secretary-general or chairperson the right to conduct straw votes – that is, to count opinions by means of informal, confidential consultations with permanent missions or delegations; among other things, this provides the opportunity to detect the way the wind is blowing. Another device, which builds on this one, is 'silence procedure'; namely, the rule that a proposal with strong support is deemed to have been agreed unless any member raises an objection to it before a precise deadline – silence signifies assent, or at least acquiescence. This procedure relies on the assumption that a member in a minority will fear that raising an objection will expose it to the charge of obstructiveness and thus to the perils of isolation. Silence procedure is employed by NATO, the OSCE, and in the framework of the Common Foreign and Security Policy of the European Union (EU) and, no doubt, in numerous other international bodies. Finally, voting itself might still be employed, although its function is the limited one of ratifying a consensus already negotiated.

It seems reasonable to conclude, therefore, that consensus decision-making is something more than ordinary negotiation: it is the unanimity system adjusted to the prejudices of the present era. Despite this, it provides no guarantee that a decision can be reached, or reached in time, or that – if one is reached in time – it will be a good one. The notorious vagueness of UN Security Council Resolution 1441 of November 2002 on Iraq, notably in its reference to the 'serious consequences' that would follow non-compliance, is a case in point.

The return of a system of decision-making in which the more powerful states were able to exert the influence to which they thought they were entitled also marked a 'crisis of multilateralism' (Aurisch: 288). At least, it marked a crisis of the kind of multilateral diplomacy by means of which, in the 1970s, the weaker states had hoped to create a New International Economic Order. It is perhaps, therefore, not surprising that the number of international organizations should have gone into sharp decline after the mid-1980s, dropping by over one third by the turn of the millennium, although the level of universal membership international organizations remained steady. The total number of NGOs, by contrast, rose by roughly the same proportion.

Summary

Multilateral diplomacy took firm root in the early twentieth century under the impact of world war and the strength of the democratic idea. It blossomed after World War II with the great expansion in the number of states and the belief of the new ones that conference diplomacy within the UN system – based on majority voting – was their best chance of securing influence. Ultimately, they were disappointed. The major

Western powers became tired of paying for programmes to which they took strong political objection and, under the name of consensus decision-making, gradually began to make their weight felt. In the 1980s, with the UN system reeling under the impact of American budgetary withholdings and the poorer states increasingly disillusioned with the meagre results obtained by their large voting majorities, a crisis of multilateralism set in. However, multilateralism is here to stay: it has weathered its crisis, and it has emerged a little leaner. It has also emerged a little more diplomatic.

Further reading

Bailey, S. D. and S. Daws, *The Procedure of the UN Security Council*, 3rd edn (Clarendon Press: Oxford, 1998).

Barder, Brian, *What Diplomats Do: The life and work of diplomats* (Rowman & Littlefield: Lanham, MD, 2014): ch. 6.

Brahimi, L., Notes to Correspondents: 'Transcript of press conference by Joint Special Representative for Syria (JSRS) Lakhdar Brahimi', Geneva, 20 December 2013 (United Nations) [www].

Buzan, B., 'Negotiating by consensus: Developments in technique at the United Nations Conference on the Law of the Sea', *American Journal of International Law*, 72(2), 1981.

'Congress', in *Encyclopedia Britannica* (1911 edn), written by Walter Allison Phillips [www].

Evans, Gareth, 'Commission Diplomacy', in Andrew F. Cooper, Jorge Heine, and Ramesh Thaku (eds), *The Oxford Handbook of Modern Diplomacy* (Oxford University Press: Oxford, 2013).

Fennessy, J. G., 'The 1975 Convention on the Representation of States in their Relations with International Organizations of a Universal Character', *American Journal of International Law*, 70, 1976.

G20 [www].

G20 Information Centre (University of Toronto) [www].

Hankey, Lord, *Diplomacy by Conference: Studies in public affairs 1920–1946* (Benn: London, 1946) [www].

IAEA [www].

Jenks, C. W., 'Unanimity, the veto, weighted voting, special and simple majorities and consensus as modes of decision in international organisations', *Cambridge Essays in International Law: Essays in honour of Lord McNair* (Stevens: London; Oceana: Dobbs Ferry, NY, 1965).

Kahler, M., *Leadership Selection in the Major Multilaterals* (Inst. for International Economics: Washington, November 2001): 23–4, 62–75, 80, 85.

Kissinger, H. A., *Years of Upheaval* (Weidenfeld & Nicolson/Michael Joseph: London, 1982): ch. 17.

Langhorne, R., 'The development of international conferences, 1648–1830', in *Studies in History and Politics*, 11, pt 2, 1981.

Laub, Z., 'The UN Security Council', CFR Backgrounders, 6 December 2013 [www].

Lehmann, Volker, 'Reforming the working methods of the UN Security Council: The next ACT', Friedrich Ebert Stiftung, August 2013 [www].

MacMillan, Margaret, *Peacemakers: The Paris Conference of 1919 and its attempt to end war* (John Murray: London, 2001).

Peters, J., *Building Bridges: The Arab–Israeli multilateral talks* (RIIA: London, 1994).

Randle, R. F., *Geneva 1954: The settlement of the Indochinese War* (Princeton University Press: Princeton, NJ, 1969).

UN Chronicle, 'The process of informals in the Fifth Committee', March–May, 2002.

Walker, Ronald A., *Multilateral Conferences: Purposeful international negotiation* (Palgrave Macmillan: Basingstoke, 2004).

Webster, Sir Charles, *The Art and Practice of Diplomacy* (Chatto & Windus: London, 1961): ch. 4.

Zamora, S., 'Voting in international economic organizations', *American Journal of International Law*, 74, 1980.

12
Summits

Today an astonishing degree of multilateral diplomacy takes place at the highest level of political authority: heads of state and government, and heads of international organizations, not forgetting the leaders of factions in civil wars. But this is multilateral diplomacy of a special kind; besides, bilateral diplomacy can also take place at the summit, and this is special as well. For these reasons, it is necessary to treat summitry separately. This chapter considers the origins of summitry, its general advantages and disadvantages, and the variations in the contribution to diplomacy – as opposed to propaganda – of the different patterns it assumes.

Summit meetings – although not so-called until the 1950s – occurred sporadically between the Bronze Age and the late Middle Ages, when they reached their pre-modern high-point. Thereafter, at least in Europe, they more or less fizzled out. This was not only because resident missions had by this time become widely established. It was also because rulers had usually proved bad diplomats; because they were more attractive than their envoys as targets for embarrassment, capture for ransom, or murder; and, above all, because in the sixteenth and seventeenth centuries the rise of the modern state was eroding the notion that their territories were their private estates and, with it, the associated idea that diplomacy was their sole prerogative.

In the nineteenth century, the Concert of Europe saw summit diplomacy flicker sporadically into life, but it did not become a significant technique again until the Paris Peace Conference following World War I. Its return was consolidated by encounters in 1938 between Hitler and British Prime Minister Neville Chamberlain. These were prompted by the latter's belief that the terrible prospect of aerial bombing of cities warranted the risks of such personal diplomacy, and that coverage by the new cinema and arrival by aeroplane would add drama to the proceedings. Despite Chamberlain's failure, the subsequent wartime conferences

of the Big Three – Roosevelt, Churchill, and Stalin – were of great importance. Thereafter, in addition to being stimulated by the same political and
technological trends promoting multilateral diplomacy (see Chapter 11),
summitry increased owing to the renewed risk of general war: even more
than in 1938, diplomacy in the nuclear age was believed to be 'too important to be left to the diplomatists' (Dunn: 5). Decolonization in Africa and
Asia, where few of the new states possessed impressive diplomatic services but most had charismatic leaders, was another propellant; and the
regional organizations that were becoming fashionable gave summitry a
natural focus. It is true that a development of recent years has threatened
to put a slight damper on the enthusiasm for summit travel. This is the
theoretical vulnerability to arrest on charges of war crimes and crimes
against humanity of serving – as opposed to retired or deposed – heads
of state, demonstrated vividly by the case of President Bashir of Sudan.
However, the evidence for this is as yet slender.

Professional anathemas

The remarkable twentieth-century return to summitry produced deep
unease among professional diplomats, causing many to recall the objections
to it of Philippe de Commynes (Box 12.1). Since summitry was an insult to
their competence and, at least, a limited threat to their careers, this might
be put down to special pleading. Most eloquent among their number was
George Ball, a US under-secretary of state during the Democratic administrations of the 1960s and acerbic author of the account in *Diplomacy for a
Crowded World* on which this section draws heavily.

Box 12.1   Philippe de Commynes

Commynes (c. 1447–1511) was a French diplomat and historian, and wrote
the best-known political and diplomatic memoirs of the late fifteenth century.
Great princes, he believed, were in general spoiled, vain, and badly educated.
Unusually suspicious because of the many false stories and groundless reports
brought to them by court intriguers, they were also too ready to believe
the worst of any prince with whom they happened to be negotiating. Most
seriously of all, summitry could place them in physical danger. Therefore, he
famously concluded, 'two great princes who wish to establish good personal
relations should never meet each other face to face but ought to communicate through good and wise ambassadors.' Commynes' attitude to summitry
might not have been entirely unconnected to the role that he was required to
play when his master, Louis XI, met Edward IV on a bridge over the Somme at
Picquigny, in order to discuss the peaceful retreat of the English invasion force
of 1475. Louis instructed Commynes to wear identical clothes to his own as a
precaution against *assassination*.

The case against summitry turns chiefly on certain assumptions about heads of state and government as a class. They are held to be poor negotiators because vain, ignorant of details, pressed for time, addicted to publicity, and prone to cultural misunderstandings; also too often overtired if not actually suffering from jet-lag, insomnia, or serious ill-health; and too readily swayed by personal likes and dislikes towards fellow leaders, as was seen only too clearly in the public treatment of President Putin of Russia at the G20 summit in Brisbane in November 2014, with the result that he left prematurely (fortunately, the Australian Prime Minister and summit host, Tony Abbott, did not go so far as to carry out his earlier threat to 'shirt-front' the Russian leader). It is also claimed that, in a deadlock in a negotiation they are leading, there is no one at home to whom the president or prime minister can claim the need to refer in order to secure fresh instructions; after all, they are themselves the ultimate authority. They are, therefore, always likely to make one or other of two mistakes: either they break off the negotiations prematurely or – on their personal promise, rather than that of a disavowable official – make unwise concessions in order to achieve a 'success'. In short, diplomacy conducted at the summit is not only likely to lead to more mistakes, but also to mistakes that are irretrievable.

Summit diplomacy – so the case against it continues – is also more likely to undervalue expert advice and written records. This leads to only the vaguest understandings, with fatal consequences when disagreements about them inevitably emerge. In any case, deals achieved by this method, and thereby in some measure personalized, tend to be weakened by the fall from office of one or other of the leaders concerned: summitry 'obscures the concept of relations between governments as a continuing process,' concludes George Ball (Ball: 40).

The examples of summit failures are legion, and are quoted sometimes with sadness, sometimes with anger, by the professionals. The mistakes made in the Treaty of Versailles were in part ascribed by some to the decision of American President Woodrow Wilson to attend at Paris in person – a 'historical disaster of the first magnitude' (Nicolson 1964: 71). Dean Acheson chooses the example of President Truman: '[I]n the privacy of his study,' he remarks, the president unwittingly altered American policy in a most sensitive area by informing British Prime Minister Clement Attlee that the United States would not use nuclear weapons without first consulting the British (Acheson: 484). William Sullivan's story is how the Shah of Iran, on a visit to the United States, told President Carter of his belief that the Organization of African Unity was an 'impotent' [powerless] body, and the president – with the ear for words of a

Southerner – agreed that it was indeed 'impohtant' [important] (Sullivan: 129). George Ball himself provides a list of summits that have been a 'source of grief' too long to record here, while David Reynolds – who might also have factored in a spineless Foreign Office – argues persuasively that the Blair–Bush meetings between 2001 and 2003 'lubricated' the disastrous decision to invade Iraq (Reynolds: 389).

But this is not the end of the case against summits. Their financial cost has rocketed over recent years because of the need to take elaborate defensive measures against the threat of disruption by anti-globalization protesters among others, as well as attacks by terrorists. A leader who proposes to visit only one of two others locked in a traditional rivalry is also stoking up trouble of a different kind, or undertakes the visit in the expectation of having to make a side payment to head it off. (When President Obama announced that he would be visiting Turkey on his way home from the G20 summit in April 2009, he immediately provoked an outcry in Greece.) A related problem is the need to return a visit paid by the leader of another state of roughly equal standing, even though this might be inconvenient. Finally, those who over-indulge the summit habit, or just find they are doomed to it, might also give insufficient time to domestic affairs – and, in consequence, lose their jobs. Among those who have suffered this fate are General Smuts in the election of 1948 that gave South Africa the hateful racist doctrine of apartheid; and Seychelles President James Mancham, overthrown by an armed coup in June 1977 while attending a Commonwealth summit in London. While the cat is away, the mice will play.

General case for the defence

Summitry has been so roundly anathematized that it is not easy to understand why it remains so common – but only at first glance. It is valued chiefly for its enormous symbolic or propaganda potential, and it is no accident that it became an art form during the middle and later phases of the Cold War, itself essentially a conflict fought by means of propaganda. Summits between Soviet and American leaders symbolized the attachment of their governments to peace, while intra-alliance summits symbolized each side's internal solidarity; President Nixon's one-hour conversation with the legendary leader of Chinese Communism, Mao Zedong, in Beijing in February 1972, was 'an earthquake' in the conflict and symbolized the fact that 'the Eastern Bloc no longer stood firm against the West' (MacMillan: 1); and the end of the Cold War was also symbolized by a summit, held in Paris in November 1990.

In democracies, summits are of special value to political leaders because they demonstrate to voters not only their international recognition but also their personal engagement with the most important current problems. For these reasons, larger states might issue summit invitations to the valued but insecure leaders of lesser ones in order to boost their position at home (Young 2008: 120–1). Add to the pot of democracy the power of television, and sprinkle its contents with exotic locations of symbolic significance, and it is clear why summit diplomacy is an irresistible dish to those with an eye on their poll ratings. Nixon simply could not pass over the opportunity to visit China in 1972 – an election year – and pose for the television cameras at every opportunity, even though Washington still did not recognize its Communist regime.

Fortunately, while summitry might well be irrelevant and even highly damaging to diplomacy, and often serves principally foreign and domestic propaganda purposes, it can also have diplomatic value – provided it is employed judiciously. To help explain this, it is useful to distinguish between three main kinds of summit: serial summits, which are part of a regular series; *ad hoc* summits, which are generally narrowly focused, one-off meetings, although it is possible they will turn out to be the first of a series; and the less ambitious high-level exchange of views, which might be part of a series but is more likely to be *ad hoc*.

Serial summits

Serial summits in important bilateral relationships usually occur annually but sometimes – as in the case of France and Germany, and the EU and Russia – twice a year, typically alternating between venues in their respective countries. Multilateral serial summits, which are more difficult to organize, sometimes meet once a year, as in the case of the summits of the relatively small BRICS group of large, fast-growing economies (Brazil, Russia, India, China, and South Africa), and the much larger Community of Latin American and Caribbean States. Usually, however, they assemble less frequently: for example, every two years in the case of Commonwealth Heads of Government Meetings (CHOGMs) and every three to four years in that of the Summits of the Americas.

The serial kind is probably the summit best suited to serious negotiation, although the extent to which this is true turns greatly on its length and frequency. Longer meetings allow subjects to be treated in greater depth and permit time for a return to the table following a deadlock, while – unless they take place against a background of political crisis – frequent summits at predetermined intervals arouse fewer public expectations and thereby subject their leaders to less pressure. Irrespective of their length and frequency, serial summits usually foster serious negotiation for the following reasons:

- By virtue of their regularity, they are likely to have developed well-understood rules of procedure.
- They help to educate leaders in international realities: they are forced to do their homework on agenda subjects in order to avoid looking foolish in front of their peers, and cannot avoid learning about the influences by which they are burdened.
- They make package deals easier: sitting astride the apex of policy-making within their own administrations, heads of state and government are well placed to make trades involving bureaucratically separate topics.
- They set deadlines (see Chapter 4) for the completion of an existing negotiation, although the certainty that the leaders will re-assemble at a fixed date somewhat weakens this effect.
- If the negotiations have been brought almost to conclusion prior to the summit, the event itself – even if brief – provides an opportunity to break remaining deadlocks because of the authority of the assembled leaders. This happened at the Brisbane G20 summit in 2014, at which the Australians finally submitted to combined US–EU pressure to add steps to reduce climate change to the agreed communiqué.

As for the other functions of diplomacy, serial summits are also well suited to information gathering, including the gathering of information on personalities; serial summiteers themselves stress this point. They are also probably the best for clarifying intentions, for these rarely appear more clearly than in the give-and-take of genuine negotiations.

On the other hand, precisely because it is the summit most suited to negotiation, the serial summit is perhaps least well suited to the promotion of friendly relations. Serious negotiation invariably generates tensions and these are almost bound to be greater at summits, as their critics have so frequently pointed out, since – except in states with genuine cabinet government, such as Britain and Israel – the protagonists can rarely pretend that their word is anything other than the last word of their governments. Besides, politicians tend to find it harder to resist point-scoring than professional negotiators, as Arab League summits are notorious for demonstrating. Summits where serious negotiation occurs also allow little time for the elaborate courtesies, observance of which is so important to the pursuit of civil relations by the resident ambassador. Having said this, serial summits would not occur if there were not an appreciation of some significant overlap of interests or strong sense of cultural affinity among the participants. This will usually ensure that tensions are not permitted to become destructive, as is demonstrated by the history of the Franco-German summits (since 2003, the 'Franco-German Ministerial Council'), the CHOGMs, and – the paradigm case of the fully institutionalized serial summit – the European Council.

Ad hoc summits

[handwritten annotations: 2-3 days, ~ negotiation, ↑ publicity]

As with the serial summit, the usefulness of the *ad hoc* version in negotiation is, to some extent, a function of its length: the longer the better. The Camp David summit between Israel and Egypt, for example, which took place in September 1978, lasted for a full 13 days, and the Wye River summit between Israel and the Palestinian Authority two decades later stretched from a planned four days to eight. On both occasions, extremely tough negotiations – brokered by American presidents – took place, and important breakthroughs were made; namely, the Camp David Accords and the Wye River Memorandum. In other words, these summits did not merely rubber-stamp agreements made earlier. As *ad hoc* summits go, however, these were the exception rather than the rule; most last no more than two or three days. Because of this and because – other things being equal – they also tend to generate more publicity than the serial summit, *ad hoc* summits are unlikely to be so useful for negotiations during the meetings themselves.

But precisely because this kind of summit is able to produce more publicity, it is well suited to gaining momentum for ongoing negotiations, as when the G20 met for the first time at summit level in late 2008 and early 2009 in order to energize the search for a consensus on the urgent steps needed to sort out the international financial chaos then reigning. Because there is no guarantee of a subsequent meeting to which discussion of an unresolved agenda item can be postponed, the *ad hoc* summit also represents a better deadline for a negotiation than the serial summit. For example, in May 1972, the prospect of the Nixon–Brezhnev summit in Moscow put huge pressure on the arms control negotiators of both sides to wrap up the first Strategic Arms Limitation Treaty in time for signature before Nixon had to return home. Similarly, the state visit to Canberra by Chinese premier Xi Jinping in November 2014, which followed immediately after his attendance at the G20 leaders' meeting in Brisbane, evidently produced the impetus for successful conclusion of the negotiations on the China–Australia Free Trade Agreement (ChAFTA) that had been going on fitfully since 2005.

Some *ad hoc* summits – particularly bilateral ones – are usually better suited to the promotion of friendly relations than the serial summit. In fact, many are designed deliberately for this purpose: to symbolize friendship and foster it by providing a format that encourages relaxed encounters between the leaders. 'Bonding' in these circumstances is the more important because so much high-level diplomacy is now conducted via telephone and (in allied relationships) video links, which can produce misunderstandings if the leaders have not previously got to know each other. Whether in practice it worked out well, a good recent example of this genre is the two-day 'informal summit' between US President Barack Obama and Chinese President Xi Jinping at the Annennberg Retreat at Sunnylands, Rancho Mirage in California, in June 2013. (Presumably, no one thought the choice of this venue could imply a fear that 'sunny' prospects for the friendship might turn out to be a 'mirage'.)

The speedy development of personal rapport is doubly important if one leader has had a close relationship with an un-seated rival of the other, as British Prime Minister Tony Blair had had with Democratic US President Bill Clinton prior to the inauguration of Republican George W. Bush in January 2001.

Where clarifying intentions and gathering information are concerned, the qualifications of the *ad hoc* summit are a mixed blessing. On the one hand, the typically low emphasis on negotiation and high emphasis on photo-calls and ceremonial will reduce the opportunities for these diplomatic purposes to be pursued. On the other, the more relaxed and less adversarial atmosphere can produce a frankness in the exchanges that suits them very well.

An important and interesting category of *ad hoc* summits is the funeral or memorial service for a major political figure attended by high-level delegations from the region concerned or, as is now common, from all over the world. It is a special case, however, because it is more or less useless for the diplomatic purpose for which, it has been argued here, the typical *ad hoc* summit is principally conceived: generating significant diplomatic momentum on one or more major issues. This is partly because of its theme and partly because of the unavoidable shortness of notice received by the countries wishing to send delegations. Furthermore, funeral summits carry risks: existing diplomatic schedules are upset, which might cause insult; and decisions on attendance and on level of attendance sometimes have to be made in the absence of perfect knowledge about what other states will be doing and of how the delegation will be received.

Nevertheless, 'working funerals' – which, at least by the 1960s, had fallen into a predictable pattern – are of considerable value to the world diplomatic system. This is partly because the shortness of notice available to the mourners has compensating advantages. It provides heads of state and government with a good excuse to break existing schedules for urgent discussions on current problems without arousing public expectations; a decision to attend is unlikely to prove embarrassing as a result of changed circumstances in the short period elapsing before the funeral takes place; and, if attendance is likely to cause controversy, there is little time for domestic opposition to mobilize.

A working funeral is of special diplomatic significance if it is the funeral of an incumbent leader. This is because it is likely to be the first opportunity not only for foreign friends of the bereaved government to confirm their relationship with the new leadership, but also for its foreign rivals to explore the possibility of a change of heart. The leaders of Warsaw Pact satellite states always attended the funerals of Soviet leaders with the former purpose in mind, while Western leaders attended them for the latter, at least in the 1980s.

The sombre and reflective atmosphere of a funeral summit, when all mourners are on their best behaviour, also provides a perfect cover for discreet consultations between foreign rivals seeking to keep their conflict within peaceful bounds or striving for a way out of an impasse. Funerals of this kind are times of political truce. It is for this reason that President Obama and his Cuban counterpart Raúl Castro were able publicly to shake hands and exchange words at the memorial service for former South African President Nelson Mandela in December 2013.

Because there is so little time for preparation or for discussions during the event, funeral summits rarely serve for serious negotiation. Their functions are diplomatic signalling, promoting friendly relations, and picking up tit-bits of information.

The high-level exchange of views

The high-level exchange of views is also usually *ad hoc*, but there the similarity usually ends. It is much more likely to be bilateral than multilateral, have a miscellaneous agenda (if it has any agenda at all), and be an altogether more modest affair. It will often last for hours rather than days, and rarely be described officially as a 'summit' at all.

Sometimes, encounters of this sort are nothing more than a courtesy call; for example, when an ailing leader visits a foreign capital for medical treatment and is there met briefly by his counterpart (Young 2008: 122–5). More often, they are visits to a number of countries on a 'foreign tour', often to a region where a major, multilateral serial summit is scheduled. Newly elected American presidents have a particular weakness for this least ambitious form of summitry, but they are not alone – and 'maiden tours' are invariably followed by others. For example, shortly after his own elevation, in late March 2013 Chinese President Xi Jinping made his own maiden tour – to Russia, Tanzania, Democratic Republic of Congo, and South Africa; and, in June, added to his 'informal summit' with President Obama, 'state visits' to Trinidad and Tobago (where he had separate meetings with the leaders of Surinam and Barbados), Costa Rica, and Mexico. In March 2014, he made his first trip to Europe.

The exchange of views summit is probably the best of all summits for cementing friendly relations. It also serves well in the negotiation of trade and investment deals. Indeed, it is now quite common to find leaders on foreign tours accompanied by the chief executives of leading companies. For example, Xi Jinping had a 200-strong business delegation in tow on his European tour in March 2014; if more modestly, French presidents do the same sort of thing, not least in Africa (Melly and Darracq: 23). Precisely because they usually have a somewhat lower profile, these 'summits' are also well-designed for the delicate task of taking up, with the host leader, serious cases of maltreatment of nationals or (for states under pressure from human rights lobbyists) those involving the human rights of prominent individuals. It is hardly surprising, however, that protests on such points tend to be decidedly muted when visits have a commercial theme, as when British Prime Minister David Cameron – at the head of a government struggling to get its country out of a prolonged recession – led a party of 120 business people to China in December 2013.

Despite its self-styling, it is not self-evident that the exchange of views is necessarily better than other summits at clarifying intentions (except in the case of those that are part of a maiden tour) and gathering information. As for serious negotiations, this kind of summit can nudge forward continuing talks – especially on commercial matters – and even rescue those deadlocked on a particular point, although it will not generally be up to the standard of the serial summit in the last regard or the *ad hoc* summit in the first.

Secrets of success

Chances sometimes have to be taken with summits, especially when the stakes are high. For example, the Americans had no firm guarantee that Nixon would be allowed to meet Mao before he left for China in 1972, and this was a gamble that courted humiliation (MacMillan: 8). But, as a rule, the key to the success of a summit is meticulous preparation by senior officials known as 'sherpas', a term that comes from the name for the locally hired guides and bearers who assist mountaineers in the Himalayas. Assisted by 'sous-sherpas', the sherpas may even have the task of arranging a series of bilateral pre-summit summits. In the case of the G7/G8 summits, these take place not only with the other participants but also with important outsiders. However, if not staged properly, pre-summit summits can backfire. For example, if they include only a small number of the most powerful participants scheduled to attend the summit proper, some of those excluded can be angered. This happened when the leaders of Britain, France, and Germany met alone immediately prior to the European Council in Ghent in October 2001.

Where a summit dealing with a negotiation is concerned, the conventional wisdom is that the preparation should be so complete that the summiteers have little more to do than sign the agreement and smile for the cameras. Although sometimes disregarded without mishap, as at the Reagan–Gorbachev summits at Geneva in 1985 and Reykjavik in the following year (Shultz 1993: 596–607), the pre-cooking of agreements is usually of great importance. This is particularly true when the summit is the highly delicate kind designed to seal a new friendship between erstwhile enemies, as in the case of the Nixon–Mao summit in February 1972. The famous Shanghai Communiqué released at the end of President Nixon's visit was substantially negotiated by Henry Kissinger on his own trip to China in the previous October, although it still took him a further 20 hours of negotiation in the wings of the summit to finalize it (Kissinger 1979: 781–4, 1074–87; MacMillan: ch. 19). Pre-cooking is also indispensable when the agenda is long, complex and urgent. Clear evidence that there had been a great deal of this in the lengthy run-up to the G20 leaders' meeting in 2014 is that the final communique was accompanied by 12 supporting documents, including detailed 'action plans' on different subjects (G20).

Prior agreement, or agreement at the outset, on what might be said to the media is another important requirement for successful summitry, as it is for any diplomatic encounter involving private discussion. A perfect example of what can happen when there is no script was provided by the joint press conference following the private meeting between Tony Blair and Syrian President Bashar Assad in Damascus at the end of October 2001. (Tony Blair was on a hurried tour of Middle East leaders designed to encourage support for military action in Afghanistan and stimulate Israeli–Palestinian diplomacy.) To the British prime minister's obvious discomfort, his host condemned the bombing of Afghanistan and said Israel rather than Syria was responsible for promoting state terrorism. The over-confident visitor was generally portrayed in the press as having been publicly humiliated.

There must also be detailed planning of the choreography of the summit. This means the pattern of meetings and events (such as visits, speeches, motorcades, 'walkabouts', joint press conferences, and so on), the mix depending on the character of the summit. Pre-planned choreography is always important but is especially so if symbolism is expected to take precedence over substance, as at the Reagan–Gorbachev summit in Moscow in 1988. In preparation for this occasion, the White House planning group worked for three months to 'write a script that would resemble an American political campaign with strong emphasis on visual impressions'. The analogy that sprang to the mind of former B-movie film star Ronald Reagan was, of course, a Cecil B. DeMille epic (Whelan: 89).

Among other requirements for successful summitry is not arousing excessive expectations. This might involve repeated prior statements that, say, a planned *ad hoc* summit will merely involve an 'exchange of views', which was the line taken by the Americans in the run-up to the Churchill–Eisenhower–Laniel summit at Bermuda in December 1953 (Young 1986: 901).

These secrets of success are necessary conditions; they are not sufficient ones. The best actors can fumble their lines when the curtain goes up, trip over a stage prop, or simply fall ill. Churchill was unwell at the Bermuda summit, while French Prime Minister Laniel took to his bed with a high temperature on the second day. Boris Yeltsin, President of the Russian Federation, apparently fast asleep, failed altogether to emerge from his Tupolev after it landed at Shannon airport in the Irish Republic in September 1994. What was going through the mind of Irish Prime Minister Albert Reynolds, who was waiting for his guest on the tarmac – complete with band, red carpet, and local dignitaries – is not difficult to imagine. Unforeseeable external events can also poison the atmosphere of a summit, or cause acute embarrassment. The shooting down over the Soviet Union of an American U-2 spy-plane two weeks before the opening of the East–West summit in Paris in May 1960 reduced this event to a fiasco. The occupation of Tiananmen Square in Beijing by pro-Democracy students prior to the Gorbachev–Deng summit in May 1989 turned this into a humiliation for the Chinese leadership: the programme had to be hastily revised and the Soviet leader brought into the Great Hall of the People through the back door (Cradock: 221). The Thai government had to use helicopters to rescue the leaders attending the 14th summit of the Association of Southeast Asian Nations in Pattaya in April 2009, following its abandonment after 'Red Shirt' activists successfully stormed the conference centre. In short, thorough preparation can minimize the risks of summitry, but not eliminate them.

Summary

Summits are sometimes highly damaging to diplomacy and, in the case of those attracting high publicity, always risky; they might also serve only foreign or domestic propaganda purposes. Nevertheless, judiciously employed and carefully prepared, they can – and do – suit diplomatic purposes as well. This is particularly true of the serial summit, an institution to which resort seems to have become reflexive following the establishment of an important international relationship. But the *ad hoc* summit and the high-level exchange of views are also of some importance to diplomacy, if only as devices to inject momentum into a stagnant negotiation. The pattern of summitry has changed in the past, and might change again. Nevertheless, there seems little reason to believe that it will go into a general decline as a mode of communication between states as it did with the rise of the resident ambassador at the end of the Middle Ages. Television, the Internet, and democracy have seen to that.

Further reading

Ball, G., *Diplomacy for a Crowded World* (Bodley Head: London, 1976): ch. 3.
Berridge, G. R., 'Funeral summits', in David H. Dunn (ed.), *Diplomacy at the Highest Level: The evolution of international summitry* (Macmillan: Basingstoke, 1996).
Berridge, G. R. (ed.), *Diplomatic Classics: Selected texts from Commynes to Vattel* (Palgrave Macmillan: Basingstoke, 2004): selections from Commynes and Bynkershoek.
Carter, J., *Keeping Faith: Memoirs of a president* (Bantam: New York, 1982).
Cohen, R., *Theatre of Power: The art of diplomatic signalling* (Longman: London, 1987).

Dunn, David H. (ed.), *Diplomacy at the Highest Level: The evolution of international summitry* (Macmillan: Basingstoke, 1996).

Eubank, K., *The Summit Conferences 1919–1960* (University of Oklahoma Press: Norman, OK, 1966).

European Council, 'The institution' [www]. This is the official website.

Feinberg, Richard, 'Institutionalized summitry', in Andrew F. Cooper, Jorge Heine, and Ramesh Thakur (eds), *The Oxford Handbook of Modern Diplomacy* (Oxford University Press: Oxford, 2013).

Gorbachev, Mikhail, *Memoirs*, trans. by G. Peronansky and T. Varsavsky, first pub. 1995 (Bantam Books: London, 1997).

Kissinger, H. A., *The White House Years* (Weidenfeld & Nicolson/Michael Joseph: London, 1979): 769, 781, 919–21.

MacMillan, Margaret, *Seize the Hour: When Nixon met Mao* (John Murray: London, 2006).

Melly, Paul, and Vincent Darracq, 'A New Way to Engage? French policy in Africa from Sarkozy to Hollande' (Chatham House: London, May 2013) [www].

Nicolson, H., *Peacemaking 1919* (Methuen: London, 1964).

Plischke, Elmer, *Summit Diplomacy: Personal diplomacy of the President of the United States* (Bureau of Governmental Research, Univ. of Maryland: Maryland, 1958) [www – Internet Archive].

Post, J. M. and R. S. Robbins, *When Illness Strikes the Leader* (Yale University Press: New Haven, CT, 1993).

Reynolds, David, *Summits: Six meetings that shaped the twentieth century* (Allen Lane: London, 2007).

Shultz, G. P., *Turmoil and Triumph: My years as Secretary of State* (Scribner's: New York, 1993): chs 30, 36, 46 and 49.

Smith, Gordon, 'Don't turn back from the summit', *Ottawa Citizen*, 25 June 2010 [www].

Thatcher, Margaret, *The Downing Street Years* (HarperCollins: London, 1993): ch. XVII, esp. the first two pages.

Whelan, J. G., *The Moscow Summit 1988* (Westview Press: Boulder, CO, 1990).

Yeltsin, B., *Midnight Diaries* (Phoenix: London, 2001): chs 8, 9, and 23.

Young, John W., *Twentieth-Century Diplomacy: A case study of British practice, 1963–1976* (Cambridge University Press: Cambridge, 2008): chs 6 and 7.

13
Public Diplomacy

Propaganda is the manipulation of public attitudes through the mass media for political ends. It might be more or less honest, more or less subtle, and sometimes directed more at achieving long-term, rather than short-term, changes in opinion. Its target might be foreign public opinion, domestic public opinion, or both. Makers of propaganda have traditionally distinguished between white propaganda and black propaganda – the former admitting, but the latter concealing, its source. 'Public diplomacy' is the modern name for white propaganda directed chiefly at foreign publics. Why has it acquired this new name? Why are the activities it embraces now so popular? What contribution is made to them by foreign ministries and diplomats posted abroad?

Rebranding propaganda

Propaganda acquired a bad reputation in the first half of the twentieth century because in World War I, and especially in the hands of the totalitarian regimes that emerged afterwards, it was particularly slippery, strident, and mendacious. As a result, most governments, although forced to resort to methods that were, in principle, identical, baulked at the idea of *publicly* admitting that they were making propaganda. Instead, they claimed, what they were engaged in was 'information work'. Ministries of Information were created, particularly during World War II, and although these tended not to outlast the duration, the inception of the Cold War in the late 1940s ensured that the residues they left were soon being used to build 'information services'. The result was that 'information sections', or 'information and cultural relations sections' (later known in the US Foreign Service collectively as 'public affairs sections'), together with their 'information officers', became an established feature of many embassies for the rest of the century; even the French employed *attachés d'information*. The United States Information Agency (USIA), with its arm's length relationship with the Department of State, the best-known supplier of such officers, was created in 1953. In the following year, a summary was published of the then still-confidential report of the Drogheda Committee on Britain's 'Overseas Information Services', which was eventually so influential on British practice (HCPP 1954). But the point is that no one involved in or discussing this *'information work'* was under any illusions that what they were really talking about was overseas *propaganda* (HCPP 1954: *passim*; Plischke: 149). The British Prime Minister, Winston Churchill, had no hesitation in describing even the cultural work of the British Council as propaganda, although others were usually more coy about this.

The point is neatly illustrated by a book called *Through the Back Door*, the memoirs of Sir Robert Marett, a British diplomat who specialized in propaganda and served as secretary to the Drogheda Committee. Its sub-title is *An inside view of Britain's Overseas Information Services*, but then the veil is pulled aside: the first part is called 'An Introduction to Propaganda'. In describing his appointment as head of the Foreign Office's 'Information Policy Department' immediately after working for Drogheda, Marett even observes that he had achieved the 'doubtful distinction' of being the 'Dr Goebbels of the Foreign Office' (Marett: 171). (Dr Joseph Goebbels was Hitler's notorious Minister for Public Enlightenment and Propaganda from 1933 until the end of the war.) In short, when it was publicly using a term such as 'information work', the political class knew that it was simply making propaganda about propaganda.

Referring to information work a decade later, the Plowden Report on the British foreign service remarked that 'It is easy to see why it was necessary to adopt the more urbane label', although it regretted that the phrase lacked the 'sense of purpose and direction' conveyed by the term 'propaganda'. It added that information officers should not think their task was merely to provide information to foreigners for its own sake. 'The Information Services,' Plowden reminded its readers, 'grew out of the need, in two world wars, to help achieve political aims by means of propaganda' (HCPP 1964: para. 260).

It might be that the term 'information' had some success in camouflaging the propaganda activities of states such as Britain and the United States as far as their broad audiences were concerned, but it is unlikely to have fooled the politically savvy. It also had another problem. In some states, such as Turkey, it aroused suspicion of information officers: since 'information' suggested 'intelligence', it implied that their business was *gathering* information rather than imparting it – espionage (Arndt: 28; Berridge 2009: 216). The consequence was that the term 'information work' gradually fell out of favour and the hunt was on for a fresh euphemism.

It was found in 1965 by Edmund Gullion – a former US Foreign Service officer, then Dean of the Fletcher School of Law and Diplomacy, and no innocent: like Plowden, he would have preferred the term 'propaganda', but for its negative connotations. He decided, therefore, to press into service the vintage phrase 'public diplomacy', which, up to this point, was nothing more than a synonym for the 'open diplomacy' allegedly exemplified by the pre-war League of Nations. With its old echoes of this idealistic enterprise, and hardly suggesting espionage, 'public diplomacy' generated particularly good vibrations. Its very vagueness was also valuable in Washington bureaucratic politics: in 1978, to the dismay of traditionalists, USIA assumed responsibility for US cultural diplomacy as well, thereby bringing all of America's overseas propaganda activities under one roof (Arndt: chs 23 and 24; Cull 2006).

In the course of the 1990s, more states adopted the new euphemism to describe their propaganda operations and, today, it is more or less ubiquitous (although 'information' has by no means disappeared). 'Public diplomacy' is, therefore, *not* a new activity, despite the commonly heard view that 'at its best' it is different from propaganda because it invites the absorption of as much influence from foreign publics as it seeks to achieve over them (Cull 2007). But listening to foreigners is one thing; giving equal weight to what they say is another. In the hard world of governments, 'public diplomacy' is simply propaganda rebranded. This is obvious from what they do under its heading, as well as from the fact that – despite heroic efforts to obscure this with a screen of semantic convolutions – they end up admitting it (Wilton: 12; Carter of Coles: 8; US Advisory Commission on Public Diplomacy: 4).

The importance of public diplomacy

While one of the aims of conventional diplomacy is to exert direct influence on foreign governments, the aim of propaganda, or public diplomacy, is usually to do this *indirectly;* that is, by appealing over the heads of those governments to the people with influence upon them. In a tightly controlled authoritarian regime these might be just 'the influential few', to borrow a phrase favoured by the Drogheda Committee; in a more loosely controlled authoritarian political system and especially in a liberal democracy, it is likely to be a great many more.

Propaganda has grown in importance since the start of World War I because the reasons to reach for it have strengthened while the means available to its practitioners have multiplied. For one thing, the spread of democracy and the need to mobilize entire populations in 'total war' both vastly increased the political importance of public opinion. For another, ideology – a simplified, quasi-religious mode of political argument peculiarly suited to propaganda – tightened its grip on governments. And then nuclear weapons appeared on the scene, making too risky anything other than a 'war of words' between states locked into an ideological rivalry – the Cold War – that was too bitter to be capable of producing serious diplomacy. And to all of this was added a steady increase in the number and quality of the means of delivering propaganda, roughly in the following chronological order:

- the printed word (and photograph), delivered to increasingly literate populations;
- short-wave radio broadcasting in indigenous languages, which reaches the illiterate and is relatively cheap and virtually impossible to block;
- satellite television; and
- the Internet and its associated 'social media' tools, such as Facebook, Twitter (Box 13.1) and blog posts.

Box 13.1 Twitter for diplomats

Enthusiasts for Twitter are right to maintain that it is one of the best 'tools' for getting through to the population of a state where the media is tightly controlled (Koenig). However, they are on weaker ground in claiming that responses to them are a good measure of the '*vox populi*' (Sandre). Twitter feeds can be useful as gauges of foreign opinion, like comments on embassy Facebook and web pages, but conclusions should be drawn from them with caution, for violent and extreme voices have a tendency to drown out the others. In any case, in light of the brevity imposed on diplomatic tweets and the haste with which they usually need to be composed, it is not easy for all but the most deft to make sure that an attractive personal voice is consistent with official policy. The result is that they risk either embarrassing blunders or studied banality. Nevertheless, diplomats who know better – and have got better things to do – are being bullied into tweeting by foreign ministries pathetically fearful of being thought out of touch. It is an open secret that some – probably most – senior diplomats in the foreign ministries and embassies of major states have someone else to write their tweets for them, which should surprise no one. By contrast, those of poorer states are more likely to have to write their own, and waste more time checking those of their junior staff. So much for 'e-diplomacy' helping to level the playing field between the rich and the poor.

In the course of the twentieth century much was also learned about the ingredients of successful propaganda – notably, that it is best used to reinforce existing attitudes and stimulate action on the part of the already well disposed, rather than to attempt changing entrenched opinions. There were often doubts about its effectiveness because of the methodological problems dogging its measurement, but these were usually overcome in the end (Berridge 1997: 138–43). This has been helped by a growing belief that propaganda has played a key role in certain dramatic developments of recent years. These include the collapse of Communism in Eastern Europe, where broadcasting by Western radio stations such as Munich-based Radio Free Europe, is believed to have been critical; the overthrow of traditional authoritarian regimes in the Middle East and north Africa during the 'Arab Spring'; and, more recently, the spread of radical Islamist thinking – not least, via the Internet, to Muslim communities in the West. As documented by the OpenNet Initiative, deep fear of the ability of propaganda to stir up and guide political opposition has led many states, especially in the Middle East and Asia, to invest in sophisticated technology to filter political content and access to communication tools out of the Internet.

It is in light of these developments that 'public diplomacy' has become not merely a fashionable phrase but also a fashionable practice – and a fashionable one over which to agonize. In the United States alone, 25 reports appeared on the subject between 2003 and 2005 (Carter of Coles: 68). In order to exploit this epic rediscovery of the wheel, foreign ministries have generally been given the lead role.

The role of the foreign ministry

Foreign ministries commonly play a number of roles in connection with propaganda. Some of these are routine, well known and usually uncontroversial:

- providing embassies with printed and other publicity materials for distribution (still in demand despite spreading access to the Internet), and training for their press and public affairs officers;
- dealing with foreign correspondents based in the capital (Box 13.2);
- putting out their own propaganda directly, notably by means of multi-language websites (with Arabic pages increasingly popular on those of Western foreign ministries), and the 'personal' blogs and tweets of ministers (often, it is reassuring to learn, written not in fact by themselves but by assistants); and

Box 13.2   'News management': convincing foreign correspondents

Making sure that foreign correspondents see things from the 'correct perspective' is particularly important because, as the Wilton Review disarmingly noted in 2002, there are good grounds for believing that their articles have a greater impact in their home countries than 'other' public diplomacy outputs (Wilton: 11, 20). News management normally includes the provision of official briefings on current events, helping to arrange interviews with ministers and officials, and laying on tours; among other things, it usually includes provision of such facilities as work-spaces and communications equipment as well, although this so readily facilitates official eavesdropping (see Chapter 10) that there are many countries (including Britain) where any serious foreign correspondent would be mad to use them. The US Department of State has 'Foreign Press Centers' in New York and Washington, the former having opened in 1946, the latter in 1968. The Chinese foreign ministry opened its own International Press Center in the year 2000. It should be noted, however, that not in all states does the foreign ministry have responsibility for the foreign press centre, and elsewhere the pattern varies. For example, in South Korea it is the task of the Ministry of Culture, Sports and Tourism; in Denmark, it falls to the lot of an independent body over which, nevertheless, the foreign ministry has influence via financial support and chairmanship of the governing board; and, in Japan, there is both a foreign ministry 'international press division' *and* a quasi-independent foreign press centre similar to the one in Copenhagen.

- perhaps funding, or helping to fund, associated broadcasting organizations and cultural and educational bodies such as the Goethe-Institut (Germany), the Confucius Institutes (China – nominally 'affiliated' with the Ministry of Education), the Alliance Française (France), the Cervantes Institute (Spain), the Dante Alighieri Society (Italy), the Camões Institute (Portugal), and the British Council (Britain), whose audiences are in the main the *next* generation of decision-makers and opinion-leaders.

Some of these tasks are also far from new. Among them, news management, at least on an organized and systematic basis, goes back only to World War I, but one favourite device goes back to the early nineteenth century. This is the selective publication by foreign ministries of documents from their archives in order to justify an earlier course in foreign or military policy. These were not only carefully chosen but also sometimes 'corrected' – a practice for which, in Britain, Lord Salisbury was notorious (Roberts 1999: 509). It even became quite common for secret diplomatic despatches to be drafted with a view to their possible later publication, the real messages being confined to 'private letters'. The one-off publications containing these selections were called 'Blue

Books' in Britain, 'Yellow Books' in France, 'White Books' in Germany, and so on.

Foreign ministries, or functionally equivalent bodies under other names, also have public diplomacy tasks that in liberal democracies are sometimes more controversial at home and raise serious public policy questions. These include the elaboration of public diplomacy strategy and relating it to foreign-policy priorities; the monitoring of implementation and measuring of performance; and, above all, the *coordination* of the activities of the various bodies engaged in propaganda to minimize duplication of effort and ensure that they are in tune with the strategy – because there is a wafer-thin line between coordination and control.

Coordination of their various public diplomacy activities usually presents no more than administrative problems for the foreign ministries of authoritarian states – even fewer of these for the council of high state and party officials from various government departments chaired by a Politburo member that governs the Chinese Language Council International (Sahlins). And, in some of these states, international broadcasting services in tune with their governments have made enormous strides in recent years: for example, Al-Jazeera (Qatar), Russia Today, and – above all – China Central Television (CCTV).

In liberal-democratic states, on the other hand, government efforts at public diplomacy coordination inevitably meet strong resistance. The usual device employed in an attempt to overcome this takes the form of an official strategy board of one sort or another that includes co-opted media representatives. There was some flirtation with such boards in the first flush of the 'War on Terror' (prolonged and continuing in the United States), but government pressure in general seems not to have been too heavy. This is fortunate because it is in large part precisely because of their reputations for independence that bodies such as the BBC World Service and the British Council produce the most effective propaganda – immensely varied, often stimulating, invariably professional, and – as far as it goes – always truthful. For many years, both of them actually relied heavily on Foreign Office financial support, but this was removed altogether from the World Service in early 2004, and the British Council today receives under 25 per cent of its income from this source.

The role of the embassy

When asked by a member of the Select Committee on Foreign Affairs of the House of Commons to comment on views it had received urging more public diplomacy, Sir John Kerr, former British Ambassador in Washington and subsequently Permanent Under-Secretary in the Foreign Office, replied:

> I think it is a very elegant re-invention of the wheel. Embassies have always had such a role. While they exist to talk privately to governments, they also exist to talk to people and populations at large, and that is *probably the modern ambassador's principal function, to be on television, to be on the radio, to accept all the platforms.* ... We are not shut away but we never really were. (FAC 2001: para. 119, emphasis added)

Sir John Kerr was right, and it is not difficult to find early examples to illustrate his point.

Sir Henry Wotton, British resident ambassador at Venice at the beginning of the seventeenth century, distributed Protestant publications among members of the political elite as a key part of his attempt to stir up the republic against the Pope; it is true that he seems not to have been acting on written instructions, but he knew he could rely on the sympathy of James I (Smith 1907: 89–90). Another example, at the end of the eighteenth century, is provided by the new French minister plenipotentiary to the United States, Citizen Charles-Edmond Genet, who was formally despatched from Paris in order to serve chiefly as a 'revolutionary missionary to the American people', rather than as an envoy in the ordinary way to its government. He behaved accordingly, showing great determination to 'excite, display, and exploit American enthusiasm for the French Revolution' (O'Brien: ch. 5). Nevertheless, as in the case of foreign ministries, it was the twentieth century before embassies became routinely involved in public diplomacy, and only in recent years that, as Sir John Kerr maintained, it has become arguably the principal role of the ambassador, as opposed to the embassy generally.

Having said this, the extent to which it is advisable for an ambassador to engage in public diplomacy varies with the political culture of the receiving state and the sensitivities of the government of the day, because it is easily construed as interference in domestic affairs. In a totalitarian state such as North Korea, where no opposition is tolerated and even the telephone directory is a state secret (Hoare 2007: 116–21), a direct appeal to the public by an ambassador would probably be their last step before buying an air ticket home. In somewhat more relaxed Russia, the government reacted strongly to the many 'tweets' to which it took exception of the non-career American Ambassador at

Moscow, Michael McFaul, in 2012 and 2013 (Lally). And even in France, remarked Sir Nicholas Henderson, a former British ambassador to that country, 'it would be thought odd and might prove counter-productive with the French government for a foreign diplomat in Paris to appear to be advancing his country's cause in public' (Henderson: 287).

But, as a rule – and provided they not enter directly into the political fray – ambassadors are able to adopt a propaganda role with much more freedom in the liberal democracies. In Washington, to which Henderson was moved in 1979, he says that 'It would be regarded there as a sign of lack of conviction in his country's case if an Ambassador did not go out of his way to promote it publicly' (Henderson: 287–8). And he famously did this with some success, putting the British point of view directly to the American people on television on a number of issues of considerable sensitivity in Washington, particularly Northern Ireland and the Falklands crisis. Ambassadors from authoritarian regimes enjoy the same rights. For example, during the Gulf War in early 1991, Iraq's ambassadors in Europe and the United States were at the forefront of Baghdad's propaganda campaign. This is perhaps one reason why Saddam Hussein did not sever diplomatic relations with the Coalition powers until three weeks after the outbreak of the war (Taylor: 97–8, 106, 181).

Resident ambassadors are well placed to engage in public diplomacy, because they are attractive to the local media as interviewees and to a variety of local bodies as speakers. After all, in the absence of a high-ranking visitor from home, they are the most authoritative representatives of their governments. They are also likely to have mastered the sound-bite and the after-dinner address; it is improbable that they will make any great fuss about having to appear at an inconvenient time; and they will expect neither a fee nor payment of their expenses.

But the ambassador is by no means the only member of the embassy with a public diplomacy role. Even small embassies usually have one officer required to devote time to handling the local media and trying to coordinate the activities of local representatives of any public diplomacy 'partners'. Such a person used to be known – and sometimes still is – as the 'press attaché'. Larger embassies might have a whole section devoted to public diplomacy, usually relying heavily on LE staff. In addition, they often have responsibility for cultural relations: in this case they are known in US embassies as the 'public affairs section', as already mentioned; and, in British embassies, as the 'press and public affairs section'. The Danish Embassy in Washington has a 'public diplomacy and communication section'. These sections are not always as large as the recent enthusiasm for public diplomacy would lead us to expect, because some diplomatic services believe that the embassy's other sections are best placed to conduct their own public diplomacy – the commercial section should handle commercial publicity, and so on.

A public diplomacy officer's role not only involves distributing publicity material, but also 'working the media'; that is, persuading local journalists to run friendly stories, the counterpart activity of what the foreign ministry should be doing at home with foreign correspondents (Box 13.2). In the past this has involved bribing individual journalists and subsidizing local newspapers, and it would be surprising if the same sort of thing does not go on in some states today. One of the reasons why the British Embassy in Turkey retained a major presence in Istanbul after it was forced – along with other embassies – gradually to shift its presence to Ankara in the 1920s, and also why the ambassador continued to spend a great deal of time in the former capital, was that this was where the editors and leader writers of the major Turkish newspapers were still to be found.

The work of an embassy's public diplomacy section is particularly prone to bursts of frenetic activity; some of them anticipated, some of them not. In the former category falls that provoked by the long-planned arrival of high-level visitors from home, which must be preceded with the sort of advance publicity ensuring their enthusiastic reception, and be accompanied by careful attention to the needs of the local media for interviews, photo-opportunities and background briefings during their stay. In short, the section must ensure that a glow of warmth and approval is left behind after the visitors' departure, and so assist other aspects of the embassy's work. As for bursts of unanticipated activity, into this category falls the action required, for example, by a furious explosion in the local media – perhaps accompanied by hostile demonstrations in the streets – provoked by criticism of some aspect of the host country's domestic habits by the press at home. Public diplomacy sections often find themselves fire-fighting for this and other reasons. The sudden increase of the workload of press officers in Denmark's embassies, especially in Muslim states, following publication of the cartoons of the Prophet Muhammad in a Danish newspaper in early 2006, is not difficult to imagine.

It will be apparent that, in contrast to the long-term outlook of cultural attachés, the horizon of the embassy's press or information officers is much closer: their task is the manipulation of public attitudes in the following hours, days, and weeks, and is obviously political. Because cultural diplomats have a quite different style of operation, and usually wish to avoid the impression of having any kind of political agenda at all, there has – at least where they are members of bodies such as the British Council – always been some resistance to the idea of serving under the embassy's physical roof. Those taking this view maintain that a separate physical presence not only makes them more approachable, but also makes it more probable that they will be able to remain in place even if the embassy is forced to depart. However, the 'coordinators' reply that appointing them to the embassy as cultural attachés makes coordination easier. They also point out that, in practice, obvious embassy affiliation does not do significant harm to the reputation of the educational bodies because foreign publics are aware that they are sponsored by the sending state anyway; that putting them under the embassy roof is more economical than having to maintain (and guard) separate premises for them; and that so locating them gives them diplomatic privileges and immunities that may well turn out to be valuable in unstable states. In recent years, the calls to coordination and economy have been difficult to resist. A compromise solution is to provide the cultural diplomats with diplomatic rank, but still permit them to operate from separate premises, although this has given the British Council offices in Russia little protection from severe police harassment in recent years.

Summary

'Public diplomacy' is what we call our propaganda; 'propaganda' is what the other side does. Irrespective of the label, its aim is to influence foreign governments indirectly by appealing over their heads to the people with influence upon them – whether the mass of the population or just 'the influential few'. Nevertheless, it varies enormously in its style as well as its targets; less so in the vehicles it employs – now chiefly shortwave radio, satellite television, and the Internet and its associated social media tools. The lead role in 'public diplomacy' is frequently given to foreign ministries, and it is probably now the most important duty of ambassadors – although, for the rest of the embassy staff, only one task among many.

Further reading

Arndt, Richard T., *The First Resort of Kings: American cultural diplomacy in the twentieth century* (Potomac Books: Washington, DC, 2005).

Berridge, G. R., *International Politics: States, power and conflict since 1945*, 3rd edn (Pearson Education: Harlow, 1997): ch. 8.

Brown, J. F., *Radio Free Europe: An insider's view* (New Academia Publishing: Washington, DC, 2013).

Cavaliero, R. E., 'Cultural diplomacy: The diplomacy of influence', *The Round Table*, 75(298), April 1986.

Childs, J. Rives, *American Foreign Service* (Holt: New York, 1948): ch. 12.

Cull, Nicholas J., 'Public diplomacy: Seven lessons for its future from its past' [www].

Cull, Nicholas J., 'The Perfect War': US public diplomacy and international broadcasting during Desert Shield and Desert Storm, 1990/1991' [www].

Cull, Nicholas J., *The Cold War and the United States Information Agency: American propaganda and public diplomacy, 1945–1989* (Cambridge University Press: Cambridge, 2008).

Hamilton, Keith, 'Historical diplomacy: Foreign ministries and the management of the past', in Jovan Kurbalija (ed.), *Knowledge and Diplomacy* (DiploFoundation: Malta, 1999).

HCPP, Cmd. 9138, April 1954: *Summary of the Report of the Independent Committee of Enquiry into the Overseas Information Services* ['the Drogheda Report'].

Koenig, Robert L., 'Tweet-errific: Ambassador, embassy adept at social media', *State Magazine*, December 2013 [www].

Koenig, Robert L., 'Using "social media" to reach Russians', *Foreign Service Journal*, January–February 2014 [www].

Lally, Kathy, 'U.S. ambassador in Moscow uses social media to bypass official line', *Washington Post*, 13 January 2013 [www].

Marett, Sir Robert, *Through the Back Door: An inside view of Britain's Overseas Information Services* (Pergamon Press: Oxford, 1968): chs 13–15.

Rana, Kishan S., *21st Century Diplomacy: A practitioner's guide* (Continuum: London, 2011): ch. 4.

Sahlins, Marshall, 'China U', *The Nation*, 18 November 2013 [www].

Taylor, Philip M., *Munitions of the Mind: A history of propaganda from the ancient world to the present era*, 3rd edn (Manchester University Press: Manchester, 2003).

Tryhorn, Chris, 'BBC is in a "soft power" battle with international broadcasters', *Guardian*, 13 November 2013 [www].

US Department of State, *Cultural Diplomacy: The Linchpin of Public Diplomacy. Report of the Advisory Committee on Cultural Diplomacy*, September 2005 [www].

14
Economic and Commercial Diplomacy

Economic diplomacy, narrowly defined, is concerned with international economic policy questions, such as how to preserve global financial stability without indefensible levels of youth unemployment and unmanageable levels of wholly defensible levels of civil unrest; and how to stimulate economic growth, particularly in the poorest countries, while arresting or at least slowing down climate change. Commercial diplomacy, on the other hand, consists mainly of assistance to the promotion of exports and foreign direct investment (FDI), and access to raw materials. This chapter will show how modern diplomacy was influenced by commerce from its earliest days, but how the priority given to economic as well as commercial diplomacy has risen more in recent years. What is the role of foreign ministries and especially embassies in this work, and how are the latter set up to cope with its varied demands? These are the questions guiding the remainder of the chapter.

Rising priorities

The invention and spread of resident diplomatic missions in the late fifteenth century had probably been encouraged by the example of the consulates earlier established by trading peoples in and around the Mediterranean world (as noted at the beginning of Chapter 8), and, from the first, they sometimes had a decidedly commercial flavour. In a few exceptional cases, major trading companies, with the blessing of their sovereigns at home, themselves established full-blown embassies, not only financing them but also appointing and sharing in the instruction of ambassadors (Box 14.1). Thereafter, although high politics came to dominate the work of most embassies until World War I, the 'trade'-averse aristocrats who usually headed them were rarely able to ignore commercial work altogether. This was because they had field responsibility for the consular posts that, in time, fell under state control; because international trade began to grow enormously in the first half of the eighteenth century; and because embassies themselves came to be given direct responsibility for the negotiation of commercial treaties – that is, the general framework in which trade was conducted in bilateral relationships.

Box 14.1 The Levant Company and the English Embassy at Constantinople

Furtherance of the distant and dangerous trade with the Levant was the main English interest in developing diplomatic relations with the Ottoman Empire. In September 1581, in compensation for the risks involved, certain London merchants – soon to be organized as the Levant Company – obtained a charter from Queen Elizabeth I that gave them its monopoly. Two years later, William Harborne, one of the merchants and a former member of parliament, was confirmed as England's first ambassador and soon secured from the Ottoman sultan trading privileges as good as those already obtained by Venice and France. For many years afterwards, the first priorities of Harborne's successors were to ensure that these privileges were honoured, seek redress for the English traders when they were not, renew them when necessary and, if possible, improve upon their terms. The priority given to commercial diplomacy by the embassy at Constantinople was reflected in the unusual procedure whereby new ambassadors were always provided not only with instructions from the government but also with articles of agreement and a separate set of instructions from the Levant Company. Gradually, the crown prised from the company the right to appoint ambassadors but it was not until the beginning of the nineteenth century that the British Embassy at Constantinople – one of the most important posts in the British diplomatic service – fell entirely under government control.

In the late nineteenth century, as international rivalry intensified for markets – as also for foreign concessions to sink mine shafts, drill for oil, build railways, and cut canals – so commercial diplomacy was given a strong fillip. Diplomats were required to interest themselves in projects such as these, especially when they were thought to have the additional advantage of serving political and strategic interests. The Suez Canal and the Berlin–Baghdad Railway are well known examples. Diplomatic missions intervened with local ministries both to support the placement of capital by their nationals on advantageous terms and subsequently to provide protection to their investments against violence, breach of contract, and hostile legislation. The latter role gave rise to the legal doctrine of 'diplomatic protection' and, inevitably, to a counter-doctrine (Box 14.2).

Box 14.2   The Calvo doctrine

The Calvo doctrine was named after the nineteenth century Argentine diplomat and jurist Carlos Calvo (1824–1906). It announced that aliens were not entitled to more favourable treatment than citizens, and hence that their states could not give them 'diplomatic protection' in the event of their receiving treatment deemed by those states to fall below an acceptable standard – the 'minimum standard of civilization', as the more developed states were wont to call it. A corollary of the Calvo doctrine was the widespread introduction into contracts between Latin American states and foreign nationals of a clause requiring the latter to waive the right to diplomatic protection in any dispute between them.

The ultimate decisiveness of economic resources in the total wars of the twentieth century, together with the massive economic losses and dislocation to which these conflicts gave rise, encouraged a strong belief among capitalist states that their diplomats should give more attention to economic as well as commercial matters; this was stiffened particularly by the huge hike in oil prices in the early 1970s. Britain is a case in point (Box 14.3). As for the 'developing countries' that subsequently emerged from the dissolving European empires, the title embraced by them is alone sufficient to indicate that they thought their own diplomats should do likewise. In this regard, they in their turn were followed by the new, generally pro-Western elites of the successor states of the USSR, anxious to replace Soviet-style Communism with market economies. Since World War II, therefore, the foreign ministries of most states have been under steadily increasing pressure to fall into line; and they have found this the more difficult to resist because of the major challenge to the continued relevance of embassies discussed in Chapter 8.

The continuing rise of the economic-commercial priority in the work of foreign ministries has been given particular emphasis in a recent Dutch report, which – among other striking facts – records that the average South Korean embassy now allocates 50 per cent of its time to this activity (Advisory Committee: 47–8). Nevertheless, there is other evidence that, as a result of the exceptional political volatility of some of the world's most sensitive regions in recent years, the climb of the economic-commercial priority in other diplomatic services – perhaps that of Seoul itself – has now peaked. Already in 2011, the British parliament was warning that 'the Government's strengthened focus on pursuing UK economic and commercial interests as part of the UK's foreign relations must not come about at the expense of the FCO's core foreign policy functions' (FAC 2011: para. 6).

Box 14.3 The new economic priority in British diplomacy

In his book on the Foreign Office published in 1955, the former permanent under-secretary, William Strang, was at pains to stress that 'It is probably no exaggeration to say that at present fully one-third of the work of the Foreign Service as a whole is preponderantly economic – or commercial, or financial – in character' (Strang: 39). A little less than a decade later the Plowden Report stated squarely that 'economic and commercial work... should be regarded as a first charge on the resources of the new Diplomatic Service' (HCPP 1964: para. 233). And in 1969, the Duncan Report on Overseas Representation (chaired by Sir Val Duncan, Chairman of the huge mining-finance house Rio Tinto Zinc Corporation) said that, in consequence of 'the long-drawn-out series of balance of payments crises,' the balance of the workload of the British Diplomatic Service 'should now reflect the clear precedence that belongs to the commercial objective in the day-to-day conduct of Britain's relations with other countries' (HCPP 1969: 10). The practical implications of this seminal report were not accepted by the FO with wild enthusiasm and in some missions political questions remained more important – but it was a sign of the times.

Multilateralism and the squeeze on the foreign ministry

Economic diplomacy, as explained at the beginning of this chapter, is concerned with international economic policy. In so far as this involves negotiations, some of its subjects with far-reaching implications are still dealt with in bilateral channels; for example, the anti-democratic Transatlantic Trade and Investment Partnership (TTIP), at the time of writing still being negotiated between the EU Commission and the United States (Monbiot), and the numerous 'free trade agreements' in which China has a strong interest – 12 signed and eight currently under discussion, according to the Chinese Ministry of Commerce (China FTA Network). However, many issues of international economic policy are also negotiated in multilateral conferences, and these require more attention because they are myriad and overlapping – and, in consequence, present a particular challenge.

The multilateral channels through which economic diplomacy is conducted stand in a continuum leading from high-level, high-profile, broad-agenda gatherings at one end, to lower-level, narrowly focused, highly technical, and little noticed – but no less important – ones at the other. For example, at the one extreme are summits such as the annual gatherings of the leaders of the G20; in the middle are the regular encounters of finance ministers and central bank governors, together with international organizations like the IMF, the WTO, and the World Bank; at the other end are bodies such as the standing committees of the central bankers' Basel-based Bank for International Settlements.

Diplomatic operations in this labyrinth of international economic forums produce an urgent need for the coordination of national positions. Nevertheless, as a rule it is only when the political implications of their agendas are serious – as in East–West economic relations during the Cold War, and at wide-ranging high level meetings such as the preliminaries to the G7/G8 economic summits – that foreign ministries and the diplomatic officers they despatch tend formally to be in charge (Woolcock and Bayne: 389, 395). Instead, responsibility for coordination as well as the lead in economic negotiations is usually given to an economic ministry or agency. For example, in the United States, where the conduct of trade and investment diplomacy was removed from the Department of State in 1962, inter-agency trade policy coordination, together with lead responsibility for all trade and trade-related investment negotiations, falls to the Office of the US Trade Representative, part of the Executive Office of the President.

In international *financial* negotiations, the formal exclusion of foreign ministries from the lead is complete (Woolcock and Bayne: 389). In Britain, for example, under an internal MoU drawn up to clarify which departments represent the country on the 17 international bodies dealing with financial matters, the Foreign Office is nowhere mentioned, while the international coordination committee established by the MoU is chaired by the Treasury representative (Bank of England). Only at G20 leaders' meetings and, via diplomats seconded to the Cabinet Office, is the Foreign Office likely to have any influence at all on international financial policy.

Embassy tasks and set-up

As already mentioned, economic diplomacy is still conducted via bilateral channels as well, and here diplomats come rather more into the picture, whether directly or by providing platforms in their embassies for officials from economic ministries and agencies. Embassy staff working in this area are engaged chiefly in *reporting* on macro-economic problems and trends in the receiving state, taxation and anti-corruption policies, and so on, especially those bearing on any current bilateral negotiations. Thus one of the tasks of the Economic Section of the Australian Embassy in Beijing was – and, despite its signature in November 2014, probably still is – working on the feasibility of a Free Trade Agreement with China. However, they might also have imposed on them one or more (usually more) other duties. The number and nature of these depends very much on local circumstances. They include:

- policing the observance of an international economic agreement, for example the International Coffee Agreement in the case of the US Embassy in Honduras;
- handling media requests for comments on policy on general economic questions;
- lecturing to business audiences and others;
- negotiating minor bilateral economic agreements, for example on direct investment, landing slots at airports, and double taxation;
- working closely with foreign aid agencies, IMF and World Bank missions, and giving economic advice to a receiving state designed to create an environment favourable to businesses from home; and
- supporting, or providing staff who double as members of, a permanent mission to an international economic organization, often the duty of an economic officer at the US Embassy in Paris in connection with the OECD, which is headquartered in the French capital.

It is also necessary to add a borderline task of economic diplomacy for the embassy. This is assisting in the implementation of smart economic sanctions; that is, sanctions that seek to have an impact only on named individuals and corporations in the power elite of a target state (as in the case of Russia in 2014), thereby minimizing their effect on its wider population. Rather like an army artillery spotter in a forward position, the embassy in this state is well placed to identify individual targets and their special points of economic and financial vulnerability; as also to report on the effects of sanctions (Office of Foreign Assets Control: 10) and recommend any necessary adjustments to their direction of fire. In addition, it can employ soothing language in advising those in the economic cross hairs on steps they might take to ameliorate sanctions and, in order to encourage the others, urge the swift 'de-listing' of those who have already begun to hold up a white flag. Finally, in order to keep the righteous onside, as well as assist those among its own nationals who wish to do business with them, the embassy can employ clear and detailed advertising of the sanctions regulations in force and what the unaffected must do in order to avoid being hit by friendly fire. In early 2014, the website of the US Embassy in Khartoum (headed only by a chargé d'affaires since 1998) was instructive in this last regard, as was that of the US Embassy in Damascus until it suspended operations in February 2012. As indicated by the fate of this embassy, and of the British Embassy in Tehran a little earlier, assisting in the implementation of smart economic sanctions is one of the most delicate and risky tasks an embassy can be asked to undertake.

Embassies tend, however, to be less engaged with economic than with commercial diplomacy; indeed, they are at its forefront. Heads of state and government, and their ministers, now commonly visit foreign countries in order to give an impetus to – and steal the credit for any successes in – commercial negotiations. But it is on embassies that the chief burden of commercial diplomacy still falls – not least in preparing and following up these visits – as well as on the trade promotion organizations (TPOs) often housed on their premises. This sort of diplomacy has, incidentally, also helped to revive the resident embassy because this activity has in general become more important to states anxious about their balance of payments as other traditional means of official support to national businesses – such as subsidies, tariffs, and tied aid – have become unpopular, and in many cases subject to control by international regimes like that of the WTO (Woolcock and Bayne: 387).

As well as 'country branding', usually at the head of the embassy's commercial diplomacy to-do list is the promotion of exports to countries with which there is a large and enduring adverse imbalance of trade. Also important is encouraging FDI, possibly in both directions. Inward direct investment has traditionally been attractive to countries suffering from a recession or 'under-development'; unlike portfolio investment, it is also not easily pulled out. But outward FDI to countries from which profits can be readily repatriated is now officially encouraged even by some developing countries, especially in Asia; it can offer easier access to markets, additional capital, cheap and docile labour, favourable tax regimes, and also be a valuable means of securing the supply of vital raw materials and energy sources. China is the most obvious case.

Among other things, embassies must send home market intelligence, provide attractive advertising of business prospects on their websites, give political briefings and support to any high-level visitors, and open doors for trade missions and companies from home, especially those small and medium-sized enterprises (SMEs) that cannot afford their own agents. If the sending state is an arms exporter, embassy service attachés are expected to promote arms sales by exploiting their contacts with the local defence establishment. When the foreign government is itself the customer, the political expertise of the embassy gained from its long experience of contacts with the various ministries is especially valuable to the representatives of large companies from home as well as SMEs (Barder: 203). Embassies might also lobby against, or for a more liberal application of, non-tariff barriers to their country's exports, and offer their assistance to the settlement of trade disputes involving their nationals.

How is the normal embassy set up to handle economic and commercial work of the sort described above? This question is best answered under the headings of organization, staffing, and location but, in passing, I shall also take the opportunity to mention the influence in the embassy of those charged with economic-commercial work.

Organization: a motley picture

Large and medium-sized US embassies tend to have both an economic section *and* a commercial section or service. The embassies of many other states also have firm echoes of this model, although the commercial section sometimes goes by a different name, typically the title of a TPO. Thus we find the commercial section in French missions described as the office of UbiFrance (literally, France *ubiquitaire*, or everywhere) and in British missions as UK Trade & Investment (UKTI). Government control and embassy housing of TPOs is actually not recommended by the World Bank as best practice for poorer states, especially those where political instability and corruption are rife. Instead, it advises that these potentially invaluable bodies should either be semi- or wholly independent of government and managed by a predominantly private sector board (Giovannucci), although this can lead to conflict with embassies.

In practice, the distinction between the economic and commercial work of embassies – like that between their economic-commercial and political work – is artificial, and not just in mini-embassies. To begin with, both activities often require embassy staff to rub shoulders with some of the same people and deal with much the same subjects. Moreover, commercial officers tend to be more effective if they have a good grasp of the economic background to their work, while the reporting of economic officers is more likely to be relevant to policy priorities if they share in day-to-day commercial and business affairs. It is for the last of these two reasons that in 1964 the British Plowden Report argued that economic and commercial work are 'two sides of the same coin' and that 'it is right in principle for economic and commercial work to be handled in the same section of our overseas Missions' (HCPP 1964: para. 234). No doubt there are good reasons why this principle has not always been observed in British embassies: for example, with London desperate for the establishment of Japanese factories in the United Kingdom's de-industrialized northern regions, it is hardly surprising that the British Embassy in Tokyo has a separate 'Inward Investment Section' as well as separate 'Commercial', 'Energy', and 'Trade Policy' sections. Nevertheless, the Plowden rule has been observed in many

British missions, and an 'economic and commercial section' can be found in the embassies of other countries, among them Argentina, China, Greece, and Switzerland. Even in some large American embassies, the distinction between economic and commercial work tends to be blurred, with economic officers often helping out the over-worked commercial section, and visiting US businessmen – for whom the staff of either section can be used as control officers (chaperones) – wanting to see members of both. In smaller US embassies, and even in some large ones such as the mission in Kabul, a so-called 'economic section' formally embraces both economic reporting *and* commercial work. (This is paralleled in the Afghan Embassy in Washington.) To cap it all, the US Department of the Treasury, which has an Office of International Affairs, maintains its own section in some large American embassies; the finance ministries of some other states do likewise in their own larger missions.

To add to this motley organizational picture, it should also be noted that some economic or commercial work is often given by a head of mission to members of quite different embassy sections; and that personal leadership on particularly important economic issues is best provided by the ambassador in order to energize the embassy's effort. Furthermore, 'task forces' headed usually by the DCM and composed of members of the economic or commercial section, and sometimes others, might be created for specific projects.

Staffing: two models

As to the question of staffing the embassy's economic and/or commercial sections, there has long been uncertainty as to whether it is best to employ specialist attachés or diplomatic service generalists. The first model has its origins in the 1880s, with the tentative appointment to a few European embassies of commercial attachés recruited from the consular service. Specialist officers are now typically individuals on temporary attachment from a department of trade or finance (and sometimes others, such as agriculture, labour, energy, and transport); and their titles indicate their provenance – 'treasury attaché', 'labour attaché', and so on. (One title less bureaucratically revealing, although it appears to be the new name for the British Foreign Office's commercial attachés, is the cringe-making 'Prosperity Officer'.)

However embarrassing the titles it generates, the specialist attaché model has the advantage of providing expert knowledge and experience to the embassy's economic and commercial sections, although – as with other specialists, such as military attachés – it has the drawback of bringing different departmental loyalties and outlooks into a mission, and thereby risks creating tensions.

The second model, which involves diverting diplomatic service officers to commercial work from, say, political duties, also has both advantages and disadvantages. Giving most diplomatic generalists a tour as a 'counsellor (commercial)' or '2nd secretary (commercial)' might well entrench more deeply in the diplomatic service an understanding of the nature and importance of economic and commercial work – *and* its connection with politics. It has also been observed that the absence of personal experience of the underworld is no obstacle to the work of a criminal barrister; and that companies from home, always nervous that their secrets will leak to rivals, will probably be more willing to take into their confidence a diplomat with no private business connections. On the other hand, this model sacrifices specialist knowledge and will usually throw more responsibility onto LE staff. In large embassies, LE staff are often specialists in particular industrial or commercial sectors and are also valued by home-country businessmen because they are usually more effective than home-based diplomats in dealing with less cosmopolitan middle-level executives. However, in addition to other disadvantages (see p. 120 above), their knowledge of the home country's exports and investment potential is in most cases bound to be limited.

In view of the entrenched distaste of diplomats for most things to do with trade and finance, it is hardly surprising that, when in the twentieth century embassies came under increasing pressure to interest themselves in such matters, their strong preference was for the first of these models. Since World War II, however, there has clearly been a wise attempt to get the best of both practices. In other words, specialist economic or commercial attachés remain prominent in embassies; but *alongside* them are now to be found diplomatic generalists holding similar briefs who are as well, if not better, qualified for them. Many diplomats are now highly educated in Economics, which is particularly true of those employed in the (pure) economic sections of US embassies; some have a period on industrial or other private sector secondment under their belts, which should give them a better understanding of what the corporate sector needs from embassies, as well as valuable contacts; and others are late entrants into the diplomatic career from backgrounds in business, banking, or accountancy, for example. In mini-embassies, sections of any sort are out of the question, and, whether specially qualified in some way or not, diplomatic generalists in such missions must multi-task, undertaking economic and commercial work as and when appropriate.

Growing influence

In view of the growing importance attached to economic and especially commercial diplomacy in the 1960s and 1970s, in these years the size of embassy staff in this area began to grow – and with it a corresponding increase in their influence. But this did not happen overnight; it also started from a very low point. Indeed, it was a telling index of low prestige that the rooms occupied by commercial officers in British embassies were evidently often cramped and poorly furnished (HCPP 1964: 252), while the importance of economic-commercial work did not fully penetrate the culture of US embassies until the 1980s (Lundy). It was 1998 before a member of the US Commercial Service, George Mu, was appointed as an ambassador, to Côte d'Ivoire.

The experience of the commercial staff of the British Embassy at Ankara was probably typical. It had already started to expand in the mid-1960s, and by 1974 its home-based element had more than doubled. It included a counsellor as its head, two first secretaries, and two attachés. In 1970 the British Consulate-General in Istanbul, which remained the business capital of Turkey, was given a second commercial officer, and in 1972 a 'commercial section' was formally noted for the first time in the British *Diplomatic Service List*.

A similar trend was observable in US embassies. A 'Foreign Commercial Service' (later 'US Commercial Service') was created by the US Department of Commerce in 1980, and the commercial element in US embassies began to dwarf the purely economic one. Sometimes this acquired provincial branches, which occasionally were 'upgraded' to consular posts, as at Pusan in South Korea in 1984.

The growth in influence of this element in the embassy was not only a function of the increase in its size; it was also assisted by the new trend for high-fliers to appear in its ranks because encouraged to believe that promotion to ambassadorial status depended on experience of commercial work. In 1969, the Duncan Report went so far as to state its expectation that the position of deputy head of mission (DCM in American terminology) in every British embassy should 'normally…be occupied by an officer specialising in commercial work' (HCPP 1969: para. 38). Accordingly, the appearance of such DCMs began to spread: to Ankara in 1970, Warsaw in 1971, Jakarta in 1972, Seoul in 1976, and Santiago in 1978. It had created a stir in the local diplomatic corps when John Fretwell was appointed counsellor (commercial) and number two at the British embassy in Warsaw in 1971 and then chargé d'affaires: 'It was,' he said later, 'one of those little shifts in diplomatic structure which seemed quite revolutionary at the time' (Fretwell).

At some embassies, the influence of an economic or commercial section is further reinforced when the receiving state is of major economic importance to the country it represents, as in the case of Saudi Arabia relative to oil importing and arms exporting states – and doubly so when for political and cultural reasons big companies are as likely as SMEs to need their help, as also in Saudi Arabia. The section's influence is also increased in hyper-suspicious authoritarian states, where commercial officers can operate more freely than political officers in making contacts and gleaning information, and so in practice serve as proxies for the latter, as – once more – in Saudi Arabia (Greenstock), and also Ba'athist Iraq (Hawley).

There has, then, been a general upward trend in the influence of the economic-commercial element of the normal embassy. It has, however, fluctuated over time, varied significantly between different diplomatic services and between individual embassies within the same service – and, together with the general economic-commercial priority, has now probably peaked.

'Location, location, location'

A popular television series for house-hunters, called 'Location, location, location', stresses the critical importance of a property's location. Forget the poorly pointed brickwork, the woodworm in the roof joists, the dry rot under the floor, and even the building's footprint. For a price, these can be corrected; the location cannot. This factor is almost equally important for the embassy's economic-commercial section.

The section is usually housed in the main embassy building (occasionally in a down town office) but this in turn is invariably located at the seat of government – the capital city. Unfortunately, in some very important states this does not coincide with its *business centre* (Box 14.4). In order that it be better placed for its purposes, it has in consequence long been the practice at some posts to locate the economic-commercial section – or a major branch office – in this city instead of in the capital, often in a consulate-general. For example, although the British Embassy in Brasilia provides some commercial services, the Director for Trade and Investment,who has primary responsibility for British commercial interests in Brazil, is based at the consulate-general in São Paulo, 500 km away by road. To take two more examples: the French Embassy in Canberra has an 'Economic Section' dealing 'mainly with legislative, market and multilateral issues', but the UbiFrance office in Australia is located in Sydney; and the embassy of the Netherlands in Delhi has a sizeable 'Economic

---

Box 14.4　Where the seat of government is not the business centre

	seat of government	business centre/s
Australia	Canberra	Sydney/Melbourne
Brazil	Brasilia	São Paulo
Canada	Ottawa	Toronto
China	Beijing	Shanghai
India	Delhi	Mumbai
Netherlands	The Hague	Amsterdam
South Africa	Pretoria/Cape Town	Johannesburg
Saudi Arabia	Riyadh	Jedda
Switzerland	Berne	Zurich/Geneva
Turkey	Ankara	Istanbul
USA	Washington	New York/Los Angeles

Department', but also a major 'Economic Cluster' in its consulate-general in Mumbai,

However, physical separation inevitably hinders coordination with other embassy sections (especially political and public diplomacy), and probably weakens the influence of the section concerned inside the embassy; and, for the first of these reasons, Busk was strongly opposed to it (Busk: 77). However, dramatic advances in communications since he wrote have reduced – although not by any means eliminated – the bearing of distance on these considerations. Therefore, in countries where the distance between the embassy and the business centre is not great and overland transport rapid and safe, as in the Netherlands, the argument that the economic-commercial section should be based exclusively in the business centre falls away. If the reverse is the case, the argument for this arrangement remains strong, although it is evident that poorer countries cannot afford it.

Summary

Economic and commercial diplomacy was a steadily rising priority in the second half of the twentieth century, but has peaked in recent years because of the surge in political volatility in key regions. In so far as economic diplomacy involves negotiations, most is conducted in a labyrinth of multilateral conferences to which – especially where finance is the subject – foreign ministries make little if any contribution. Embassies handle some economic diplomacy, including – by a stretch of the definition – the fine-tuning of smart sanctions. However, together with TPOs – and branch offices in the case of richer states – they are more heavily involved in commercial work. Whether all of this activity should be administered via traditional sections or transient projects – or some compromise between the two – is now a live issue.

Further reading

Advisory Committee on Modernising the Diplomatic Service, *Modernising Dutch Diplomacy: Progress Report, Final Report* (May 2014) [www]: 9–10, 47–8.

Bank for International Settlements, 'BIS Activities' [www].

Bank of England, 'Memoranda of Understanding' (MoU: International Organisations) [www].

Barder, Brian, *What Diplomats Do: The life and work of diplomats* (Rowman & Littlefield: Lanham, MD, 2014): 203–8.

Berridge, G. R., *British Diplomacy in Turkey, 1583 to the Present: A study in the evolution of the resident embassy* (Martinus Nijhoff: Leiden, 2009): introduction, chs 2, 4, 10.

Brief History of US Diplomacy: 'Commercial Diplomacy' [www].

Busk, Sir Douglas, *The Craft of Diplomacy: How to run a diplomatic service* (Praeger: New York, 1967): 71–84 ('The Commercial Section'); obviously dated but floats some general points still relevant to this topic as well as being historically valuable.

Cargill, Tom, 'More with less: Trends in UK diplomatic engagement in Sub-Saharan Africa', *Africa Programme Paper* AFP PP 2011/3 (Chatham House: London, 2011) [www].

Giovannucci, Daniele, 'National trade promotion organizations: Their role and function' (The World Bank Group: 2013) [www].

Hamilton, K. and R. Langhorne, *The Practice of Diplomacy: Its evolution, theory and administration*, 2nd edn (Routledge: London, 2011): 121–4, 172–8.

Jones, R. A., *The British Diplomatic Service, 1815–1914* (Colin Smythe: Gerrards Cross, 1983): App. A (Military and Commercial Attachés).

Krebsbach, Karen (ed), *Inside a U.S. Embassy: How the Foreign Service works for America* (AFSA: Washington, DC, 1996): 18–20 (Economic Officer); 36–9 (Commercial Officer).

Office of the US Trade Representative, 'History of the USTR' [www].

Rana, Kishan S. and Bipul Chatterjee (eds), *Economic Diplomacy: India's experience* (CUTS International: Jaipur, 2011).

Staley, E., *War and the Private Investor: A study in the relations of international politics and international private investment* (Doubleday: Garden City, 1935): ch. 6.

Strang, Lord, *The Foreign Office* (Allen & Unwin: London, 1955): 66–8, 109–11.

UK Department for Business Innovation and Skills, 'Sanctions, embargoes and restrictions' [www].

UK Trade & Investment [www].

UK Trade & Investment, *Annual Report and Accounts 2013–2014* [www].

UN Comtrade Database [www].

UN, *International Trade Statistics 1900–1960* [www].

'UN Security Council Sanctions Committees' [www]. This site also has an excellent list of links to key UN documents.

'United States Commercial Service', *Wikipedia* [www].

Woolcock, Stephen and Nicholas Bayne, 'Economic diplomacy', in Andrew F. Cooper, Jorge Heine, and Ramesh Thakur (eds), *The Oxford Handbook of Modern Diplomacy* (Oxford University Press: Oxford, 2013).

World Trade Organization, 'Historical Trends': Table A1 [www].

Part III
Diplomacy without Diplomatic Relations

Introduction to Part III

In some bilateral relationships, ordinary communications – including those usually maintained by means of ordinary embassies – cannot be employed because the parties are not in diplomatic relations (see Introduction to Part II). This might be because one party is not recognized by the other as a *state*, frequently because it has seceded from another by means with worrying implications for international norms and the integrity of other states, or because priority attaches to good relations with its spurned parent. Those from whom recognition of statehood has been to varying extents withheld, include – among a few others – Abkhazia, Kosovo, Nagorno-Karabakh, South Ossetia, Transnistria, and the Turkish Republic of Northern Cyprus (TRNC). Diplomatic relations might also be absent because one party is not recognized by the other as the *government* of the state over which it claims to rule, even though the state itself enjoys widespread recognition. Although this is now less common than it used to be (Young 2008: 199–207), this was the misfortune of the PRC for many years, notably at the hands of the United States: from 1949 until 1979 Washington recognized China as a state but insisted on recognizing as its legitimate government the regime of the anti-Communist Kuomintang (the Republic of China), although in practice the writ of the latter ran little beyond the island of Taiwan. Finally, diplomatic relations might not exist because one party, while continuing to recognize the other as a state and not denying the legitimacy of its government, has simply *severed* those relations, whether as a protest at some policy, as a more general expression of distaste for its regime, or because of an outbreak of fighting.

However, even if states go to war, they usually wish to prevent the fighting from escalating out of control, especially in this age of weapons of mass destruction. Unless led by homicidal psychopaths or street thugs of limited intelligence, they normally desire to restrict its geographical extent as well, secure the humane treatment of prisoners of war, and eventually edge towards a restoration of peace and, in due course, normality. If in war there is an urgent need for a minimum of diplomatic communication, the requirement for it might be no less urgent in fractured relations still below this threshold – because there is still time to prevent the parties crossing it. In recent years, the relationship between the United States and Iran has been very much an example of this sort of situation.

When diplomatic relations are in abeyance but the parties maintain an interest in communicating with each other, this might be achieved by a variety of means, some of which have already been touched upon; for example, telecommunications (Chapter 7), contacts in the diplomatic corps of third states where both have embassies (Chapter 8), and meetings in the wings of international organizations of which they are both members (Chapter 11). The final part of the book will discuss three other, more important methods: disguised embassies, special missions, and mediation by different kinds of third party. The last two of these methods are sometimes put to use in tackling difficult issues in the relations between states still in diplomatic relations, but are most badly needed, most severely tested, and thus most worthy of investigation in those dangerous cases where the states in question do not enjoy such a formal link.

Which is the best of these three means, or combination of them, to employ? Aside from consideration of the personalities in charge of them – which might in fact be decisive – the answer to this cardinal question depends chiefly on the reasons for the absence of diplomatic relations, the nature of the interests at stake in preserving effective contact, and whether diplomatic relations have only just collapsed or are already in prospect of restoration. These considerations will be much to the forefront in the following chapters.

15
Disguised 'Embassies'

Regular, flag-flying resident embassies cannot be employed in the absence of diplomatic relations, but diplomatic functions might still be performed – sometimes very fully – by irregular resident missions, some more heavily disguised than others. This chapter will consider the advantages and disadvantages of each of these disguised missions, and why one is preferred to another in different circumstances. It will also consider the debateable question as to whether any of them can properly be described as embassies by another name, which is why the word 'embassies' is placed in inverted commas in the title of this chapter.

To begin with, though, it is important to stress that disguised embassies are not to be confused with so-called 'shadow embassies'; that is, embassies partially re-assembled at home to provide policy advice on the states from which they have been either ejected or voluntarily removed (Smith 2009: 851–2). These probably have a limited shelf-life and, in any case, seem to be rare. Nor do disguised embassies include 'listening posts' – resident embassies or consulates in states adjacent to the hostile country – although these are more common and of greater value than shadow embassies. The British Embassy in Amman in Jordan was used to watch Iraq during the years of Saddam Hussein, and the Americans still use their massive consulate-general at Dubai in the UAE to keep an eye on Iran. Such missions are normally able to glean intelligence from exiles, traders, or persons applying to them for visas. In 2013, the US mission in Dubai processed 25,000 applications from Iranian citizens for non-immigrant visas alone (OIG 2014a: 14; also Rice: 313–314, 626). From time to time, as was certainly true of the British Embassy in Amman, they might even be able to send diplomats across the border (Chaplin: 39, 66–7; Prentice: 71). But the general diplomatic value of such missions is extremely limited and even the information they can report is patchy. The real disguised 'embassies', therefore, are those actually located *inside* the state with which there are no diplomatic relations. And of these there are more than might be imagined. They include interests sections, consulates, representative offices, and front missions – the last being analogous to the 'front organizations', typically businesses of one sort or another, employed to conceal espionage activities.

Interests sections

The interests section is a modification of the old institution of the protecting power, which originated in the sixteenth century with the successful assertion by Christian rulers – in particular His Most Christian Majesty, the King of France – of the right to protect co-religionists of any nationality in 'heathen' lands such as the Ottoman Empire. In the nineteenth century, the need for diplomatic protection was increased by the great expansion in trade and travel, and the growing tendency to expel enemy consuls on the outbreak of war. Protecting powers to rival France were not slow to come forward. Apart from considerations of religious and racial solidarity, prestige accrued to any state able to demonstrate its influence by assuming this responsibility. Those with neutralist traditions, such as Switzerland and Sweden, became especially active as protecting powers, although others have also been important. Among these are Austria (a permanent neutral after 1955), Belgium, Spain and – especially in the Americas – the United States. The practice was duly codified in the Vienna Convention on Diplomatic Relations (Box 15.1).

Although the institution of the protecting power certainly proved useful to those enjoying protection, it also had drawbacks for them. The protecting power's embassy could not be expected to have any special familiarity with their interests (especially if they were complicated), or to look upon the interests of the protected power as necessarily equivalent to those of its own state. Employing a protecting power was also attended by the general drawbacks of relying on a third state (see Chapter 17), as well as by the possibility of having to pay it a political price to take on what could well prove to be a delicate, even dangerous, job. When the US Embassy in Kampala was forced to close for security reasons in 1973, the protection of American interests in Uganda by the West German ambassador was only secured after protracted and difficult negotiations (Keeley: 1995).

Box 15.1   Protecting powers and the VCDR (1961)

Article 45

If diplomatic relations are broken off between two States, or if a mission is permanently or temporarily recalled:

(a) the receiving State must, even in case of armed conflict, respect and protect the premises of the mission, together with its property and archives;
(b) the sending State may entrust the custody of the premises of the mission, together with its property and archives, to a third State acceptable to the receiving State;
(c) the sending State may entrust the protection of its interests and those of its nationals to a third State acceptable to the receiving State.

Article 46

A sending State may with the prior consent of a receiving State, and at the request of a third State not represented in the receiving State, undertake the temporary protection of the interests of the third State and of its nationals.

The consequence of these drawbacks, allied to the practice adopted by a number of new states in the 1960s of severing diplomatic relations for chiefly symbolic reasons, was that the original institution of the protecting power was significantly modified. The practice quickly developed of formally closing embassies but – with the assent of the host state – arranging for a handful of diplomats to be left behind and attached to the embassy of a protecting power. (Where the animosity was too great or conditions too dangerous, the old system still had to be used, and still is today; for example, in Pyongyang, North Korea, where the Swedish mini-embassy protects Australian, Canadian, and US interests without benefit of any staff from these states. In such circumstances, the section concerned – if the embassy is big enough to support any sections – is still called an 'interests section'.) The beauty of the modified practice was that it permitted resident diplomacy to remain in the same hands while, simultaneously, making it possible to claim that relations with an unsavoury government had been 'severed'. The burden of work placed on the protecting power – which in any case seems usually to have been financially compensated by the protected state – was also reduced. And any hostility otherwise attracted to its own embassy was avoided if – as became common – the diplomats composing the interests section continued to work *in their own embassy building*, even if they were not allowed to do this immediately and restrictions might be put on which parts of the premises could be used, as in the case of the British Interests Section in Kampala (Berridge 2012a: 6–8).

An interests section, then, with rare exceptions, is a group of resident diplomats of one state working under the flag of a second on the territory of a third. The first ones were established by West Germany in Cairo, and Egypt in Bonn, in May 1965, when the Egyptians broke diplomatic relations with the Germans in retaliation for the decision of the latter to open them with Israel. (Similar sections had been seen in World War I, but were staffed by consuls, Berridge 2009: 124–8.) Shortly afterwards, Britain was allowed to adopt the same practice in order to maintain contact with the more important of the nine states that broke off relations with London in protest at the refusal of the Wilson government to put down, by force, the rebellion in Southern Rhodesia. Some of these states, which also included Egypt, reduced their embassies or high commissions in London to interests sections.

As its advantages became apparent, the interests section then spread rapidly. It was first used by the United States in the aftermath of the Six-Day War in the Middle East in 1967, when a number of Arab states severed relations with Washington, alleging that it had supported Israel's attack on Egypt. Interests sections also appeared in Washington, two of which have been of enduring importance – one belonging to Iran, based in the embassy of Pakistan, and the other to Cuba, which has enjoyed the protection of the Swiss embassy since the Czechs renounced the task in 1991. The new device also proved particularly useful to Israel, especially in Africa, where over 20 states severed relations with it at the time of the Yom Kippur War in 1973 (Klieman: 63–4).

Although, at first, a reaction to a break in diplomatic relations, interests sections have also been used since as a tentative first step towards their restoration. For example, the United States had severed relations with Cuba in January 1961 but, during a brief thaw in 1977, a Cuban interests section was allowed to open in the Czech Embassy in Washington and a US interests section in the Swiss Embassy in Havana. The Cuban section was bombed by anti-Castro Cuban exiles in July 1978, and no further improvement in US–Cuban relations occurred, but the interests sections remained in place. With this example in mind, in 2007, Condoleezza Rice, dissatisfied with her listening post in Dubai and handicapped by the withering away of Iran expertise in the US Foreign Service, was keen to establish an interests section in Tehran in order to gain 'firsthand knowledge of the terrain' – but on this occasion nothing came of the idea (Rice: 626–7; *Al-Monitor*).

Interests sections might have become popular since the mid-1960s, and on the upside as well as the downside of diplomatic relations (James: 1992). But are they really – as American diplomats with experience of them sometimes claim – embassies in all but name? In fact, this is rarely, if ever, the case, although they sometimes come close to it. How close depends on the degree of animosity prevailing at the time of the break, the importance of the interests likely to be damaged by a break taken to extremes, and the attitude of the chief of mission of the protecting power.

Interests sections are usually very small. For example, the 19-strong British Embassy in Argentina was replaced at the time of the Falklands War in 1982 by an interests section containing only two British diplomats, while, two years later, the 18-strong British Embassy in Libya was replaced by an interests section similarly reduced. US interests sections have had similar experiences. The American Embassy in Cairo was the biggest US mission in the Middle East at the time of the Six-Day War in 1967, occupying premises and grounds that gave it an atmosphere 'something like a university campus'; however, the interests section that replaced it was initially limited to a mere four diplomats (Bergus: 70–1).

But it is not because they are very small and, therefore, extremely limited in what they can do, that interests sections are rarely embassies in all but name; after all, there are mini-embassies, as we have seen (Chapter 8). Instead, it is because, although legally part of the protecting power's embassy, they generally operate under formal or tacit agreements that not only interpret the VCDR harshly but also fail to observe some of its key provisions.

For example, it is one thing for these agreements to place very low limits on overall staff size and severe restrictions on their freedom of movement, as in the case of that under which the Iraqis were permitted to establish an interests section under Algerian protection in Washington in May 1991, following the earlier fight with Saddam Hussein over Kuwait (US Department of State 1991: 347). Such restrictions are harsh but not illegal. It is quite another to insist, as is usual, that the interests section's work be limited to consular affairs, and effectively prohibit the continuation of other sections (typically, the more sensitive ones, such as political and defence); to deny an interests section any access to the receiving state's foreign ministry (or any other ministry), which is the 'major inhibition' under which the British Interests Section in the Swiss Embassy in Buenos Aires laboured for many years after the Falklands/ Malvinas War (HCPP 1987: 53); to require prior approval of *all* appointments to the interests section rather than simply that of the head of mission, which seems to be standard practice; and to forbid an interests section to have regular, confidential communications with its own foreign ministry, which was the regime imposed on the British Interests

Section in the French Embassy in Kampala by the otherwise indulgent chief of the French mission (Berridge 2012a: 9). Such restrictions on a genuine embassy would not be permitted under the Vienna Convention on Diplomatic Relations (1961).

The typical experience of an interests section in an actively hostile environment, albeit one exacerbated by American provocation (OIG 2007: 1, 24), is summed up by that of the US Interests Section in Cuba (USINT):

> The COM [Chief of Mission] and DCM must deal with an implacably hostile government ... in the absence of many formal authorities available to an Ambassador at an ordinary embassy. Official contact in Havana is minimal; with rare exceptions, officers cannot travel outside city precincts. The Cuban government obstructs or violates the terms of agreement for operating USINT and its Cuban counterpart in Washington. (OIG 2007: 7)

It is true, on the other hand, that interests sections set up in more benign circumstances, such as a thaw in hitherto frozen relations or the aftermath of a purely symbolic break, are likely to resemble a regular embassy more closely. When Egypt reluctantly severed relations with Britain over Southern Rhodesia in December 1965, large numbers of staff were permitted to remain in the new interests sections; the political section of the British Embassy in Cairo was closed, but the counsellor was allowed to stay on under cover of responsibility for consular affairs; and, in London, even two assistant military attachés were permitted to stay put in the guise of 'medical advisers' (Kear 2001: 77–9). A similar state of affairs appears to have obtained in the interests sections employed to cope with the symbolic severance of relations with Egypt by most Arab states following the Camp David accords in 1978.

As for USINT – still located in the former embassy building, which was renovated in the early 1990s – this might not always have been operating in benign circumstances, but things were better when it was created in 1977. The atmosphere has also improved in recent years, an index of which is a surge in the numbers of Cubans leaving for the United States and American tourists (over half a million a year) visiting the island. The Cubans recognize that USINT carries an enormous consular burden, and – while generally it still operates under significant restrictions – permit it to function 'in a considerably more normal fashion than previously possible'. The result is that it is huge, with 51 US direct-hire staff (an agreed upper limit) and roughly 400 LE employees (OIG 2014b).

According to the Department of State website, there were 24 diplomatic staff at the Cuban Interests Section in Washington in 2014.

Consulates

There is a long tradition of employing consulates as the usual device for conducting resident diplomacy in the absence of diplomatic relations, although there was uncertainty over its legality until this was confirmed by the VCCR in 1963 (Box 15.2) and fortified by its provision – subsequently adopted in other important consular conventions – that the encouragement of 'friendly' relations is a normal consular function (Lee and Quigley: 541–3). For most states, this has only been an occasional ploy in recent years, but it was a common one for South Africa during its apartheid-inflicted diplomatic isolation. Why should states still occasionally prefer to talk to their enemies via consulates now there is wide acceptance of interests sections staffed by *diplomats* of a sending state? This method does in fact have many advantages:

- It avoids the drawbacks of the interests section's reliance on a third party: indebtedness, possible misunderstandings, and the difficulty of keeping secrets from it.

Box 15.2   Diplomatic acts and the VCCR (1963)

Article 2
Establishment of consular relations
1. The establishment of consular relations between States takes place by mutual consent.
2. The consent given to the establishment of diplomatic relations between two States implies, unless otherwise stated, consent to the establishment of consular relations.
3. The severance of diplomatic relations shall not ipso facto [by virtue of that fact] involve the severance of consular relations ...

Article 17
1. In a State where the sending State has no diplomatic mission and is not represented by a diplomatic mission of a third State, a consular officer might, with the consent of the receiving State, and without affecting his consular status, be authorized to perform diplomatic acts. The performance of such acts by a consular officer shall not confer upon him any right to claim diplomatic privileges and immunities.

- It usually draws little public attention, because typically unostentatious and popularly thought to do little more than issue visas and provide relief to feckless backpackers. By contrast, the interests section is known to be more political and, more often than not, remain in the former embassy building. It is salutary in this connection that, in 1988, the US administration resisted Congressional pressure to open an interests section in Hanoi on the grounds that it would represent the establishment of a US diplomatic presence in Vietnam and be seen as 'a major political victory by Hanoi' (House of Representatives: 41).
- For states with greater resources, consular posts might also come in multiples; spread around an important receiving state, they are better placed than the interests section to discharge functions such as intelligence-gathering, and not hindered in this respect by the kind of restrictions often imposed on these sections.
- With the general integration of the consular and diplomatic services that occurred in the course of the twentieth century (see Chapter 9), consular officers today will usually have had previous diplomatic experience.
- The assumption of diplomatic functions does not confer *diplomatic* privileges and immunities on consular officers (Boxes 9.1 and 15.2), but the gap between those enjoyed by diplomats and those grudgingly given to consuls has narrowed – so, in practice, this is not a great handicap.
- Finally, it is important to note that consular representation might also be a convenient method of conducting limited relations in the special case of unrecognized states, when these states were created out of provinces of larger ones in which external powers happened already to have consulates. This is possible because of the international norm, albeit rather shaky and perforce carefully worded in the fifth edition of *Satow's Guide to Diplomatic Practice* (note my italicization), that 'neither the retaining nor the replacing of consular officials *necessarily* constitute recognition' (Gore-Booth 1979: 213; see also Roberts 2009: 252). Here, important examples are provided by consular posts in Hanoi during the Vietnam War, North Vietnam having been effectively sliced off from the rest of the country following the Geneva Conference in 1954; in Elisabethville, for several years after the secession of Katanga province from the Congo Republic in 1960; and in Jerusalem today, for the purposes of conducting relations with the Palestinian National Authority in the West Bank and Gaza (Box 15.3).

Box 15.3   The consulates in Jerusalem

The peculiar position of the consulates in Jerusalem, which conduct relations with the Palestinian National Authority in the West Bank and Gaza, was neatly summarized in a UN report in 1997:

> Particular mention should also be made of the continued presence in Jerusalem of an international *sui generis* consular corps, commonly referred to as the 'Consular Corps of the Corpus Separatum'. Nine States have maintained consulates in Jerusalem (East and West) without, however, recognizing any sovereignty over the City. Unlike consuls serving in Israel, the consuls of those States do not present a consular letter of authorization to the Foreign Ministry and do not receive accreditation by the President of Israel. They do not pay taxes and have no official relations with Israeli authorities. In their activities, they respect common protocol rules designed to prevent any appearance of recognition of sovereign claims to the City.

The nine states with consular posts in Jerusalem are Belgium, France, Greece, Italy, Spain, Sweden, Turkey, UK, and USA. In addition, there is an apostolic delegation of the Holy See in the city, and a number of states have honorary consulates there. The website of the US consulate-general states that, throughout its history, its staff 'has included Christians, Muslims, and Jews, demonstrating that people of different faiths and nationalities can work together in peace in this region'.

Source: The Status of Jerusalem (United Nations: New York, 1997). Prepared for, and under the guidance of, the Committee on the Exercise of the Inalienable Rights of the Palestinian People.

Representative offices

In some cases of diplomatic difficulty when business-like relations are still desired, interests sections cannot be employed and consular posts are problematical. This is most common when one party continues to grant recognition to a rival of the other. For example, when the United States and the PRC wanted to consolidate their *rapprochement* in 1973, interests sections could not be contemplated because their employment would have amounted to a denial of a firmly held American position; namely, that 'Chinese interests' in the United States were *already* protected by the Washington embassy of the Republic of China ('Taiwan'). As for consular posts, Chou En-lai, the PRC Prime Minister, regarded these as insufficiently political to advertise the new Sino-American relationship and, therefore, inadequate for the purpose of deterring any Soviet attack (Kissinger 1982: 61). In such circumstances, an increasingly common expedient is now the representative office, sometimes also known as a 'liaison office'. This is a mission that looks like and operates much like an embassy, the only difference being its informality.

liaison offices = rep. offices

According to Henry Kissinger, the liaison offices exchanged between the United States and the PRC were embassies in all but name. 'Their personnel would have diplomatic immunity; they would have their own secure communications; their chiefs would be treated as ambassadors and they would conduct all exchanges between the two governments. They would not become part of the official diplomatic corps,' he adds, 'but this had its advantages since it permitted special treatment without offending the established protocol orders.' Both countries sent senior and trusted diplomats to head these offices. According to Kissinger, the establishment of diplomatic relations with the PRC on 1 January 1979 produced nothing more than an entirely nominal change to the resident missions in Beijing and Washington (Kissinger 1982: 62–3).

Representative offices have proved particularly useful to so-called international 'pariahs' (whether sending or receiving states), as well as to entities struggling for recognition. These include the TRNC; Taiwan, although many of its representative offices are called the 'Taipei Economic and Cultural Office' ('Taipei' – the capital – rather than 'Taiwan', to avoid implying that there are two Chinas); the Palestinian National Authority, which hosts numerous representative offices in Ramallah, Jericho and Gaza; and – in the past – the Republic of South Africa. At the time of writing, France and Estonia are willing to accept only a representative office from North Korea.

Front missions

As their name implies, front missions are the most heavily disguised of the irregular resident missions: on the surface, altogether innocent of diplomatic purpose – but, beneath it, pursuing their political work with zeal. Distinct from the representative office by virtue of their genuine cover function, front missions come in all shapes and sizes. Trade missions or commercial offices are an old favourite, and a natural ploy for a trading state. This was the device by which the PRC and Japan maintained representation in each other's capitals prior to normalization in 1972 (Beer: 170–1), and that employed at the end of the 1950s by Britain as a half-way house to the restoration of diplomatic relations with Egypt following the Suez crisis (Parsons: 41–2). It was also used by Britain to preserve relations with Taiwan, a very important trading partner, after it was obliged to close its Tamsui consulate in 1972. A few years after this, the Anglo-Taiwan Trade Committee was established and, in 1989, it acquired a visa handling unit. This was a front mission that might have been heavily disguised relative to other kinds of irregular resident mission, but it was thinly disguised relative to other front missions: by 1992 its entire senior staff, including its 'Director', were British Diplomatic Service officers 'on secondment' (HCPP 1993: 11, 14 Annex A). Israel, and Taiwan itself, have also made widespread use of commercial offices for diplomatic purposes, as did South Africa during the apartheid era.

Information or tourist offices, travel agencies, scientific missions, and cultural affairs offices, are also favourite covers for diplomatic activity. In the late 1960s and early 1970s, the North Vietnamese disguised their diplomats in London, who were well known to the Foreign Office, as journalists (Young 2008: 215–216). The Holy See's apostolic delegate, whose mission in a foreign country is formally (and largely) religious, also serves as a saintly cover for diplomacy in states where the Vatican is unable to accredit a nuncio or pro-nuncio. The apostolic delegate served this purpose in Britain until 1979, and in the United States until as late as 1984 (Berridge 1994: 54–6).

Some front missions have gathered so many responsibilities of the kind commonly associated with diplomatic posts that, apart from their names, they are little different from representative offices. For example, in 1993 the privately managed Anglo-Taiwan Education Centre was taken over by the British Council and merged with the Trade Committee to form the 'British Trade and Cultural Office'.

Front missions are of most value where visible relations between unfriendly states could lead to acute embarrassment on one or both sides. However, precisely because they have to preserve their cover by pursuing work normally important in its own right, their time and resources remaining for diplomatic activity can be comparatively slender. Furthermore, while the staff of some trade missions gained partial immunities after 1945 (Peterson 1997: 117), it seems unlikely that – with some important exceptions – many front missions enjoy anything like full diplomatic, or even consular, immunities. This means that their staff must be unusually circumspect in their activities. Their access to local officials is also liable to be restricted and might have to be conducted through intermediaries (Cross: 257–8).

Summary

If there is a desire to preserve some degree of communication by resident means in the absence of diplomatic relations, alternatives to the regular embassy have to be found that can achieve the purpose without undue embarrassment. These are interests sections, consulates, representative offices, and front missions. The similarities of these disguised 'embassies' to regular embassies vary greatly. Except for the representative office, all labour under handicaps that the normal embassy does not experience. Even a large interests section occupying its own building operates under formal or tacit agreements that not only interpret the VCDR harshly but also fail to observe some of its key provisions.

Further reading

Al-Monitor, 'Study recommends US interests section in Tehran', 18 February 2014 [www].

Berridge, G. R., *Talking to the Enemy: How states without 'diplomatic relations' communicate* (Macmillan: Basingstoke, 1994): chs 1, 3.

Berridge, G. R. and Nadia Gallo, 'The role of the diplomatic corps: the US–North Korea talks in Beijing, 1988–94', in Jan Melissen (ed.), *Innovation in Diplomatic Practice* (Macmillan: Basingstoke, 1999).

Berridge, G. R., 'The British Interests Section in Kampala, 1976–7', January 2012 [www].

Cross, Charles T., *Born a Foreigner: A memoir of the American presence in Asia* (Rowman & Littlefield: Lanham, MD, 1999): ch. 19 (Taiwan).

Franklin, W. M., *Protection of Foreign Interests: A study in diplomatic and consular practice* (US Government Printing Office: Washington, DC, 1947).

Hertz, Martin F. (ed.), *The Consular Dimension of Diplomacy* (University Press of America: Lanham, MD, 1983).

James, Alan, 'Diplomatic relations and contacts', *The British Yearbook of International Law 1991*, Volume 62 (Clarendon Press: Oxford, 1992).

Kear, Simon, 'The British Consulate-General in Hanoi, 1954–73', *Diplomacy and Statecraft*, 10(1), March 1999.

Kear, Simon, 'Diplomatic innovation: Nasser and the origins of the interests section', *Diplomacy and Statecraft*, 12(3), September 2001.

Kissinger, Henry A., *Years of Upheaval* (Weidenfeld & Nicolson: London, 1982): 60–3.

Lee, Luke T. and John Quigley, *Consular Law and Practice*, 3rd edn (Oxford University Press: Oxford, 2008): ch. 36.

Lockhart, R. H. Bruce, *Memoirs of a British Agent* (Putnam: London, 1932), book 4.

Lowe, V., 'Diplomatic law: protecting powers', *International and Comparative Law Quarterly*, 39(2), April 1990.

Newsom, David E. (ed.), *Diplomacy under a Foreign Flag: The protecting power and the interests section* (Hurst: London, 1990).

OIG, *Inspection of Consulate General Jerusalem*, March 2011 [www].

OIG, *Inspection of U.S. Interests Section Havana, Cuba*, May 2014 [www].

Shaw, M. N., *International Law*, 6th edn (Cambridge University Press: Cambridge, 2008): ch. 9, on recognition.

Wylie, Neville, 'Protecting powers in a changing world', *Politorbis*, 40(1), 2006 [www].

Young, John W., *Twentieth-Century Diplomacy: A case study of British practice, 1963–1976* (Cambridge University Press: Cambridge, 2008): ch. 9.

16
Special Missions

Special missions are missions sent abroad to conduct diplomacy with a limited purpose and usually for a limited time. Led by special envoys, their employment was the normal manner of conducting foreign relations until resident diplomacy began to take root during the late fifteenth century. Advances in air travel led to their resurgence in the anxious days preceding and following the outbreak of World War II, and, since then, it has been unstoppable. Special missions are a feature of normal diplomatic relationships, but they are particularly valuable to the diplomacy between hostile states, not least in breaking the ice between them – as when American National Security Advisor Henry Kissinger flew secretly to Beijing, capital of the PRC, in July 1971. What are the advantages of special missions used in the absence of diplomatic relations? How are they variously composed? When should they be sent in public, and when in secret?

The advantages of special missions

Special missions may be designed to supplement activity by disguised embassies or play a larger role in their absence. They also come in many guises themselves, but most provide maximum security for the secrecy of a message, which, in the circumstances, might be of considerable sensitivity. In this respect their function is identical to that of a diplomatic courier, but their higher status underlines the importance attached to the message by the sending state, and this – together with the special knowledge of the mission's members – makes it more likely that it will command respect.

The procedures of special missions, and the privileges and immunities of their members, were clarified and marginally reinforced in the second half of the twentieth century by what is commonly known as the 'New York Convention' (Box 16.1). This alarmed many states because customary international law had 'essentially' restricted the privileges and immunities of special missions 'to immunity from criminal jurisdiction and inviolability of the person' (Wood 2012); that is, it had *not* treated them as generously as resident embassies. The New York Convention was, accordingly, seen as a Third World instrument and, even today, has been ratified by only 38 states – not including the United States. Nevertheless, even as between the states that are parties to it, it permits flexibility in the use of special missions. As for the rest, as Sir Michael Wood observes, 'in most circumstances' the rules on special missions and other official visitors continue to be found in customary international law (Wood 2012). The customary law also has the advantage of extending the class of those entitled to immunity beyond the narrow formula of the New York Convention; namely, to specialized *permanent* missions sent by one state to another, such as aid or military missions, and special missions to and from an authority not constituting a state.

Box 16.1   The New York Convention on Special Missions (1969)

The Convention on Special Missions was unfinished business for the ILC in the codification and development of diplomatic law. It was adopted by the UN General Assembly on 8 December 1969, and entered into force on 21 June 1985. Narrowly defining special missions as those sent by *one state to another* on a *temporary* basis, it says that – with the consent of the receiving state – special missions can be despatched even though neither diplomatic nor consular relations exist between the states concerned; and that – on the grounds that any mission might be better than none at all – a receiving state must be allowed to insist that the members of a special mission should have unusually limited privileges and immunities. Otherwise, advancing well beyond the customary international law, it says that – with certain exceptions – their privileges and immunities should be identical with those enjoyed by the staff of regular embassies in the VCDR (1961). On the other hand, it also provides that the prior agreement of the receiving state must be obtained to both the size and – as with interests sections – named members of a special mission; and that its functions must be determined by mutual consent.

The variety of special missions

Special missions vary in form at least as much as disguised resident missions, but they can be classified fairly simply by their political weight and nature of appointment. There are four main kinds: unofficial envoys (high and low level); and official envoys (high and low level).

Unofficial envoys

Unofficial envoys are recruited from outside government or, at least, from outside the foreign policy and military establishments, and are informally tasked. If they are high-level envoys – typically friends or political cronies of government leaders – they are commonly known as 'personal envoys'. Employment of individuals of this sort has long been favoured by American presidents, but their use is by no means unique to the United States. In the 1960s, British Prime Minister Harold Wilson sent his close political ally, Harold Davies, on a peace mission to North Vietnam (Young 2008: 100) and, for almost a decade, one of Wilson's successors, Tony Blair, used Lord Levy as his personal envoy to the Middle East (Box 16.2).

Box 16.2 About Lord Levy: Tony Blair's personal envoy to the Middle East and Latin America

Lord Levy, a multi-millionaire businessman, was the Labour Party's chief fundraiser and a close friend of Tony Blair, whom he partnered at tennis. By reason of his great success in delivering funds for the party he was popularly known as 'Lord Cashpoint', and subsequent to his appointment as the PM's personal envoy in 1999 as 'Lord Fix-it' (unfortunately he never did). It was reported in 2007 that he had made 121 visits to 24 states, including 24 to the Palestinian National Authority (*Mail Online*, 4 January 2007). The following written exchange between Tony Blair and the Conservative frontbench spokesman on foreign affairs, Cheryl Gillan, on 5 February 2001, illustrates some interesting points about such envoys.

Mrs Gillan: To ask the Prime Minister, ... concerning messages carried by Lord Levy, for what reason such messages could not be carried by Ministers and diplomats.

The Prime Minister: The purpose of asking Lord Levy to convey such messages as my personal envoy was to signal my personal interest in our relations with the countries. He was accompanied throughout by our ambassadors to the countries concerned and by a Foreign and Commonwealth Office official.

Mrs Gillan: To ask the Prime Minister ... what his policy is on the payment of travel expenses by Lord Levy while travelling as his personal envoy

The Prime Minister: Lord Levy has always paid his own travel expenses when travelling as my personal envoy.

Source: Hansard 2001.

Low-level unofficial envoys are usually known as 'private envoys'. Good examples of these are Landrum Bolling, the private American citizen used by US President Jimmy Carter to make contact with the PLO in September 1977 (Quandt: 101–2), and Ya'acov Nimrodi, the private Israeli arms dealer employed by Israeli Prime Minister Shimon Peres to respond to feelers (carried by agents of similar standing) from moderates inside the Iranian government in 1985 (Segev: 2–3).

Unofficial envoys, whether personal or private, have the great advantage of flexibility and are, therefore, the kind often employed on the most sensitive missions. As we have seen, they can be chosen from any walk of life; they can also be given any rank or title, or none at all; and their instructions and credentials can take any form desired (Wriston: 220). If they are rich, like Lord Levy, so much the better: they can pay their own travel expenses. Personal envoys have the great advantage of being known to enjoy the complete confidence of their leaders and, therefore, of being able to command maximum attention, although a high-level reception will normally need to be negotiated prior to departure. Such envoys also convey the maximum degree of flattery to the recipient of the message, and generate the conviction that any message returned will go direct to the top.

If flattery is not desired and disavowal is an important option in the event that a secret mission is exposed, the more peripheral figure of the private envoy will normally be preferred, even though establishing the credentials of this individual might be more difficult. This was probably one of the motives for choosing Bolling as the US emissary to the PLO, and was certainly the reason why Peres used Nimrodi to deal with the Iranians: 'he chose a private merchant so that he could deny any connection with the matter should there be a snafu [situation normal: all fucked up] or early revelation' (Segev: 23).

Unofficial envoys have the additional advantage that they can be used by political leaders to bypass the foreign service of their own country. They may want to do this for any number of reasons; for example, to take the credit for any diplomatic breakthrough themselves; or because they regard the foreign service as politically hostile, incapable of radical thinking, prone to leaking or just plain incompetent. At the end of the 1960s, South African Prime Minister John Vorster employed Eschel Rhoodie, secretary of the Department of Information, as a personal envoy in his adventurous diplomacy in West Africa and elsewhere, because he was convinced that the Department of Foreign Affairs lacked imagination and was paralysed by an obsession with protocol (Rhoodie).

There is usually a price to be paid for the use of unofficial envoys, particularly personal ones. They tend to create resentment in the foreign ministry at home and if – as is often the case – it has not been kept fully in the picture, problems might occur in implementing any new policy agreed. Personal envoys can also make serious mistakes if they act in the absence of professional scrutiny. This is a dilemma, because giving them foreign ministry minders might defeat the object of sending them in the first place.

Official envoys

The more common type of high-level envoy is the official species ('special envoys', in US parlance); that is, those recruited from within the political establishment and formally appointed. It is only in exceptional circumstances – not because of their capacity for exceptional insights – that presidents or prime ministers themselves visit states with which their governments do not have diplomatic relations, as when President Nixon made his epic journey to Beijing in February 1972 ('Gee, this is a great wall!'). Instead, it is senior political advisers, diplomats, or other civil servants (including intelligence officers) who are usually selected; and occasionally generals, war heroes, former presidents and government ministers, and – although not in Zimbabwe – opposition politicians. Despite the elevation of most such individuals, they are often not well known and can 'carry out the most delicate mission without drawing attention' (Young 2008: 101). If they are inside or not far from the inner circle of a leader or foreign minister, they will also carry similar weight to a personal envoy, without the same tendency to make mistakes or cause disaffection in the bureaucracy – the misadventures of Colonel Oliver North and US National Security Advisor Robert McFarlane, in the Iran–Contra affair in the mid-1980s, notwithstanding (*Tower Commission Report*: vii). A better and certainly more successful example is provided by US Director of National Intelligence James Clapper, who flew secretly to North Korea in November 2014 and – amid great publicity – returned a few days later with two previously detained American nationals. A special envoy was particularly valuable on this occasion since the United States did not have a disguised embassy of any description in Pyongyang, and the Swedish embassy protecting its interests had only two full-time home-based staff and Canadian and Australian interests to look after as well.

A high-level official envoy more typical than Clapper was Harold Beeley, the quiet, pragmatic Arabist in the British diplomatic service, who had been previously ambassador at Cairo and, in 1967, was

treading water as representative to the UN disarmament conference in Geneva. In October, he was whisked away from Switzerland and sent for 'path-finding talks' with President Nasser of Egypt; in December, Anglo-Egyptian diplomatic relations were restored, with Beeley himself once more ambassador (Young 2008: 210). Some high-level official envoys soon become well known precisely because of the international dramas in which they have been involved. Henry Kissinger was one such individual, but more on him later.

Some high-level official envoys are appointed as roving ambassadors, or 'ambassadors-at-large'. As with some personal envoys, these are individuals given the task of visiting a number of countries, usually within the same region. In the past, roving ambassadors were often employed to spread the word about the policies of a new government suspicious of the loyalties of the diplomats it had inherited, and it would be surprising if they were not still sometimes used for this purpose. Normally diplomats of great experience and seniority ('seasoned' is the adjective commonly applied), they are more often today a feature of the diplomacy of a major power wanting to promote a settlement of a regional conflict, and be seen to be doing so. Unlike a president or foreign minister, such 'trouble-shooters' have the time to gain a command of the necessary detail; and, unlike any ambassadors in states in the region with which diplomatic relations are enjoyed, they are in a better position to coordinate the broad approach needed (Fullilove: 15, 18).

Malcolm MacDonald, a veteran British politician and diplomat, was an envoy of this sort, and helped to negotiate the restoration of diplomatic relations between Britain and a number of East African states in the late 1960s (Young 2008: 102–4, 211–12). One of the first moves of newly elected President Obama, in January 2009, was to appoint a number of similar special envoys, one of whom, Stephen Bosworth, visited North Korea. Among his other appointments, probably the most thankless, announced in March 2014, was that of Daniel Rubinstein as 'US Special Envoy for Syria'. This was the more necessary because, in the same month, the Obama administration – having closed its Damascus embassy in February 2012 and entrusted protection of its interests to the Czechs – ordered immediate closure of President Assad's embassy in Washington and even all of Syria's honorary consulates in the United States. However, there were evidently no *immediate* plans to make Rubinstein the default link to the government in Damascus, but rather to any other government or moderate militia capable of helping to bring it down.

As for low-level official envoys sent to unfriendly regimes, or to meet their counterparts in third countries, rumours about them often circulate and are occasionally confirmed; although usually only when government archives are opened up many years later. This is because they are employed for the most delicate initial contacts and are often intelligence officers. In practice probably more often middle than low level, they are used because they are easier to control and relatively obscure. If they are exposed, the significance of their missions can also be more plausibly played down; they can even be disavowed altogether, although less convincingly than private envoys.

To go secretly or openly?

When special missions are employed in diplomacy between hostile states, they are often despatched in secret – especially when contacts are at an early stage. Indeed, because of their 'tradecraft', senior intelligence officers are themselves commonly employed in this capacity (see Chapter 10); and it was a source of regret to the Tower Commission that the CIA was not used to run the arms-for-hostages initiative into Iran in the mid-1980s (*Tower Commission Report*: vii).

The first reason for the preference for secret emissaries is the avoidance of sabotage. Public knowledge that a special mission to a hostile state is planned, especially if it is a high-level one rumoured to be seeking a *rapprochement*, is likely to spread alarm among factions at home and allied governments abroad whose interests are locked into the status quo. Advance warning of what is afoot permits them time to marshal their forces and nip it in the bud. The fear of an outcry from die-hard anti-Communists at home (especially in the well-organized, pro-Taiwan 'China lobby'), as well as vigorous opposition from Japan and Taiwan itself, was the given reason for the intense secrecy cloaking Henry Kissinger's first mission to Beijing in July 1971 in order to explore the possibility of a summit spectacular between President Nixon and Chairman Mao (Kissinger 1979: 725; MacMillan: 179–80). The anxiety to avoid sabotage has also encouraged the employment of secret envoys in contacts between Israel and its Arab neighbours, a tradition that goes back to the activities of the Arab experts of the Jewish Agency before World War II, notably Elias Sasson (Shlaim: 11–12).

The second reason for sending a special envoy in secret is the need to avoid the damage to one's prestige that might result from appearing to the world as a supplicant at the seat of the rival's power, particularly if the mission produces no tangible benefit. Any power in relative decline will be readily persuaded by this argument, and – although it was not admitted – was probably another reason for Washington's insistence on the secrecy of Kissinger's first visit to Beijing, because at the time it was clearly in retreat in Vietnam and its gold reserves were being decimated. If secrecy is impossible or for other reasons inadvisable, another way of minimizing the risk to prestige is for special envoys from both states to meet on neutral ground – for example, in Geneva, where US Secretary of State James Baker met his Iraqi counterpart, Tariq Aziz, in a televised last-minute attempt to avert fighting in the Gulf in April 1991; or at working funerals (see Chapter 12); or in the setting of the diplomatic corps of a third state, as when in the early 1970s Henry Kissinger flew to Paris to meet the Chinese ambassador, and Le Duc Tho of North Vietnam flew there to meet Kissinger.

There are also reasons for despatching envoys in secret that have nothing to do with diplomatic considerations; they are rooted, instead, in either the personalities or domestic political needs of those sending the mission. It is, for example, notorious that Richard Nixon also had re-election on his mind when he insisted on the secrecy of Kissinger's first visit to the PRC. Secrecy right through to the end of the trip meant that he could produce a *coup de théâtre* by springing the news of it on the world on Kissinger's return, and also ensure that as much public attention as possible was focused on his own plans to visit China (Ball: 22).

When the risk of sabotage and loss of prestige is judged to be minimal – perhaps because a previous secret trip had been successful, as with Kissinger's visit to China in July 1971 – the advantages of publicly announcing a special mission and, indeed, encouraging maximum media coverage, might become overwhelming. Kissinger's second visit to Beijing, in October 1971, was made openly. The Chinese, who had been suspicious of the American insistence on secrecy for the first visit, appear to have been more insistent with regard to openness on this occasion. In any case, it would have been difficult for the Americans to conceal because their party needed to be much larger, and it flew in Air Force One in order to familiarize the Chinese with its handling in preparation for the president's own arrival (MacMillan: 205).

The United States also publicly sent numerous special missions headed by high-ranking official envoys to the Socialist Republic of Vietnam in the years prior to the restoration of diplomatic relations in 1995. Among these were former Chairman of the Joint Chiefs of Staff General John Vessey, and Assistant Secretary of State for East Asian and Pacific affairs Winston Lord, who alone had made five trips to Hanoi in the first Clinton administration (Lord). This enabled the administration to advertise its efforts on the highly emotional prisoners of war/missing in action question, while simultaneously maintaining the formal diplomatic isolation of Vietnam (Berridge 1994: 56–8). In April 2002, and again in January 2003, South Korea publicly sent a high-level official envoy, Lim Dong-won, to North Korea in an attempt both to highlight its attachment to, and keep alive at a time when it seemed imperilled, Seoul's 'Sunshine Policy'.

Special missions are sometimes announced beforehand because, while secrecy might be preferred, there is no faith in either the determination or the capacity of the other side to preserve it. In such circumstances, it is generally best to have one's own justification of the mission made known, especially to one's friends, as soon as possible.

So-called pariah states, like the TRNC and North Korea, and those on the US Department of State's list of 'State Sponsors of Terrorism' (in 2014, Cuba, Iran, Sudan, and Syria), are nearly always anxious both to despatch and receive special envoys in public. It simultaneously advertises their protestations of good citizenship and the fact that they are weighty players with which the world has no alternative but to deal. If they are not widely recognized, either as states or as legitimate governments, the public despatch and receipt of special envoys might also grant them a degree of de facto admission to this coveted status. While all of this is going on, their enemies become demoralized. These reasons explain why the white South African government, then pursuing its policy of 'dialogue' with black Africa in increasingly difficult circumstances, was so delighted to receive a *public* special envoy from the Ivory Coast in October 1971. And also why the Sudanese regime of Omar al-Bashir, for whom the International Criminal Court had just issued an arrest warrant for war crimes and crimes against humanity, took a degree of comfort from the widely reported arrival in Khartoum in April 2009 of a US special envoy in order to 'engage' it on the question of Darfur.

Summary

Special missions come in many guises and operate under a permissive legal regime. Among *unofficial envoys*, personal envoys are perhaps the best suited to underlining a leader's own interest in a particular policy, although high-level *official envoys* can do likewise without the same liability of the former to make mistakes and prompt bureaucratic disaffection; this is why they are more common. Low-level envoys, whether private or official, are relatively invisible and are, therefore, best for the most delicate, initial contacts. Private envoys of this sort are the most easily disavowed if discovered, while lowly official envoys – often intelligence officers – are most easily controlled and most adept at concealment. In the conduct of diplomacy without diplomatic relations, special missions are particularly valuable in the absence of disguised resident missions.

Further reading

Bartos, M., 'Fourth report on special missions', *Yearbook of the International Law Commission*, (1967), Volume II, UN Doc. A/CN. 4/SER A/ 1967/ Add. 1.

Berridge, G. R., *Talking to the Enemy: How states without 'diplomatic relations' communicate* (Macmillan: Basingstoke, 1994): ch. 6.

Convention on Special Missions, 8 December 1969, United Nations, *Treaty Series*, 1400 (UN: 2005) [www].

Farnsworth, Eric, 'Back to smart diplomacy', *Poder 360*, September 2008 [www].

Fullilove, M., 'All the presidents' men', *Foreign Affairs*, March/April 2005.

James, A., 'Diplomatic relations and contacts', *The British Year Book of International Law 1991* (Clarendon Press: Oxford, 1992).

Johnson, Chalmers, 'The patterns of Japanese relations with China, 1952–1982', *Pacific Affairs*, 59(3), Autumn 1986.

MacMillan, Margaret, *Seize the Hour: When Nixon met Mao* (John Murray: London, 2006): chs 12, 13.

Naland, John K., 'U.S. Special Envoys: A flexible tool', *USIP PeaceBrief*, 102, 15 August 2011 [www].

Roberts, Sir Ivor (ed.), *Satow's Diplomatic Practice*, 6th edn (Oxford University Press: Oxford, 2009): ch. 13.

Ryan, Michael H., 'The status of agents on special mission in customary international law', *Canadian Yearbook of International Law*, 16, 1978.

Wood, Sir Michael, 'Convention on Special Missions, New York, 8 December 1969', *Audiovisual Library of International Law* (United Nations: 2012) [www].

Yearbook of the International Law Commission (1967), II: 344–68 [www].

Young, John W., 'The Wilson government and the Davies peace mission to North Vietnam', *Review of International Studies*, 24, 1998.

Young, John W., *Twentieth-Century Diplomacy: A case study of British practice, 1963–1976* (Cambridge University Press: Cambridge, 2008): ch. 5.

17
Mediation

Mediation has a long and generally honourable record in the history of diplomacy. It is by definition multilateral and can occur, as in the momentous talks on the Middle East at Camp David in September 1978, at the summit. To this extent, it raises questions identical to those discussed in Chapters 11 and 12. But mediation requires separate treatment because it raises separate questions and is so important. It is particularly necessary in long, bitter disputes in which the parties are unable to compromise without seriously jeopardizing the domestic positions of their leaders. It is usually needed the more when the parties retain the most profound distrust of each other's intentions, where cultural differences present an additional barrier to communication, and where at least one of the parties refuses to recognize the other.

The presence of mediation in international conflicts, and also in civil wars, is extensive, although only occasionally does it attract great attention: some form of *official* mediation alone was enjoyed by 255 of the 310 conflicts between 1945 and 1974 (Princen: 5). At the time of writing, it seems even more difficult to find conflicts in which intermediaries – unofficial, as well as official – are not participating in one way or another. What does mediation involve? What motivates the mediator? What are the intermediary's ideal attributes? Should the start of a mediation effort wait until the time for a settlement is ripe? And what are the drawbacks of involving third parties in disputes?

The nature of mediation

Mediation is a special kind of negotiation designed, at the least, to manage and, at the most, to promote the settlement of a conflict, although what might constitute 'success' in such endeavours is inevitably controversial

(Kleiboer: 361–2). In this negotiation a distinctive role is played by a third party; that is, one not directly involved in the dispute in question. It must be substantially *impartial* in the dispute – at least, once the negotiation has started and on the issue actually on the agenda. Certainly, the third party must want a settlement but *any* settlement with which the parties themselves will be happy. As to its role, in a mediation – which is not to be confused with being a 'facilitator' or provider of 'good offices' (Box 17.1) – the third party searches actively for a settlement and, for this reason, is sometimes described as a 'full partner' in the negotiations. Typically, this means drawing up an agenda, calling and chairing negotiating sessions, proposing solutions, and – where the third party is a powerful state – employing threats and promises in order to promote agreement. In short, mediation is the active search for a negotiated settlement to an international or intrastate conflict by an impartial third party.

Box 17.1   Good offices, conciliation, and arbitration

A third party acting as a facilitator or provider of good offices has a more limited role than a mediator, usually involving no more than helping to bring the parties in conflict into direct negotiations. At this point it withdraws, although it will usually remain in the wings in case the talks threaten to founder and it is needed again. In short, its role is limited to the prenegotiation stage. Modern social-psychological versions of this traditional approach emphasize that an enduring settlement is one at which the parties must arrive themselves, and reflect basic attitude changes. It is quite common for a good offices mission to turn into a mediation, but the activities remain distinct. Unfortunately, this does not prevent many mediations from being described as missions of 'good offices', and the separate chapters on 'Good Offices' and 'Mediation' disappeared from the later editions of *Satow's Guide to Diplomatic Practice*. Mediation should also be distinguished from *conciliation*. This is the attempt to resolve a dispute by having it examined in depth by an independent commission of inquiry or conciliation commission. This then offers its recommendations for a settlement, which are non-binding. This had a short heyday in the period between World Wars I and II. *Arbitration* is the same as conciliation, except that the recommendation is binding. It is akin to, but not the same as, judicial settlement.

Providing good offices might be more passive than mediation, but is sometimes its starting point. It is, moreover, by no means just a question of providing the parties with a channel of communications and, perhaps, a secure and comfortable venue for their talks. Ideally, the third party will also assist with the interpretation of messages and be able to show one or both parties how the style, as well as the content, of a message from one party can be made more palatable to the other. It should also provide reassurance to each party that the other means what it says and is sincere in seeking a negotiated settlement. This seems to have been at least one of the roles played by the government of General de Gaulle in the earliest stage of the Sino-American *rapprochement* in 1969. The French leader was a figure who still enjoyed enormous international respect and whose reassurances, in consequence, were trusted (Nixon: 370–4; Hersh: 351–2).

Via the communications they have exchanged through the facilitator, the parties to a conflict might conclude that there is a basis for negotiation between them. In this eventuality, the third party can facilitate this by arranging for a neutral venue for the talks. (This is not essential: in the final Iranian hostages negotiations in 1980, the Americans shuttled between Washington and Algiers, the Algerians shuttled between Algiers, Tehran, and Washington, and the Iranians stayed complacently at home.) This might be on the third party's own territory, or it might be elsewhere. For example, the US-mediated talks between Israel and Syria in early 2000 were held at Sheperdstown in West Virginia, and then shifted to Turkey in 2008 following Ankara's assumption of the role of third party. Talks mediated by the UN are commonly held at its headquarters in New York or Geneva, as in the latter case were those between the Syrian government and 'coalition' of internal factions ranged against it commencing in 2012.

Having brought the parties together, the subsequent role of the third party depends on a variety of factors. These include its own motives, influence, diplomatic skill, and standing with the parties; and whether or not the latter have been brought to a stage where they can bear it to be known that they are talking face to face with their enemies.

A third party might lack significant influence with the rivals and find that, in any case, they are soon prepared to talk directly. This was the case in the Sino-American *rapprochement* in the early 1970s, in which Pakistan had emerged as the most important provider of good offices and then withdrew to the wings. Conversely, the influence of the third party might be considerable, especially if it has the support of other important players. Furthermore, the parties in dispute might not only find it impossible to meet without the face-saving presence of the third party, but also require a constant stiffening of their resolve to continue talking. In such circumstances, third parties – by this point, full-blown mediators – have the chief responsibility for driving the negotiations forwards. To reassure the rivals that calamity will not follow noncompliance with any agreement reached, the mediator may also provide tangible guarantees – a vital feature of American mediation in the Arab–Israeli conflict in the 1970s (Touval 1982: chs 9 and 10). The mediator can make a final contribution to face-saving on the part of one or both of the antagonists by going along with an agreement that suggests, by its packaging, that the concessions it contains have been granted to the mediator rather than to the opponent. In the Tehran hostages negotiations in 1980, for example, the final agreement took the form of a 'Declaration of the Government of the Democratic and Popular Republic of Algeria' – *not* of an 'Agreement between Iran and the United States'.

Different mediators and different motives

Mediators resemble those brokers in the worlds of commerce and finance who act as middlemen between clients in order to turn a profit (*FRUS*: 532; Touval 1982: 321). In early modern Europe, resident ambassadors eagerly sought this role in the expectation of valuable gifts from foreign monarchs grateful for their assistance in helping to bring peace to their conflicts. This was especially good business for ambassadors in Constantinople, where diamond snuff boxes and sable furs often changed hands in the constant cycle of war and peace-making on the frontiers of the Ottoman, Russian, and Austro-Hungarian empires. Today, the nature of the profit sought by mediators still depends on who they are and what kind of dispute they are trying to mediate, but ambassadors seeking the role for personal gain are no longer prominent among them. First, then, who are today's mediators? It is most useful to divide them simply into official and unofficial categories, or into 'track one' and 'track two'. (The attempt to identify additional tracks under the aegis of the concept of 'multitrack diplomacy' trivializes the key distinction between states and the rest, and merely confuses matters.)

Track one

The most important mediators in international relations are states, whether acting singly or collectively, or via the international organizations that are largely their creatures. The major powers, which held a virtual monopoly over mediation until the twentieth century, generally pursue it for one or more of the following main reasons:

- To defuse crises that threaten the global stability, including global economic stability, in which they have such an important stake. This is particularly true of major power mediations in the oil-rich Middle East.

- To sustain or increase their prestige. It is to the interest of a great prince, wrote Callières, to procure peace between quarrelling sovereigns 'by the authority of his mediation. Nothing,' he concluded, 'is more proper to raise the reputation of his power, and to make it respected by all nations' (Callières: 73). This is as true today as when it was written in the early eighteenth century.
- In the case of conflicts within alliances or looser associations of states in which the major powers play leading roles, to maintain their internal solidarity and pre-empt offers of 'assistance' from outside. These have been key factors leading the United States and Britain to interest themselves in the Cyprus dispute, which involves two of the most important members of NATO's southern flank – Turkey and Greece.

Small states such as Algeria, Vatican City (the Holy See), and the Sunni Muslim Gulf state of Qatar, together with middle powers such as Turkey and South Africa, periodically take a hand in international mediation for similar reasons, particularly their interest in *regional* stability and influence. Among the middle powers, however, Switzerland and Austria should be mentioned as special cases by virtue of their permanent neutrality.

Permanent neutrality provides Austria and Switzerland with a motive, as well as an opportunity, to supply good offices and – more so in the case of the former – play the role of mediator as well. This is the need to deflect the free-rider criticism of their neutrality. By their unusual diplomatic exertions in the cause of peace, they are able to take the edge off the complaint that, like non-unionized workers who take the pay rises secured by trade unions without paying subscriptions and standing on picket lines, they enjoy the security provided by NATO without contributing to its military strength.

Following its admission to the EU in 1995, and shortly afterwards NATO's Partnership for Peace, Austria's status of permanent neutrality became questionable, and even Switzerland's has been slightly diluted following its entry into the United Nations (a collective security body) in September 2002. Nevertheless, their reputations still provide them with an outstanding qualification to provide good offices or engage in international mediation. Supporting their positions, Geneva hosts the European headquarters of the UN, and Vienna has a purpose-built International Centre for the use of UN agencies, opened in 1979.

Switzerland and Austria are both frequently employed by states in conflict as protecting powers (see Chapter 15) – which, in practice, is usually a discreet mediating role, although in theory it is not. It is true, nevertheless, that Switzerland has tended to confine itself to the provision of good offices, as in its discreet promotion of low-level contacts between Israel and Syria in 2004–7; this is because it has a particularly purist conception of neutrality, and is aware that genuine mediation involves the kind of active diplomacy that risks the charge of partiality towards one side at the expense of the other. By contrast, Austria has prided itself on its 'active neutrality', especially when it was led by Dr Bruno Kreisky (Box 17.2).

Box 17.2 Dr Bruno Kreisky

Kreisky, a Jewish but anti-Zionist socialist, was Austrian Minister of Foreign Affairs from 1959 until 1966, and federal Chancellor from 1970 until 1983. He took a strong interest in the Arab–Israeli conflict in the mid-1970s, and was the first Western statesman to recognize the PLO, allowing it to open an information office in Vienna. In 1977, he also hosted a famous encounter in the city between South African Prime Minister John Vorster and US Vice-President Walter Mondale, and later visited Tehran on behalf of the Socialist International in an unsuccessful attempt to break the impasse in the hostages crisis at the US embassy (Stadler: 16–17). According to Henry Kissinger, Kreisky was 'shrewd and perceptive ... [and] ... had parlayed his country's formal neutrality into a position of influence beyond its strength, often by interpreting the motives of competing countries to each other' (Kissinger 1979: 1204).

Finally, it is important to note that states also mediate in international and intra-state conflicts under the authority of the charters of the international organizations they have established. As well as the United Nations, these include regional bodies such as the OAS and the AU. With councils dominated by their weightiest members, it is hardly surprising that the interests of the latter should be most influential in shaping the mediations in which these intergovernmental bodies are involved. Nevertheless, their secretariats are not entirely puppets. The secretary-general of the UN, for example, now has some limited capacity to engage in independent mediation. This derives, in part, from the tradition going back to the Middle East crisis of 1956, in which the Security Council gave then Secretary-General Dag Hammarskjöld the right to use his discretion in seeking fulfilment of the purposes and principles of the UN Charter and the Council's decisions (Bailey and Daws: 119–20; de Soto: 350). It is reinforced by the express and implied provisions of the Charter, especially Article 99, which entitles the secretary-general to 'bring to the attention of the Security Council any matter which in his opinion may threaten the maintenance of international peace and security'. Successive secretaries-general have pointed out that they cannot form an opinion of the sort envisaged in this article without the ability to appoint staff, authorize research, make visits, and engage in diplomatic consultations (Bailey and Daws: 111–13). Since 2006, the world body has had a 'mediation support unit', although it remains handicapped by the lack of its own intelligence-gathering arm.

It is because track one mediators stand to earn a profit from brokering a settlement to a conflict – whether in cash or in kind, and whether it arrives indirectly in the shape of increased prestige or directly from the erstwhile antagonists – that states and others have an incentive to dispense with them as soon as possible. Payments for mediation services can be considerable. For example, the Americans found themselves having to 'tilt' to Pakistan in the latter's conflict with India in the early 1970s partly by way of payment of a debt to Pakistani president Yahya Khan for acting as intermediary in the early approaches to Beijing. Using mediators also causes delays in communications between rivals, increases the number of foreigners who share their secrets, and carries the risk that messages might be garbled in transmission. Not surprisingly, as early as mid-1970 both Nixon and Kissinger were anxious 'to get rid of all the middlemen' in their developing relationship with China (Kissinger 1979: 722–3; Hersh: 364). This is rarely easy.

Track two

Mediation by private individuals and NGOs was known in the United States as 'citizen diplomacy' until it was christened 'track two' by the American diplomat Joseph Montville in 1981. It has increased rapidly over recent decades. Prominent among private individuals engaged in these activities have been well-connected businessmen such as the legendary Armand Hammer (Box 17.3) and 'Tiny' Rowland, the former managing director of the mining-finance house Lonrho, whose diplomatic playground was central Africa. Such people are prompted by any mixture of corporate interests, political ambitions, and charitable instincts – and, perhaps, just by a simple desire to show off. Among NGOs, religious bodies have long been important and new ones are constantly emerging. The Quakers, with their strong pacifist leaning, have been energetic in this work since the seventeenth century, while the Rome-based religious order of Sant'Egidio came to prominence for its role in the ending of the civil war in Mozambique in the early 1990s. However, secular NGOs dedicated to conflict prevention and resolution, as it is known in trade jargon, are now also extremely numerous. Sometimes referred to as track two professionals, a good example is the Carter Center, set up by former US President Jimmy Carter.

Box 17.3   Armand Hammer: citizen-diplomat

Armand Hammer, who died in 1990, was an American tycoon whose Russian father had emigrated to the United States in the late nineteenth century. During the Cold War he received much carefully engineered publicity for his attempts as a citizen-diplomat to promote East–West *détente*, although less so for his efforts on behalf of Soviet Jews at the instigation of Israel. Exploiting to the full his huge experience of the Soviet Union, his vast wealth, and his remorseless energy, Hammer seemed to open doors in Moscow that others found closed. He certainly had political achievements to his credit. However, there were many in the US Department of State who did not trust him, and some of his efforts on behalf of East–West *détente* were rendered superfluous by the fact that diplomatic relations between the superpowers were never actually broken off.

Multiparty mediation

So far, and despite occasional hints to the contrary, it has been assumed in this chapter that mediation is an activity carried out by a single party. However, the involvement of more than one mediator – whether in track one or track two – is now so common as probably to be the norm. Multiparty mediation can be simultaneous or sequential, coordinated or uncoordinated.

When two or more parties are trying *simultaneously* to facilitate or mediate the settlement of a conflict but make no attempt to coordinate their activities, it is usually because they are in competition: rival brokers seeking the sole contract. This was the situation in the early stages of the Sino-American *rapprochement* at the beginning of the 1970s. But, sometimes, mediators see numerous advantages in coordinating their actions and, for this purpose, accept the assistance of a self-selecting group of 'friends'. Such groups – which go by a variety of names – usually have four or five members, as in the case of the Contact Groups on Namibia and Bosnia created in 1977 and 1994 respectively, and the 'Quartet' on the Middle East formed in 2002. The more recent Action Group for Syria had considerably more (Box 17.4) – but still far fewer than the Friends of Syria, the membership of which reached a high point of 114 when it met at Marracech in December 2012 (it later boiled down to a 'core group' of 11 members). When there are only two mediators, as for example in the original UN/EU mission to broker a settlement in Bosnia, the designation 'joint mediation' is more common. A joint effort of this sort between the UN and the regional organization with the closest interest in the dispute concerned was the model proposed by the then UN secretary-general.

Box 17.4 Action Group for Syria

This group was formed in the middle of 2012, following the appointment in February of former UN Secretary-General Kofi Annan as Joint Special Envoy of the UN and the League of Arab States for Syria. It was a response to the worsening crisis in the country, the absence of a consensus in the Security Council on what to do about it and, in consequence of this, the rapid emergence of a very large anti-Assad ginger group of chiefly Western and Gulf states called the Friends of Syria. On 30 June 2012, when the much smaller but politically more broad-based Action Group announced itself in the 'Geneva Communiqué', it comprised the secretaries-general of the UN and the Arab League; the foreign ministers of China, France, Russia, UK, USA, Turkey, Iraq (as chair of the Arab League summit), Kuwait (as chair of the Arab League's council of foreign ministers), and Qatar (as chair of the Arab follow-up committee on Syria of the Arab League); and the EU high representative for foreign and security policy. The Action Group was chaired by the joint envoy of the UN and the Arab League. (In this role, Kofi Annan was replaced in August by Lakhdar Brahimi, who endured it until May 2014.) The glaring absence from membership of this group was Iran.

As for *sequential* multiparty mediation, this is predicated on the notion that conflicts have life cycles with levels of violence that rise and then fall, and that certain kinds of mediator are more appropriate to one stage in this cycle than another. Only one mediator is active in the conflict at any one time, but – as in a relay race – makes a deliberate 'handover' to one thought more suitable to the new stage considered imminent (Crocker et al.: 10). This sort of mediation was seen in Haiti in the early 1990s, where responsibility started with the OAS, then passed to the UN, and finally – when the threat of real force seemed necessary – came to rest with the United States (McDougall). It is important to stress, however, that not all mediations in which different parties take turns in trying to settle a conflict are examples of this species of multiparty mediation. There is, for example, no evidence that the attempt to mediate a settlement between Israel and Syria – first by the United States in 2000, then by Switzerland in 2004–7, and finally by Turkey in 2008 – was in any way orchestrated.

The ideal mediator

The attributes of the ideal mediator vary according to the nature of a conflict. For example:

- The (Roman Catholic) Holy See is, in principle, well suited to the mediation of a conflict between two Catholic states, provided the exertion of material power over them is not required.
- Small states are appropriate to conflicts involving one or more major powers, since threats by a third party in such circumstances would probably be at best useless and at worst dangerous – and deferring to a small state's suggestions is easily presented as an act of grace by a major power, thereby enhancing, rather than diminishing, its prestige.
- The UN often seems best for the mediation of conflicts that appear intractable, but are of relatively marginal concern to the major powers.
- Track two bodies are particularly suited to mediations in which at least one of the parties believes that track one intervention would give too much legitimacy to its rival, or in which the major powers favour progress but, for one reason or another, cannot risk direct involvement themselves.
- As for the major powers, and at the risk of appearing tautological, they are usually the most suitable to the mediation of conflicts that are amenable only to power.

The ideal mediator also appears to vary with the stage of the conflict cycle – as remarked in the discussion of sequential multiparty mediation – and with the stage of the mediation. It is a common observation that a track two party can have a key role in prenegotiations, but must stand down in favour of a more muscular track one party once the mediation is properly launched. This is an oversimplification, as the Oslo channel (which produced the historic agreement between Israel and the PLO in September 1993) and other mediations have demonstrated. Be that as it may, whatever the nature of the conflict or the stage it has reached, all mediators should share certain characteristics in addition to routine diplomatic skills, which include the ability to generate 'creative formulas' (Crocker 1999: 243).

First, mediation, by definition, requires a third party that is impartial on the issue of the moment, even if – generally speaking – it does not hold the parties to the conflict in equal affection. Impartiality enables the third party to be trusted by both parties. This is important if they are to believe that the mediator will convey messages between them without distortion, that its reassurances about their mutual sincerity are well founded, and that their confidences will be kept. It is also important if they are to believe that any compromises it proposes will be of equal benefit to both, and that it will implement any guarantees if this is required by any defaulting on the settlement achieved – irrespective of which party is guilty. It is true that a third party with close ties to only one of the antagonists might be attractive as a mediator to the other because the role will require the third party to draw away somewhat from its traditional relationship. This can also strengthen the hand of such a mediator, once the mediation has started, by enabling it to play on the fears of desertion of the one and the hopes of consolidating a new friendship on the part of the other (Touval 1982). The fact remains, however, that the party not hitherto enjoying friendly relations with the third party is only likely to accept it as a mediator on two conditions. It must believe, first, that it will be impartial on the issue actually on the table and, second, that it is able to deliver its traditional friend. It was on these conditions that the Egyptians accepted American mediation with the Israelis in the late 1970s. The notion of a biased intermediary (Ross: 228–9; Touval 1982: 10–16) is a contradiction in terms.

Second, there is the value to the mediator of influence or more effective power relative to the parties. It is unlikely that this will be of great importance if the 'mediation' is confined to the provision of good offices, provided ripeness does not need engineering. However, it is clearly valuable – possibly vital – to a genuine mediation if the parties remain uncertain as to whether it is in their interests to settle; it is even more so if it is necessary to provide guarantees against the consequences of any subsequent non-compliance with a settlement's terms. Mediator influence has many sources. It can derive from a record of past success and the lack of alternative mediators acceptable to both parties at a critical point, which seems to have helped Algeria during the Tehran embassy hostages negotiations in 1980. It can even derive from spiritual authority, as in the case of the Holy See. It seems most effective, however, when it is based on the ability to manipulate tangible rewards and sanctions, including increased or reduced levels of economic and military aid. Thus, Jimmy Carter said that he was wary of 'buying peace' in the Camp David negotiations between Egypt and Israel – but he did. Israel received from Washington US$3 billion in concessional loans to fund the building of new airfields in the Negev to compensate for the ones they would have to surrender in Sinai (Quandt: 241); while by 1980–81, the year following signature of the Egypt–Israel Peace Treaty, Egypt was the top recipient of US official development assistance (Berridge 1997: table 7.2).

Whatever the source of the mediator's influence relative to the parties, it will also be increased to the extent that it is allied to that of other states or track two bodies pushing in the same direction. For example, America's influence in the Angola/Namibia negotiations in 1988 was clearly enhanced by the support of a considerable list of states – among them the Soviet Union, Britain, Portugal, and the African Frontline States – together with members of the UN and OAU secretariats. If, as in this case, the external patrons of the parties to the conflict are all on the list, the latters' game is usually up. (This is why it was a serious mistake to exclude Iran from the Action Group on Syria.) The parties to the conflict will also find the cost of any subsequent default raised because the ranks of those directly affronted by it will have been multiplied. In principle, maximizing power relative to the parties can be achieved by multiparty mediation in the form of a contact group but, in practice, the disadvantages of this form of mediation tend to weaken it, as we shall see later. Track two bodies usually acknowledge that their own efforts are most effective when conducted in support of those of track one, although such cooperation can be difficult to organise.

Third, the ideal mediator should be able to give continuous attention to a conflict, for intractable conflicts are not settled overnight. Continuous involvement produces familiarity with the problem and key personalities, enables relationships of personal trust to develop that reinforce calculations of interest, and fosters a routine that reduces the likelihood of false expectations being generated. It also makes possible procedural breakthroughs, and even breakthroughs of principle – which, in turn, make seizing a propitious moment for settlement that much easier. This is where track two diplomats and the secretariats of international organizations, notably the UN, tend to have the edge over states, especially in the mediation of disputes where major power interest is, at most, moderate. This applies even to stable political regimes like that of the United States. Such states might have foreign ministries capable of pursuing consistent policies over long periods, but electoral cycles tend to condemn their mediations to being episodic rather than continuous affairs. This has been a marked feature of American mediation in the Middle East.

Finally, the ideal mediator should have a strong incentive to obtain a settlement. Different kinds of mediator, as already noted, tend to have different motives, but none of them is indifferent to the implications of the role for their prestige – and this argues for a lead mediator, rather than a contact group, albeit one informally assisted by 'friends'. Aside from the fact that this arrangement speeds up and simplifies decision-making, it is uniquely energizing because it guarantees all of the credit for success, and – barring a damaging change in circumstances that no one could foresee – all of the blame for failure. It is probably no accident, therefore, that the real breakthroughs tend to come when one of the members of a contact group seizes the reins of the mediation, frees itself of the need to work within a consensus, and puts its prestige directly on the line. This is well illustrated by the success of American mediation in south-western Africa in the late 1980s subsequent to Washington's withdrawal from the Western Contact Group on Namibia. It is also demonstrated by its even more spectacular success at Dayton, Ohio, in November 1995, following President Clinton's decision to take the lead in Bosnian diplomacy from the Bosnia Contact Group.

In sum, the attributes of the ideal mediator are one thing; the attributes of the ideal form of mediation are another. Single mediation is better than mediation via the divided responsibility of a contact group; but, in some conflicts, an orchestrated *sequence* of different, single mediators is better than both. In all cases, the support of 'friends' is usually indispensable.

The ripe moment

Provided there is to hand an ideal mediator appropriate to a particular dispute, mediation is most likely to succeed in the circumstance in which any negotiation is most likely to succeed. This is when the antagonists have both arrived at the conclusion that they will probably be better off with a settlement than without one – when, in other words, the situation is 'ripe' for a settlement. (This can be engineered by a prospective mediator, especially if it is a major power; for example, by manipulating the flow of arms to a client that is a party to the dispute.) But does this mean that no move to launch a mediation should be contemplated before this point is reached? In fact, the doctrine of the ripe moment should not be interpreted too strictly.

It is certainly true that the attempt to get a mediation going before the time is propitious will probably fail, especially if it is ambitious and conducted with much fanfare. It can also be counter-productive: the leaders and domestic groups on which political support for negotiations rests will be at least temporarily discredited, the view that the conflict is intractable will be strengthened, and one or both of the parties to the conflict might take provocative measures in reaction to the failure. On the other hand, if the mediation is initially low key (track two, for example) and its goals modest, useful advances on procedure, in the building of trust, and even on broad principle can be made that will make seizing the opportunity that much easier when the time really is ripe for substantive negotiations. Besides, diagnosing 'ripe moments' is not exactly a scientific exercise, and it is not always possible to tell if these circumstances exist until they are put to the test; that is, by negotiation.

Having secured the agreement of the parties to collaborate with its efforts, the mediator needs to judge whether it is best to seek a comprehensive solution to the dispute, or approach it in a step-by-step manner (see Chapter 3); and then employ a judicious combination of carrots and sticks, together with deadlines and press manipulation in order to sustain diplomatic momentum (see Chapter 4). A fair share of luck is also needed. This is because a local incident or change of regime in one of the parties can sour the atmosphere at a critical juncture, while the eruption of a major international crisis can, at best, distract attention from the dispute in question and, at worst, seriously alter the calculation of interests on which one or more of the parties – including the mediator – had previously agreed to proceed.

Summary

International mediation is the active search for a negotiated settlement to an international or intrastate conflict by a third party. Mediators come in all shapes and sizes, as well as singly and – more often than not – in groups. Their ideal attributes vary chiefly with the conflict in question and the stage of the mediation. However, all should be perceived as impartial while playing their role; they should also have influence relative to the parties, the ability to devote sustained attention to the dispute, and a strong incentive to achieve a settlement. This incentive will usually be greater if one mediator has sole responsibility, not least because its prestige will be at stake. Mediators are brokers looking for profit; the lure of direct talks between the hostile parties is, therefore, usually strong.

Further reading

Action Group for Syria Final Communiqué 30 June 2012 [www].
Bailey, Sydney D. and Sam Daws, *The Procedure of the UN Security Council*, 3rd edn (Clarendon Press: Oxford, 1998): ch. 3 (1), 'Secretary-General'.

Bercovitch, J., 'International mediation and intractable conflict', January 2004 [www].

Berridge, G. R. (ed.), *Diplomatic Classics: Selected texts from Commynes to Vattel* (Palgrave Macmillan: Basingstoke, 2004): index references to 'mediation'.

Christopher, W. and others, *American Hostages in Iran: The conduct of a crisis* (Yale University Press: New Haven, CT, 1985).

Crocker, C. A., Fen Osier Hampson, and Pamela Aall (eds), *Herding Cats: Multiparty mediation in a complex world* (US Institute of Peace Press: Washington, DC, 1999).

Doucet, Lyse, 'Troubled path to talks with Taliban', *BBC News*, 20 June 2013 [www]

Holbrooke, Richard, *To End a War* (Random House: New York, 1998).

Kleiboer, Marieke, 'Understanding success and failure of international mediation', *Journal of Conflict Resolution*, 40(2), June 1996 [www]. A lengthy trailer for the book; very acute.

Kleiboer, Marieke, *The Multiple Realities of International Mediation* (Lynne Rienner: Boulder, CO, 1998).

Lindsley, L., 'The Beagle Channel settlement: Vatican mediation resolves a century old dispute', *Journal of Church and State*, 29(3), 1987.

Mitchell, George J., *Making Peace* (Heinemann: London, 1999): on the Good Friday agreement.

Quandt, W. B., *Camp David: Peacemaking and politics* (Brookings Institution: Washington, DC, 1986).

Ross, Dennis, *Statecraft: And how to restore America's standing in the world* (Farrar, Strauss: New York, 2007): chs 10 and 11.

Smith, Amy L. and David R. Smock, *Managing a Mediation Process* (USIP: Washington, DC, 2008) [www].

Touval, S., *The Peace Brokers: Mediators in the Arab–Israeli conflict, 1948–1979* (Princeton University Press: Princeton, NJ, 1982).

United Nations Department of Political Affairs, 'Mediation Support' [www].

United Nations, *Guidance for Effective Mediation* (UN: New York, 2012) [www].

USIP, *The Peacemaker's Toolkit* [www]. This extremely valuable site provides free PDF downloads of numerous 'best practice' handbooks on key aspects of mediation, including the timing of mediation, working with 'groups of friends', and track two.

Whitfield, Teresa, *Working with Groups of Friends* (USIP: Washington, DC, 2010) [www]. Clear and authoritative.

Wilkenfeld, J., K. Young, D. Quinn, and V. Asal, *Mediating International Crises* (Routledge: London, 2005).

Conclusion: The Counter-Revolution in Diplomatic Practice

In examining the different functions of diplomacy and how they are pursued, this book has traced in some detail what elsewhere I have called a 'counter-revolution in diplomatic practice' (Berridge 2005). As a broad trend, this rejuvenation of some of the key features of traditional diplomacy has gone unnoticed – partly because it has been masked by the attachment of new labels to old procedures, and partly because the novel has a greater fascination than the tried and tested. For those who care to look, however, the evidence of this counter-revolution is unmistakable.

There has emerged a quiet, almost resigned acceptance that resident embassies are not the anachronism they were thought to be in the 1960s and 1970s. Instead, they are still the state's first line of defence abroad; daily integrated more into policy-making by secure, instant communications; the key vehicle for routine negotiations; essential support to special envoys; and nearest thing to a mind-reader bolted onto the side of a host government. With the great increase in the flow of people across frontiers, the value of consular posts has also been rediscovered, and the old institution of the honorary consul, or consular agent, is flourishing once more. Propaganda – with which diplomats have often been uneasy, but with which they came to terms in the middle of the twentieth century – has been reinvented, and even returned to war-time proportions; for governments to describe this as 'public diplomacy' and allege that it is something new is understandable but should be seen as a rebranding exercise designed to pull the wool over our eyes. As the importance of coordinating foreign activities – among them, propaganda – has been reasserted, so, too, has the foreign ministry bounced back, or a functionally equivalent body placed over its shell. Summitry has also played its part in the counter-

266

revolution, for its serial – as opposed to its *ad hoc* – form has become by far its most important; this, as with the new respect for the resident mission, signifies further recognition of the value of *continuous* contact between states – a cardinal principle of the old, French system of diplomacy. Greater reliance on special envoys is a return to a medieval reflex. In multilateral diplomacy, the twentieth century's experiment with taking decisions by voting after a public debate has been liquidated by the rejuvenation of secret negotiation, among the many benefits of which is a working Great Power concert called the UN Security Council. As for the so-called 'new actors in diplomacy' – in particular, international NGOs – they are neither new nor engaged fully in diplomacy, a professional activity akin to the law or medicine: they are either free-booting amateurs, or para-diplomats with valuable but limited usefulness and no special immunities; in both cases, they long pre-date the appearance of the diplomatist. The main point here, though, is that the more experienced track two 'diplomats' now appreciate that to make a real contribution to diplomacy they must work with, and not parallel to, the professionals.

It is true that the counter-revolution in diplomatic practice I have described is, fortunately, only a partial one. For example, in the art of negotiation, there is now more manipulation of publicity to assist this all-important activity, more informality in the packaging of any agreements issuing from it, and – in following them up – far greater reliance on a variety of devices (some new) for their expert and systematic monitoring. As for change in the modes of diplomacy, consensus decision-making contains a few new tricks as well as old ones, and thereby represents a new version of secret negotiation in multilateral diplomacy; summitry has been extensively institutionalized; nationally staffed interests sections have become the norm; special envoys are now transported so frequently and quickly that this change in degree might be said to represent a change in kind; and telecommunication between governments at all levels has been truly revolutionized. In other words, planes carrying VIPs have not been grounded, the tablets of diplomats have not been dropped into bins, the secure telephones of other government departments and garrulous presidents have not been disconnected, and twittering – unlike birdsong in this respect, as also in its lack of harmony – has not got into the habit of diminishing as dawn passes into morning. In short, there *is* innovation in diplomacy; indeed, there has already been a great deal of it. But innovation is one thing; the complete transformation often claimed as a fact or heralded as imminent is quite another.

What we have witnessed in recent years is not the complete transformation of diplomacy but, rather, the more – occasionally less – intelligent application of new technology and new devices to support tried and tested methods, with the added advantage that this has helped to integrate the many poor and weak states into the world diplomatic system. What we have now is neither an old nor a new diplomacy but, instead, a blend of the two, which has produced a mature diplomacy. It is also one fortified by a respected legal regime.

This development is fortunate because, while power remains dispersed between states – while there remains, in other words, a states-system – international diplomacy, bilateral or multilateral, direct or indirect, at the summit or below, remains essential. If anything alone makes this glaringly obvious, it is the inventiveness that has gone into preserving resident diplomacy when diplomatic relations do not exist. Only professional diplomacy can continuously foster pursuit of interests held in common, and settle remaining arguments over interests that conflict. If violence breaks out, diplomacy remains essential if the worst excesses are to be limited and the ground prepared against the inevitable day of exhaustion and revised ambition.

References

Acheson, D. (1969) *Present at the Creation: My years in the state department* (Norton: New York).

Adelman, K. L. (1989) *The Great Universal Embrace: Arms Summitry – a skeptic's view* (Simon & Schuster: New York).

Advisory Committee on Modernising the Diplomatic Service (2014) *Modernising Dutch Diplomacy: Progress report, final report* (May) [www].

Aid, M. (2007) 'Eavesdroppers of the Kremlin: KGB sigint during the Cold War', in Karl de Leeuw and Jan Bergstra (eds), *The History of Information Security: A comprehensive handbook* (Elsevier: Amsterdam).

Albright, David and Christina Walrond (2013) 'Iran's critical capability in 2014: Verifiably stopping Iran from increasing the number and quality of its centrifuges', *ISIS Report*, 17 July [www].

Albright, Madeleine (2003) *Madam Secretary: A memoir* (Macmillan: London).

Alexander, Michael (2005) *Managing the Cold War: A view from the front line*, ed. and introduced by Keith Hamilton (RUSI: London).

Algosaibi, G. A. (1999) *Yes, (Saudi) Minister! A Life in Administration* (London Centre of Arab Studies: London).

Al-Jazeera (2012) 'Kofi Annan proposes Syria "unity government"', 28 June [www].

Al-Monitor (2014) 'Study recommends US interests section in Tehran', 18 February [www].

Andrew, Christopher (1985) *Secret Service: The making of the British intelligence community* (Heinemann: London).

Andrew, Christopher and Vasili Mitrokhin (1999) *The Mitrokhin Archive: The KGB in Europe and the West* (Penguin: London).

Arndt, Richard T., *The First Resort of Kings: American cultural diplomacy in the twentieth century* (Potomac Books: Washington, DC, 2005).

Ashrawi, Hanan (1995) *This Side of Peace: a personal account* (Simon & Schuster: New York).

Aurisch, K. L. (1989) 'The art of preparing a multilateral conference', *Negotiation Journal*, 5(3).

Australian Government: Department of Foreign Affairs and Trade (2005) 'Australia China FTA negotiations: First round of negotiations', 26 May [www].

Australian Government: Department of Foreign Affairs and Trade (2009) 'New Australian Embassy, Jakarta, Indonesia', June [www].

Australian Government: Department of Foreign Affairs and Trade (2011) 'Proposed construction of a new Australian Embassy complex including Chancery and Head of Mission residence in Bangkok, Thailand', September [www].

Bailey, S. D. and S. Daws (1998) *The Procedure of the UN Security Council*, 3rd edn (Clarendon Press: Oxford).

Baker, James A. (1999) 'The road to Madrid', in C. A. Crocker, F. O. Hampson, and P. R. Aall (eds), *Herding Cats: Multiparty mediation in a complex world* (USIP: Washington, DC).

Ball, G. (1976) *Diplomacy for a Crowded World* (Bodley Head: London).

Bank of England (n.d.) 'Memorandum of Understanding: International organisations' [www].

Barder, Brian (2014) *What Diplomats Do: The life and work of diplomats* (Rowman & Littlefield: Lanham).

BBC Monitoring Scheme (2013) March [www].

Beer, Lawrence W. (1969) 'Some dimensions of Japan's present and potential relations with Communist China', *Asian Survey*, 9(3), March.

Bergus, D. C. (1990) 'U.S. diplomacy under the flag of Spain, Cairo, 1967–74', in D. D. Newsom (ed.), *Diplomacy Under a Foreign Flag* (Hurst: London).

Berridge, G. R. (1987) *The Politics of the South Africa Run: European shipping and Pretoria* (Clarendon Press: Oxford)

Berridge, G. R. (1989) 'Diplomacy and the Angola/Namibia Accords', *International Affairs*, 65(3).

Berridge, G. R. (1991) *Return to the UN: UN diplomacy in regional conflicts* (Macmillan: Basingstoke).

Berridge, G. R. (1994) *Talking to the Enemy: How states without 'diplomatic relations' communicate* (Macmillan: Basingstoke).

Berridge, G. R. (1997) *International Politics: States, power and conflict since 1945*, 3rd edn (Prentice Hall/Harvester Wheatsheaf: Hemel Hempstead).

Berridge, G. R. (2009) *British Diplomacy in Turkey, 1583 to the Present: A study in the evolution of the resident embassy* (Martinus Nijhoff: Leiden).

Berridge, G. R. (ed.) (2004) *Diplomatic Classics: Selected texts from Commynes to Vattel* (Palgrave Macmillan: Basingstoke).

Berridge, G. R. (2005) 'The counter-revolution in diplomatic practice', *Quaderni di Scienza Politica*, 1, April.

Berridge, G. R. (2012a) 'The British Interests Section in Kampala, January 2012' [www].

Berridge, G. R. (2012b) *Embassies in Armed Conflict* (Continuum: New York).

Berridge, G. R. (2013a) *A Diplomatic Whistleblower in the Victorian Era: The life and writings of E. C. Grenville-Murray* [www].

Berridge, G. R. (2013b) 'A weak diplomatic hybrid: U.S. Special Mission Benghazi, 2011–12', January [www].

Binnendijk, H. (ed.) (1987) *National Negotiating Styles* (Center for the Study of Foreign Affairs, Foreign Service Institute, US Department of State: Washington, DC).

Blair, Tony (2010) *A Journey* (Hutchinson: London).

Blix, Hans (2004) *Disarming Iraq* (Bloomsbury: London).

Boutros-Ghali, B. (1999) *Unvanquished: A U.S.–U.N. saga* (I.B. Tauris: London).

Bower, Tom (1995) *The Perfect English Spy: Sir Dick White and the secret war, 1935–90* (Heinemann: London).

Brahimi, L. (2013) Notes to Correspondents: 'Transcript of press conference by Joint Special Representative for Syria (JSRS) Lakhdar Brahimi', Geneva, 20 December (United Nations) [www].

Browne, N. W. (ca. 1980) 'British policy on Iran, 1974–1978' (FCO) [www].

Bull, H. (1977) *The Anarchical Society: A study of order in world politics* (Macmillan: Basingstoke).

Busk, Sir Douglas (1967) *The Craft of Diplomacy: How to run a diplomatic service* (Praeger: New York).

Butler Review (2004) *Review of Intelligence on Weapons of Mass Destruction. Report of a Committee of Privy Counsellors* (The Stationery Office: London), HC 898 [www].

Buzan, B. (1981) 'Negotiating by consensus: Developments in technique at the United Nations Conference on the Law of the Sea', *American Journal of International Law*, 72(2).

Callières, F. de (1994) *The Art of Diplomacy*, ed. by H. M. A. Keens-Soper and K. Schweizer (Leicester University Press: Leicester).

Campbell, Duncan 'How embassy eavesdropping works' [www].

Carter, J. (1982) *Keeping Faith: Memoirs of a president* (Bantam: New York).

Carter of Coles, Lord (2005) *Public Diplomacy Review* [www].

Chaplin, Edward (2009) Evidence of to the Iraq Inquiry, 1 December [www].

Chesterman, Simon (2005–6) 'The spy who came in from the Cold War: Intelligence and international law', *Michigan Journal of International Law*, 27.

China FTA Network [www].

Church Committee (1976) *Foreign and Military Intelligence. Book I. Final Report of the Select Committee to Study Governmental Operations with respect to Intelligence Activities. United States Senate* (U.S. Government Printing Office: Washington) [www].

Cohen, R. (1987) *Theatre of Power: The art of diplomatic signalling* (Longman: London).

Cohen, R. (1997) *Negotiating Across Cultures: International communication in an interdependent world*, rev. edn (US Institute of Peace Press: Washington, DC).

Coles, J. (2000) *Making Foreign Policy: A certain idea of Britain* (Murray: London).

Collett, Peter, *The Book of Tells: How to read people's minds from their actions* (Transworld: London, 2003).

Cordesman, Anthony H. (2012) 'The death of Ambassador Chris Stevens, the need for "expeditionary diplomacy," and the real lessons for U.S. diplomacy', *CSIS*, 11 October [www].

Cowper-Coles, Sherard (2011) *Cables from Kabul: The inside story of the West's Afghanistan campaign* (HarperPress: London).

Cowper-Coles, Sherard (2012) *Ever the Diplomat: Confessions of a Foreign Office mandarin* (HarperPress: London).

Cradock, P. (1994) *Experiences of China* (Murray: London).

Crocker, C. A. (1999) 'Peacemaking in Southern Africa: The Namibia–Angola settlement of 1988', in Crocker, C. A., F. O. Hampson, and P. R. Aall (eds), *Herding Cats: Multiparty mediation in a complex world* (USIP: Washington, DC).

Crocker, C. A., F. O. Hampson, and P. R. Aall (eds) (1999) *Herding Cats: Multiparty mediation in a complex world* (USIP: Washington, DC).

Cross, C. T. (1999) *Born a Foreigner: A memoir of the American presence in Asia* (Rowman & Littlefield: Lanham, MD).

Cull, Nicholas J. (2006) '"Public diplomacy" before Gullion: The evolution of a phrase', USC Center on Public Diplomacy [www].

Cull, Nicholas J. (2007) 'Public diplomacy: Seven lessons for its future from its past' [www].

Dalton, Robert E. (1994) 'International documents of a non-legally binding character', US Department of State, Memorandum, 18 March [www].

Daugherty, William J. (2004) *Executive Secrets: Covert action and the presidency* (University of Kentucky Press: Lexington, KY).

Deeks, Ashley S. (2008) 'Avoiding transfers to torture', *Council on Foreign Relations Special Report*, no. 35, June.

de Soto, A. (1999) 'Ending violent conflict in El Salvador', in Crocker, C. A., F. O. Hampson, and P. R. Aall (eds), *Herding Cats: Multiparty mediation in a complex world* (USIP: Washington, DC).

Dickie, J. (1992) *Inside the Foreign Office* (Chapman & Hall: London).

Dunham, Lawrence [US] Assistant Chief of Protocol (2002) Remarks by at the Consular Corps General Meeting, Las Vegas, 14 March [www].

Dunn, D. H. (ed.) (1996) *Diplomacy at the Highest Level: The evolution of international summitry* (Macmillan: Basingstoke).

Edwards, R. D. (1994) *True Brits: Inside the Foreign Office* (BBC Books: London).

Erdos, Chris, 'Heart of darkness', *Foreign Service Journal*, 85(4), April 2008 [www].

EU (2014) *Factsheet on E3/EU +3 nuclear negotiations with Iran*, EU14–020EN, 17 January, Brussels [www].

Evans, Gareth (2013) 'Commission diplomacy', in Andrew F. Cooper, Jorge Heine, and Ramesh Thaku (eds), *The Oxford Handbook of Modern Diplomacy* (Oxford University Press: Oxford, 2013).

FAC (1998–9) *Sixth Report* [www].

FAC (1999) *Minutes of evidence*, 25 May [www].

FAC (2001) *Minutes of evidence*, 24 April [www].

FAC (2007) *First Report*, 7 November [www].

FAC (2011) 'The role of the FCO in UK government', *Seventh Report of Session 2010–12, Volume I*, 12 May, HC 665 [www].

FAC (2013) *Fourth Report: The FCO's human rights work in 2012*, 8 October [www].

FCO (2011) *Consular Strategy 2010–13*, 4 August [www].

Fennessy, J. G. (1976) 'The 1975 Convention on the Representation of States in their Relations with International Organizations of a Universal Character', *American Journal of International Law*, 70(1).

Franck, T. M. and E. Weisband (1979) *Foreign Policy by Congress* (Oxford University Press: New York).

Fretwell, John (1996) interview *BDOHP* [www].

FRUS, 1955–1957, Vol. 11, China (1986) (US Government Printing Office: Washington, DC), Robert Murphy, memo of 29 April 1955.

Fullilove, M. (2005) 'All the presidents' men', *Foreign Affairs*, March/April: 13–18.

G20 Leaders' Communiqué (2014) Brisbane Summit, 15–16 November [www].

Giovannucci, Daniele, 'National trade promotion organizations: Ttheir role and function' (The World Bank Group: 2013) [www].

Glennon, M. J. (1983) 'The Senate role in treaty ratification', *American Journal of International Law*, 77.

Gore-Booth, P. (1974) *With Great Truth and Respect* (Constable: London).

Gore-Booth, Lord (ed.) (1979) *Satow's Guide to Diplomatic Practice*, 5th edn (Longman: London).

Gotlieb, A. (1991) *I'll be with you in a minute, Mr. Ambassador: The education of a Canadian diplomat in Washington* (University of Toronto Press: Toronto).

Greenstock, Jeremy (2004) Interview *BDOHP* [www].

Grenville, J. A. S. and B. Wasserstein (1987) *The Major International Treaties since 1945: A history and guide with texts* (Methuen: London).

Guicciardini, Francesco (1890) *Counsels and Reflections*, trans. by N. H. Thomson (Kegan Paul: London), first published ca. 1530.

Haass, R. N. and M. Indyk (2009) 'Beyond Iraq: A new U.S. strategy for the Middle East', *Foreign Affairs*, January/February.

Hankey, Lord (1946) *Diplomacy by Conference: Studies in public affairs, 1920–1946* (Benn: London) [www].

Harrison, S. (1988) 'Inside the Afghan talks', *Foreign Policy*, Fall.

Hawley, Donald (2007) interview *BDOHP* [www].

HCPP (1943) *Proposals for the Reform of the Foreign Service*, Cmd. 6420.

HCPP (1954) *Summary of the Report of the Independent Committee of Enquiry into the Overseas Information Services*, April, Cmd. 9138 ['Drogheda Report'].

HCPP (1964) *Miscellaneous No. 5 (1964). Report of the Committee on Representational Services Overseas appointed by The Prime Minister under the Chairmanship of Lord Plowden 1962–63*, Feb., Cmnd. 2276 ['Plowden Report'].

HCPP (1969) *Miscellaneous No. 24 (1969). Report of the Review Committee on Overseas Representation 1968–1969. Chairman: Sir Val Duncan*, July, Cmnd. 4107 ['Duncan Report'].

HCPP (1987) *Fifth Report from the Defence Committee, Session 1986–87. Defence Commitments in the South Atlantic. Report, together with the Proceedings of the Committee, Minutes of Evidence and Appendices*, 13 May, 408.

HCPP (1993) *Memorandum by the FCO: Taiwan. FAC, Relations between the UK and China in the period up to and beyond 1997: Mins. of Evidence*, 14 July, 842-i.

Hearings before the Committee on Foreign Relations United States Senate Eighty-Eighth Congress First Session Part I February 4 and 6, 1963: Activities of Nondiplomatic Representatives of Foreign Principals in the United States (1963) (US Government Printing Office: Washington, DC).

Henderson, N. (1994) *Mandarin: The diaries of an ambassador, 1969–1982* (Weidenfeld & Nicolson: London).

Henkin, L. (1979) *How Nations Behave: Law and foreign policy*, 2nd edn (Columbia University Press: New York).

Herman, Michael (1996) *Intelligence Power in Peace and War* (Cambridge University Press: Cambridge).

Herman, Michael (2011) 'What difference did it make?' *Intelligence and National Security*, 26(6), December.

Hersh, S. M. (1983) *Kissinger: The price of power* (Faber: London).

Hoare, J. E. (2007) 'Diplomacy in the East', in Paul Sharp and Geoffrey Wiseman (eds), *The Diplomatic Corps as an Institution of International Society* (Palgrave Macmillan: Basingstoke).

Hoare, Sir Samuel (1946) *Ambassador on Special Mission* (Collins: London).

Hocking, B. and D. Spence (eds) (2002) *Foreign Ministries in the European Union: Integrating diplomats* (Palgrave Macmillan: Basingstoke).

Hoffacker, Lewis, 'Murder in an embassy, Part I – "I am not losing my mind", Moments in U.S. Diplomatic History [www].

Hoffacker, Lewis, 'Murder in an embassy, Part II – Paranoid Psychotic or Faked Insanity? Moments in U.S. Diplomatic History [www].

Home Office (2011) *Review of Counter-Terrorism and Security Powers. Review Findings and Recommendations*, Cm 8004, January [www].

Horne, Alexander, Melanie Gower and Joanna Dawson (2014) 'Deportation of individuals who may face a risk of torture', *Standard Note*: SN/HA/4151, House of Commons Library, 10 February [www].

House of Representatives (1989) *Hearing before the Subcommittee on Asian and Pacific Affairs of the Committee on Foreign Affairs, 28 July, 1988: The implications of establishing reciprocal interests sections with Vietnam* (US Government Printing Office: Washington, DC).

ILC (1960) *Yearbook of the International Law Commission*, Volume I (UN Publications).

ILC (1961) *Yearbook of the International Law Commission*, Volume I (UN Publications).

ILC (n.d.) 'Consular intercourse and immunities' [ch. 2], in *Report ... to the General Assembly on its work, 1 May–7 July 1961* [www].

ISC (1999) *Sierra Leone*, April, Cm 4309 [www].

ISC (2009) *Annual Report 2007–2008*, March, Cm 7542 [www].

ISC (2010a) *Annual Report 2008–2009*, March, Cm 7807 [www].

ISC (2010b) *Annual Report 2009–2010*, March, Cm 7844 [www].

ISC (2011) *Annual Report 2010–2011*, July, Cm 8114 [www].

ISC (2012) *Annual Report 2011–2012*, July, Cm 8403 [www].

ISC (2013) *Annual Report 2012–2013*, 10 July, HC 547 [www].

James, A. M. (1992) 'Diplomatic relations and contacts', *The British Yearbook of International Law 1991* (Clarendon Press: Oxford).

Jazbec, Milan (2001) *The Diplomacies of New Small States: The case of Slovenia with some comparison from the Baltics* (Ashgate: Aldershot).

Jeffery, Keith (2010) *MI6: The history of the Secret Intelligence Service, 1909–1949* (Bloomsbury: London).

Kear, S. (2001) 'Diplomatic innovation: Nasser and the origins of the interests section', *Diplomacy and Statecraft*, 12(3), September.

Keeley, R. V. (1995) 'Crisis avoidance: Shutting down Embassy Kampala, 1973', in J. G. Sullivan (ed.), *Embassies under Siege* (Brassey's for the Institute for the Study of Diplomacy: Washington, DC).

Kennan, G. F. (1967) *Memoirs, 1925–1950* (Hutchinson: London).

Kish, John, ed. David Turns, *International Law and Espionage* (Martinus Nijhoff: The Hague, 1995): ch. 2 ('Diplomacy and Espionage').

Kissinger, H. A. (1979) *The White House Years* (Weidenfeld & Nicolson and Michael Joseph: London).

Kissinger, H. A. (1982) *Years of Upheaval* (Weidenfeld & Nicolson and Michael Joseph: London).

Kleiboer, Marieke (1996) 'Understanding success and failure of international mediation', *Journal of Conflict Resolution*, 40(2), June [www].

Klieman, A. (1988) *Statecraft in the Dark: Israel's practice of quiet diplomacy* (Jaffee Center for International Studies: Tel Aviv).

Koenig, Robert L. (2014) 'Using "social media" to reach Russians', *Foreign Service Journal*, January–February [www].

Kuehn, Felix, and Alex Strick van Linschoten (2013) 'Negotiating with the Taliban: Insights from before 2001', August [www].

Lakoff, G. and M. Johnson (1980) *Metaphors We Live By* (University of Chicago Press: Chicago).

Lally, Kathy (2013) 'U.S. ambassador in Moscow uses social media to bypass official line', *Washington Post*, 13 January [www].

Lantis, Jeffrey S. (2009) *The Life and Death of International Treaties: Double-edged diplomacy and the politics of ratification in comparative perspective* (Oxford University Press: Oxford).

Lee, Luke T. and John Quigley (2008) *Consular Law and Practice*, 3rd edn (Oxford University Press: Oxford).

Lehmann, Volker (2013) 'Reforming the working methods of the UN Security Council: The next ACT', Friedrich Ebert Stiftung, August [www].

Liverani, Mario (2001) *International Relations in the Ancient Near East* (Palgrave: Basingstoke): intro. and ch. 10.

Lord, Winston (1995) *Statement on U.S. Policy toward Vietnam, Laos and Cambodia and the POW/MIA Issues before the House Committee on National Security, Subcommittee on Military Personnel*, December 14 (Electronic Research Collection East Asia and Pacific Bureau) [www].

Lundy, Walter A. (2005) interview *FAOHC* [www].

MacMillan, Margaret (2006) *Seize the Hour: When Nixon met Mao* (John Murray: London).

Marett, Sir Robert (1968) *Through the Back Door: An inside view of Britain's Overseas Information Services* (Pergamon Press: Oxford).

Mattingly, G. (1965) *Renaissance Diplomacy* (Penguin Books: Harmondsworth).

Mazzetti, Mark (2013) 'How a single spy helped turn Pakistan against the United States', *The New York Times Magazine*, 9 April [www].

McDougall, B. (1999) 'Haiti: Canada's role in the OAS', in C. A. Crocker, F. O. Hampson, and P. R. Aall (eds), *Herding Cats: Multiparty mediation in a complex world* (USIP: Washington, DC).

Meier, S. A. (1988) *The Messenger in the Ancient Semitic World* (Scholars Press: Atlanta).

Melly, Paul, and Vincent Darracq (2013) 'A New Way to Engage? French policy in Africa from Sarkozy to Hollande' (Chatham House: London) [www].

Metcalfe, Eric (2009) 'The false promise of assurances against torture', *Justice Journal*, 6(1), June [www].

Meyer, Christopher (2005) *DC Confidential: The controversial memoirs of Britain's Ambassador to the U.S. at the time of 9/11 and the Iraq War* (Weidenfeld & Nicolson: London).

Meyer, Sir Christopher (2009) Evidence of to the Iraq Inquiry, 26 November ('Morning Session transcript') [www].

Miller, M. (1976) *Plain Speaking: An oral biography of Harry S Truman* (Coronet: London).

Mitchell, George J. (1999) *Making Peace* (Heinemann: London).

Mitrany, David (1943) *A Working Peace System: An argument for the functional development of international organization* (RIIA: London).

Monbiot, George (2014) 'The British government is leading a gunpowder plot against democracy', *Guardian*, 4 November [www].

Munn-Rankin, J. M. (1956) 'Diplomacy in Western Asia in the early second millennium B.C.', *Iraq*, 18.

National Commission on Terrorist Attacks Upon the United States (2004) *The 9/11 Commission Report: Final Report of the National Commission on Terrorist Attacks Upon the United States (9/11 Report)* (U.S. Government Printing Office: Washington, DC) [www].

Newhouse, John (2009) 'Diplomacy, Inc.: the influence of lobbies on US foreign policy', *Foreign Affairs*, May/June.

Nicholas, H. G. (1975) *The United Nations as a Political Institution*, 2nd edn (Oxford University Press: London).

Nicol, D. (1982) *The United Nations Security Council: Towards greater effectiveness* (UNITAR: New York).

Nicolson, H. (1954) *The Evolution of Diplomatic Method* (Constable: London).

Nicolson, H. (1964) *Peacemaking 1919* (Methuen: London).

Nixon, R. M. (1979) *The Memoirs of Richard Nixon* (Arrow: London).

O'Brien, Conor Cruise (1996) *The Long Affair: Thomas Jefferson and the French Revolution* (Sinclair-Stevenson: London).

Office of Foreign Assets Control (2009) *Report to Congress: Effectiveness of U.S. Economic Sanctions with respect to Sudan* (January) [www].

OIG (2007) *Report of Inspection: U.S. Interests Section Havana, Cuba*, July [www].

OIG (2014a) *Inspection of Embassy Abu Dhabi and Consulate General Dubai, United Arab Emirates*, May [www].

OIG (2014b) *Inspection of U.S. Interests Section Havana, Cuba*, May [www].

Parsons, A. (1984) *The Pride and the Fall: Iran 1974–1979* (Cape: London).

Patterson, Jr., Bradley H. (2000) *The White House Staff: Inside the West Wing and beyond* (Brookings: Washington, DC).

Peters, J. (1994) *Building Bridges: The Arab–Israeli multilateral talks* (RIIA: London).

Peterson, M. J. (1997) *Recognition of Governments: Legal doctrine and state practice, 1815–1995* (Macmillan: Basingstoke).

Philby, Kim (1969) *My Silent War* (Panther: St Albans).

Picavet, C.-G. (1930) *La Diplomatie Française au Temps de Louis XIV (1661–1715): Institutions, mœurs et coutumes* (Librairie Félix Alcan: Paris).

Pietrowicz, Nick (2013) 'The value of fortress embassies', *Foreign Service Journal*, February [www].

Pifer, Steven (2014) 'Ukraine crisis impact on nuclear weapons', *CNN*, 4 March [www].

Pillar, Paul (2012) 'The preconditions game and talks with Iran', *The National Interest*, 31 January [www].

Platt, D. C. M. (1971) *The Cinderella Service: British consuls since 1825* (Longman: London).

Plischke, E. (1967) *Conduct of American Diplomacy*, 3rd edn (Van Nostrand: Princeton, NJ).

Pope, Laurence (2014) *The Demilitarization of American Diplomacy: Two cheers for striped pants* (Palgrave Macmillan: Basingstoke).

Powell, Jonathan (2010) Evidence of to the Iraq Inquiry, 18 January [www].

Prentice, Christopher (2010) Evidence of to the Iraq Inquiry, 6 January [www].

Princen, T. (1992) *Intermediaries in International Conflict* (Princeton University Press: Princeton, NJ).

Putnam, R. (1984) 'The Western economic summits: A political interpretation', in C. Merlini (ed.), *Economic Summits and Western Decision-making* (Croom Helm: London).

Quandt, W. B. (1986) *Camp David: Peacemaking and politics* (Brookings Institution: Washington, DC).

Queller, D. E. (1967) *The Office of Ambassador in the Middle Ages* (Princeton University Press: Princeton, NJ).

Radsan, A. John (2006–7) 'The unresolved equation of espionage and international law', *Michigan Journal of International Law*, 28.

Ragsdale, L. (1993) *Presidential Politics* (Houghton Mifflin: Boston).

Ramsey, Michael (2013) 'Is the agreement with Iran unconstitutional?' *The Originalism Blog*, 25 November [www].

Rana, Kishan (2000) *Inside Diplomacy* (Manas: New Delhi).

Rana, Kishan (2004) *The 21st Century Ambassador* (DiploFoundation: Malta).

Randle, R. F. (1969) *Geneva 1954: The settlement of the Indochinese war* (Princeton University Press: Princeton, NJ).

Reagan, R. (1990) *An American Life* (Hutchinson: London).

Regan, Donald T. (1989) *For the Record: From Wall Street to Washington* (Harcourt: San Diego, CA).

Reynolds, David (2007) *Summits: Six meetings that shaped the twentieth century* (Allen Lane: London).

Rhoodie, E. (1983) *The Real Information Scandal* (Orbis: Pretoria).

Rice, Condoleezza (2011) *No Higher Honor: A memoir of my years in Washington* (Crown: New York).

Roberts, Andrew (1999) *Salisbury: Victorian titan* (Weidenfeld & Nicolson: London).

Roberts, Sir Ivor (ed.) (2009) *Satow's Diplomatic Practice*, 6th edn (Oxford University Press: Oxford).

Rona, Gabor (2004) 'The ICRC's status: in a class of its own', 17 February [www].

Ross, Dennis (2007) *Statecraft: And how to restore America's standing in the world* (Farrar, Straus and Giroux: New York).

Rozen, Laura (2014) 'Three days in March: New details on how US, Iran opened direct talks', *Al-Monitor*, 8 January.

Sahlins, Marshall (2013) 'China U', *The Nation*, 18 November [www].

Sandre, Andreas (2013) *Twitter for Diplomats* (DiploFoundation and Istituto Diplomatico: Geneva) [www].

Satow, Sir E. (1922) *A Guide to Diplomatic Practice*, 2nd edn (Longman: London).

Saunders, H. (1985) 'We need a larger theory of negotiation: The importance of pre-negotiating phases', *Negotiation Journal*, 1.

Sawers, Sir John (2009) Evidence of to the Iraq Inquiry, 10 December [www].

Schaller, Christian (2013) 'Spies', in Rüdiger Wolfrum (ed.), *Max Planck Encyclopedia of Public International Law* (Oxford University Press: Oxford).

Scott, Len (2004) 'Secret intelligence, covert action, and clandestine diplomacy', *Intelligence and National Security*, 19(2).

Segev, S. (1988) *The Iranian Triangle: The untold story of Israel's role in the Iran–Contra affair* (Free Press: New York).

Seldon, Anthony (2013) 'Power returns to the Foreign Office', *The House Magazine*, July.

Shaw, Malcolm N. (2008) *International Law*, 6th edn (Cambridge University Press: Cambridge).

Sheinwald, Sir Nigel (2009) Evidence of to the Iraq Inquiry, 16 December [www].

Sherman, Wendy R. (2014) Remarks at a Symposium on P5+1 Iran Nuclear Negotiations, Center for Strategic and International Studies, Washington, DC, 23 October [www].

Shlaim, Avi (1990) *The Politics of Partition: King Abdullah, the Zionists and Palestine, 1921–1951* (Oxford University Press: Oxford).

Shultz, G. P. (1993) *Turmoil and Triumph: My years as secretary of state* (Scribner's: New York).

Shultz, G. P. (1997) 'Diplomacy in the information age', keynote address at the Virtual Diplomacy Conference, April [www].

Shurtleff, Len (2007) 'A Foreign Service murder', *Foreign Service Journal*, 84(10), October [www].

SIAC (2007a) Appeal No.: SC/02/05, Date of Judgment: 8 February. [All of SIAC's open judgments, which provide some diplomatic background, can be accessed via the Commission's website: click 'decisions>outcomes'.]

SIAC (2007b) Appeal No.: SC/15/2005, Date of Judgment: 26 February.

SIAC (2007c) Appeal No.: SC/42 and 50/2005, Date of Judgment: 27 April.

SIAC (2007d) Appeal No.: SC/32/2005, Date of Judgment: 14 May.

SIAC (2007e) Appeal No.: SC/59/2006, Date of Judgment: 2 November.

Simpson, S. (1967) *Anatomy of the State Department* (Houghton Mifflin: Boston).

Smith, G. S. (1999) *Reinventing Diplomacy: A virtual necessity* [www].

Smith, L. P. (1907) *The Life and Letters of Sir Henry Wotton*, vol. 1 (Clarendon Press: Oxford).

Smith, Raymond F. (2009) 'Is it a pearl or a kidney stone? Intelligence reform and embassy reporting, from Moscow to Baghdad', *Intelligence and National Security*, 24(6).

Spiegel Online International (2013) 'Embassy Espionage: The NSA's Secret Spy Hub in Berlin', 27 October [www].

Stadler, K. R. (1981) 'The Kreisky phenomenon', *West European Politics*, 4(1).

Stearns, M. (1996) *Talking to Strangers: Improving American diplomacy at home and abroad* (Princeton University Press: Princeton, NJ).

Stein, Janice G. (1989) 'Getting to the table: The triggers, stages, functions, and consequences of prenegotiations', *International Journal*, 44(2).

Stockwell, John (1979) *In Search of Enemies: A CIA story* (Futura: London).

Strang, Lord (1955) *The Foreign Office* (Allen & Unwin: London).

Straw, Jack (2010) Evidence of to the Iraq Inquiry, 8 February [www].

Sullivan, W. H. (1981) *Mission to Iran* (Norton: New York).

Summary Report of the 6th Review Meeting of the Contracting Parties to the Convention on Nuclear Safety, 24 March–4 April 2014, Vienna, Austria [www].

Talmon, Stefan (2013) 'Tapping the German chancellor's cell phone and public international law', *Cambridge Journal of International and Comparative Law*, 6, November [www].

Taylor, P. M. (1992) *War and the Media: Propaganda and persuasion in the Gulf War* (Manchester University Press: Manchester).

Thatcher, M. (1993) 'The Downing Street Years', *Booknotes Transcript* [www].

Thatcher, M. (1995) *The Downing Street Years* (HarperCollins: London).

Touval, S. (1982) *The Peace Brokers: Mediators in the Arab–Israeli Conflict, 1948–1979* (Princeton University Press: Princeton, NJ).

Touval, S. (1989) 'Multilateral negotiation: An analytic approach', *Negotiation Journal*, 5(2).

Tower Commission Report (1987) (Bantam Books/Times Books: New York).

Trevelyan, H. (1973) *Diplomatic Channels* (Macmillan: London).

UN Secretariat (2013) *Assessment of Member States' advances to the Working Capital Fund for the biennium 2014–2015 and contributions to the United Nations regular budget for 2014*, ST/ADM/SER.B/889 (13 December) [www].

US Advisory Commission on Public Diplomacy (2008) *Getting the People Part Right: A report on the human resources dimension of public diplomacy* [www].

US Department of State (1991) *Dispatch*, 2(19), 13 May [www].

US Department of State (2013) Daily Press Briefing, 9 July [www].

US Department of State (2014a) 'Background Briefing on the Implementation Plan of the P5+1 and Iran's First Step Nuclear Agreement', 13 January [www].

US Department of State (2014b) Daily Press Briefing ('Iran'), 14 January [www].

Vance, C. (1983) *Hard Choices: Critical years in America's foreign policy* (Simon & Schuster: New York).

Vattel, Emmerich de (1758) *Le Droit des Gens* (Neuchâtel) [English trans. www].

Ware, R. (1990) 'Treaties and the House of Commons', *Factsheet*, FS.57 (Public Information Office, House of Commons: London).

Webster, Sir Charles (1961) *The Art and Practice of Diplomacy* (Chatto & Windus: London).

Weizman, E. (1981) *The Battle for Peace* (Bantam: Toronto).

Whelan, J. G. (1990) *The Moscow Summit 1988* (Westview Press: Boulder, CO).

Wilton, Christopher, J. Griffin, and A. Fotheringham (2002) *Changing Perceptions: Review of public diplomacy* ['Wilton Review'], [www].

Wood, J. R. and J. Serres (1970) *Diplomatic Ceremonial and Protocol: Principles, procedures and practices* (Macmillan: London).

Wood, Sir Michael (2010) 'The rights and responsibilities of occupying powers', second statement to the Iraq Inquiry, 28 January [www].

Wood, Sir Michael (2012) 'Convention on Special Missions, New York, 8 December 1969', *Audiovisual Library of International Law* (United Nations) [www].

Woolcock, Stephen and Nicholas Bayne (2013) 'Economic Diplomacy', in Andrew F. Cooper, Jorge Heine, and Ramesh Thakur (eds), *The Oxford Handbook of Modern Diplomacy* (Oxford University Press: Oxford).

Wriston, H. M. (1960) 'The special envoy', *Foreign Affairs*, 38(2).

Young, J. W. (1986) 'Churchill, the Russians and the Western Alliance: The three power conference at Bermuda, December 1953', *English Historical Review*, 101(401).

Young. J. W. (2008) *Twentieth-Century Diplomacy: A case study of British practice, 1963–1976* (Cambridge University Press: Cambridge).

Young, Kenneth T. (1968) *Negotiating with the Chinese Communists: The United States experience, 1953–1967* (McGraw-Hill: New York).

Zartman, I. W. and Berman, M. (1982) *The Practical Negotiator* (Yale University Press: New Haven, CT).

Index